Spatial Planning Systems of Britain and France

Spatial Planning Systems of Britain and France brings together a wide selection of comparative essays seeking to articulate the fundamental similarities and differences between the spatial planning systems in Great Britain and France: two countries that are near neighbours and yet have developed very different modes of planning in terms of their structure, practical application and underlying philosophies.

Drawing on the outcomes of the Franco-British Planning Study Group, and with a foreword by Vincent Renard of the École Polytechnique and Director of Research at CNRS in Paris, the book begins by providing a detailed rationale for the research and its contemporary significance in modern Europe. Chapters will offer a comparative investigation of the basic contexts for planning in both countries, including its administrative, economic, financial and legal implications, and will move on to illustrate themes such as urban policy and transport planning through detailed analysis and case studies.

From these investigations the book brings together planning concepts from both a national and European perspective, looking particularly at two current issues: the effects of urban growth on small market towns and the use of public–private partnerships to implement development projects.

Spatial Planning Systems of Britain and France will prove invaluable to policy makers and practitioners in both countries at a time when national policy is beginning to look towards practice in other countries and actively seek informed discussion of how different States tackle particular issues.

The book is published simultaneously in English and French opening up a wider debate between the English-speaking and Francophone worlds.

Philip Booth is Reader in Town and Regional Planning at the University of Sheffield, UK.

Michèle Breuillard is a Research Fellow at the Centre for Administrative, Political and Social Studies and Research (CERAPS), University of Lille 2, and the National Centre for Scientific Research (CNRS), France.

Charles Fraser is the former Head of Town Planning at London South Bank University, UK, and is currently Visiting Research Fellow of the University.

Didier Paris is Professor of Planning at the Science and Technology University, Villeneuve d'Ascq, Lille, France.

Spatial Planning Systems of Britain and France

A comparative analysis

Edited by Philip Booth,
Michèle Breuillard,
Charles Fraser and Didier Paris

Routledge
Taylor & Francis Group

LONDON AND NEW YORK

First published 2007
by Routledge
2 Park Square, Milton Park, Abingdon, Oxon OX14 4RN

Simultaneously published in the USA and Canada
by Routledge
270 Madison Ave, New York, NY 10016

*Routledge is an imprint of the Taylor & Francis Group, an informa
business*

© 2007 Philip Booth, Michèle Breuillard, Charles Fraser and
Didier Paris for selection and editorial matter; individual chapters,
the contributors

Typeset in Sabon by
HWA Text and Data Management, Tunbridge Wells
Printed and bound in Great Britain by
Biddles Ltd, King's Lynn, Norfolk

British Library Cataloguing in Publication Data
A catalogue record for this book is available from the British
Library

Library of Congress Cataloging-in-Publication Data
Spatial planning systems of Britain and France : a comparative
analysis / Philip Booth ... [et al.].
    Includes bibliographical references
    1. City planning – Great Britain. 2. City planning – France.
    3. Urban Policy – Great Britain. 4. Urban policy – France.
    5. Regional planning – Great Britain. 6. Regional Planning
    – France. I. Booth, Philip, 1946–
HT169.G7S66 2007
307.1´2160941–dc22   2006034328

ISBN10: 0–415–42951–X (hbk)
ISBN10: 0–203–96224–9 (ebk)

ISBN13: 978–0–415–42951–1 (hbk)
ISBN13: 978–0–203–96224–4 (ebk)

Contents

Contributors

Mark Baker is a Senior Lecturer in Planning Policy and Practice and the current Head of Planning and Landscape within the School of Environment and Development at Manchester University. He is a chartered town planner with previous professional experience in UK local and central government. His teaching and research interests focus on the operation of the UK planning system and especially regional and strategic planning.

Paul Boino is Professor at the Planning Institute of the University of Lyon 2. His work relates to themes connected with the process of metropolitanisation.

Philip Booth is Reader in Town and Regional Planning at the University of Sheffield. For much of the past twenty years his research has focused on the public control of private development. Much of this work has been in the form of comparative studies of planning and urban policy in France and Britain and has resulted in articles and books including *Controlling Development: Certainty and Discretion in Europe, the USA and Hong Kong* (UCL Press 1996) and *Planning by Consent: the Origins and Nature of British Development Control* (Routledge 2003).

Michèle Breuillard is a Research Fellow at the Centre for Administrative, Political and Social Studies and Research (CERAPS), University of Lille 2 and National Centre for Scientific Research (CNRS). Her main research interests are institutional and political aspects of local government, decentralisation and devolution in the UK and France. Recent projects include Franco-English comparisons of local democracy and services. An original member of the FBPSG she is also a member of other transnational research groups.

Jean-Paul Carrière is Professor of Planning and Deputy Director of the Department of Planning in the École Polytechnique of the University de Tours and is also a member of the CITERES research team. He has more than 120 publications to his name including the book *Atlantic Cities: Peripheral Towns or Metropolitan Cities for Tomorrow* with Stuart

Farthing. He was recently the scientific coordinator of the Atlantic Spatial Development Perspective.

Stuart Farthing is a Principal Lecturer in the School of Planning and Architecture at the University of the West of England, Bristol. Since the mid-1990s he has developed research with colleagues in the École Polytechnique of the University of Tours and recently published with Jean-Paul Carrière, *Atlantic Cities: Peripheral Towns or Metropolitan Cities for Tomorrow*. Until recently he was engaged with the Atlantic Spatial Development Perspective.

Charles Fraser was formerly Head of Town Planning in the Faculty of the Built Environment at London South Bank University. His main interest was in comparative housing systems and urban regeneration. Since 1998 he has been a Visiting Research Fellow at London South Bank University and has been engaged in managing and participating in EU Interreg projects from the university and from France as well as comparative studies for the IBG and other agencies. He is a co-author of *Urban Regeneration in Europe* (Blackwell 2003) and numerous articles in French and British journals.

Gay Fraser's career has been in Spatial Planning and Urban Policy in central and local government and in consultancies both in the UK and overseas. In particular she worked on the English Urban Policy White Paper for DETR and on urban affairs in Europe, representing the UK on the Member States Urban Working Group.

Marie Fournier is a Researcher in the CITERES team in the Department of Planning at the École Polytechnique of the University of Tours. She studied at Aberdeen and Tours and is currently conducting research on small and medium-sized towns in Western Europe.

Matthieu Galey is a Doctoral Student at University of Paris II Panthéon-Assas and a former lecturer and researcher at University of Paris XI. His work focuses on the interaction of property ownership and the environment and the legal and institutional structures of environmental policy. His doctoral thesis is concerned with 'Judicial techniques for environmental protection in English Law'.

Howard Green is currently Senior Advisor to the Vice-Chancellor at Staffordshire University and professor of Urban Planning. He graduated from Cambridge in 1969 and gained a PhD under Professor Peter Hall at Reading University in 1974. He has recently added a degree in French to this. His current research covers both urban policy in Europe and postgraduate education. In 2005 he published *Doctoral Study in Contemporary Higher Education* with Professor Stuart Powell. He is an original member of the Franco-British Planning Study Group.

Reg Harman is an Independent Consultant in Transport Policy and is a Visiting Research Fellow in the Centre for Transport and Society at the University of the West of England, Bristol. He has conducted research into professional education and training in transport and prepared courses on transport for the Open University. He has worked on a number of major transport studies and has a particular interest in the relationship between planning and transport in European countries. He has served as a member of the EU Libertin and Transforum groups of experts.

Pascal Hoffmann is a Senior Official of the Caisse des Dépôts et Consignations in Lille.

Alain l'Hostis is a Researcher in the field of Spatial Planning at the National Institute for Research on Transport Security in Lille. His work is focused on the relationship of transport and planning in France and other European countries. He is developing tools for the creation of urban networks.

Florence Lerique is Senior Lecturer at the University of Bordeaux IV Montesquieu. She completed her thesis on legal aspects of Urban Policy at Lille University. She now participates in the research work of GRIDAUH at the University of Paris and teaches a course on Urban Policy at masters level at Bordeaux University.

Philippe Ménerault is Director of Research at INRETS (National Institute for Research on Transport Security), where he is in charge of several research groups concerned with the interaction of transport systems and local urban development at different geographic scales. He has written widely on these topics in France, the UK and Spain.

Florence Menez is a civil servant in the French Ministry of Public Works, Transport and Housing. She is currently a PhD student at the University of Lyon preparing a thesis on private/public partnerships, comparing work in Lyon with other European examples.

Alain Motte is Professor in Urban and Regional Planning at Paul Cézanne University (Aix-Marseille-France). He is chairing a masters programme in Urban Planning. He has been Head of Department in Grenoble and Aix-en-Provence and Director of the Research Centre in Urban Planning. His current research interests are in Metropolitan Planning in France and Europe.

Suzy Nelson is Senior Lecturer in Urban Studies and course leader for the MA in Urban Regeneration at the University of Westminster, London. Her doctoral work was concerned with the relationships of agencies concerned with urban redevelopment in London and Paris. She is currently researching the process of the intensification of development in London.

Didier Paris is Professor of Planning at the Science and Technology University, Villeneuve d'Ascq, Lille where he is director of the TVES (Land, Cities, Environment and Society) research unit which is concerned with Metropolitan Development and Change. He is co-author with J.F. Stevens of *Lille et sa Region Urbaine* in 2000, with N. El Hagar and I. Sharour of *Villes en Debat*, and with B. Dolez, *Métropole en Construction*.

Stéphane Sadoux is currently a PhD student at the Planning Institute of the University of Grenoble having completed his previous planning studies at Newcastle-upon-Tyne and Grenoble. He was previously a Project Development Officer with the Town and Country Planning Association and the Association's representative at the European Environmental Bureau in Brussels.

Richard Stephenson is a professional town planner who after completing doctoral studies at Oxford Brookes University taught at the Department of Town and Regional Planning at Sheffield University. After marrying into a French family he has moved to the University of Franche-Comté where he coordinates a masters degree in Planning and European Development.

Olivier Sykes is a Lecturer in the Department of Civic Design at the University of Liverpool. His main interests are European influences on the practice of spatial planning in European states. Recent research, funded by ESPON, has been on spatial strategies for the north-west of England.

Hichem Trache is currently Director of the Urban Design course and a lecturer at the School of the Built Environment, University of Nottingham. He has undertaken extensive research on many aspects of European affairs and is currently involved in an URBACT project on the use of private sector funds to regenerate urban neighbourhoods. He is also an urban design advisor for Nottingham City Council.

Roelof Verhage is a Lecturer in the Institute of Planning at the University of Lyon 2. His research focuses on the relationship of private and public actors in the process of urban development. His main interests are in urban regeneration and land policy, often in a cross-national comparative perspective.

Foreword

In the field of town planning, Franco-British comparison is, as the journalists say, very much an 'old chestnut', one of those recurring topics that are always interesting and never short of substance, but one that can give the impression that the writers are repeating themselves.

Yes, the British and French 'town planning systems' are radically different, radical in the true sense of the word, in that their roots dig down into different histories and have developed along paths, whether institutional, legal, or economic as well as those of urban form properly speaking, which are themselves far apart. The same is true for the nature and content of property rights, for one an indivisible and absolute right, for the other a 'bundle of rights'. The chapter by Matthieu Galey and Philip Booth, dedicated to articulating the interplay of land, land markets and planning, presents a particularly precise and stimulating analysis of the two systems. This attempts to explain by reference to historical origins why the two countries use such different sets of tools and methods of operation in order to pursue the same sets of objectives, namely the public interest in the context of private property rights.

All the same, one is struck by the limited quality and quantity of truly comparative studies. There are certainly numerous works in which the British and French systems are presented alongside each other, often with those of other continental countries, or are the subject of limited sectoral analysis, such as the comparison of a British 'Local Plan' and a 'POS' or 'PLU' in France, PFI and public-private partnerships French style, or yet again the discretionary character of the UK planning permission compared to the 'permis de construire' in France in dealing with third parties. But few works (and such as they are they have been well recorded at the beginning of this book) have a truly comparative 'design objective', in the sense of a truly systematic analysis in which each element of the system can only be understood in reference to the totality of its elements, and where the comprehension of the totality is afforded by the illumination of the interaction between these elements.

One cannot find a better example among these elements than the question of the relationships between the public and private actors in spatial planning. This can only be comprehended by integrating the understanding of the methods of judicial regulation, the pattern of the interplay of the actors and the role of negotiation and contract in the decision-making process, three points on which the British and French systems present profound differences. Several chapters bring interesting insights on this point, and the comparative case study of the renovation of Wembley stadium and the construction of the Stade de France at St-Denis in the chapter by Charles Fraser and Pascal Hoffmann, 'The financing of development', is particularly illuminating.

This systematic approach to the comparative analysis appears equally clearly in the examination of the different levels of public authorities, up to European level which contributes to clarifying the decision making process, not so much in the detailing of regulations as in the method of granting planning permission. This question is well illustrated by the analysis of the role of 'planners', of elected representatives and of the independent agents in the nature of their individual decision making more than in their place in the planning process. This appears to be particularly important in everything to do with urban regeneration.

The quality of this work also comes from the mutual enrichment of the different chapters: the fruit of the longstanding collaboration of the group members on the analysis of these subjects. In contrast to countless collective efforts which are often no more than assemblies of loosely coordinated texts, here we have a really progressively structured volume, in the manner of a seminar which has been pursued over several years on both sides of the Channel, with an intelligence and a tenacity which must be recognised. This is the product of the studies of the Franco-British Planning Study Group. Each chapter is thus written by two (sometimes three) contributors, coming from both sides of the Channel, and one knows only too well the difficulties of such an exercise, but here it has largely been crowned with success.

It is by no means certain that the planning systems of the two countries are converging very rapidly. This book is manifestly an important advance in understanding simultaneously the logic of the structures of both of them and the conditions for their possible rapprochement. The last chapter, aptly entitled, 'So near, yet so far', finally opens up some interesting perspectives not merely on the simple transfer of tools from one country to the other (and one is aware of the risks of failure in a different context), but also on mutual understanding and the coming together of modes of regulation, notably in the context of the European Union.

Vincent Renard
Director of Research, CNRS, Paris

Preface

At several points during the writing of this volume it has appeared as if the United Kingdom and France were about to re-engage in the conflict that marked their relationship throughout the eighteenth century and part of the nineteenth. Newspapers scream about Waterloo and the perfidious French on one side and about the lack of commitment by the British to the European ideal on the other. Sadly these headlines could have been written at any time in the last half century, encompassing the dramatic 'Non' of President de Gaulle to British entry to the then 'Common Market', Margaret Thatcher's famous handbag act at the Rambouillet summit in 1983, to the rivalry for the 2012 Olympic Games in 2005. But why? Why do two countries which are so close to each other geographically appear to be so far apart at times in their view of major issues in Europe and in the world at large?

In truth the confrontational headlines more often than not report the 'man bites dog' instances of disagreement at high level and conveniently forget the realities of much of the interaction between the two countries: the fact that well over 80,000 British citizens now live in France and a greater number of French citizens live and work in the UK, that France is still a favourite holiday destination for Britons, that virtually every player in the French national football team is now based in the UK, that every day businessmen and professionals and academics from both countries are engaged in co-operative ventures, often funded by EU Structural Funds. In reality many more people are exploring the differences between the two countries, going beyond the level of understanding each other to learn and draw on one another's experience, because it is perceived that cross-national co-operation and comparison can be mutually beneficial.

The Franco-British Planning Study Group is just one small example of this process of dialogue. The Group was formed at the annual Association of European Planners (AESOP) conference at Nijmegen in the Netherlands in 1997, when four British town planning academics, enjoying an Oranjeboom at the end of a day's proceedings, began to discuss the aspect of planning comparisons which interested them most, the French planning system. They decided that the conversation should continue back in the United Kingdom, where it had never taken place, and that others who might share this interest be invited to join in. Every UK planning school was circulated to seek out those who might wish to take part and consequently open exploratory meetings were held in Sheffield and London at the end of 1997. Some 15 colleagues came to these and several more expressed an interest in contributing to such an academic exchange: there are now some 30 members. Their interests cover virtually every aspect of planning and land-use management from the basic development control system to regeneration finance and national parks. A programme of informal seminars in various centres was set in motion, based on voluntary participation. The creation of the original network very soon revealed the fact that every British academic had his or her own network of French contacts and some of these contacts began to participate in the seminars. This had two consequences. First, it revealed that there was a parallel situation in France where many academics had an interest in British Urban Planning and management of urban affairs but they equally often had little contact with each other and had no internal national network to bring them together. The group began to provide a forum for inter-French contact as well. Second, as the group became bi-cultural it was invited to hold some of its meetings in France and the first visit to Lille was held in 1998. The group is now clearly a Franco-British group with members mainly but not exclusively in the academic world in Besançon, Bordeaux, Bristol, Dundee, Lille, Liverpool, London, Lyon, Manchester, Nottingham, Paris, Sheffield and Stoke-on-Trent as well as other smaller centres.

A six-monthly programme of seminars over the last seven to eight years has encompassed a series of topics covering land policy, regionalisation and devolution, regeneration finance, government structures and competences, transport and legislative evolution. Much has been said and argued and many good lunches and dinners have been consumed. The papers produced and the debates, many of a high quality on matters of practical purpose and policy, have so far been for the ears of the group only and have not been transferred to a wider professional and academic audience. A primary purpose of this volume is in part to put the substance of this work into that wider world. The aspiration is that the wider readership will extend beyond the walls of academia and include policy makers and practitioners who are increasingly examining European practice for inspiration to deal with what can be demonstrated to be common problems.

The emphasis of the work however is not to describe what is happening in each country's professional practice but to compare practice and to examine in more depth the nature of the similarities and differences which arise, with a view to achieving a better understanding of the rationale, indeed the philosophy behind each. To this end each chapter is written by at least two authors, one French, one British, and the authors have been asked to meet certain common targets in terms of content and structure. To begin with, all have been asked to avoid the siren call of long historical descriptions of the evolution of their particular field, except where it was felt necessary for illumination of current practice. Authors were also asked to clarify the meanings of terms which might be used loosely and appear to have simple translations into the practice of the other culture; the search for a term to include both the British 'town planning' and the French 'urbanisme', is a case in point and its resolution has bedevilled the selection of an appropriate title for the volume. In addition, each set of authors have been asked to go beyond the comparison of practice, to provide some explanation of their conclusions in terms of both the contexts in which practice occurs, financial and economic, land laws and administrative structures and, where evident, the underlying social philosophies which have led to the development of these contexts over the period of the evolution of the two systems of land management.

The book will thereby conclude the work of the formative years of the group and provide a platform for more focused study and policy formulation by the many new (and younger) members who are beginning to take up its mission to enhance the quality of professional and academic exchange between British and French planners and related professionals. It will be, hopefully, the end of one stage in the group's evolution and the beginning of a new one.

Michèle Breuillard and Charles Fraser

Abbreviations and acronyms

AGMA	Association of Greater Manchester Authorities
AO	Autorité Organisatrice
APVF	Association des Petites Villes de France
AT	Aménagement du Territoire
BR	British Railways
CA	Communauté d'Agglomération
CDC	Caisse des Dépôts et Consignations
CEC	Commission of the European Community/European Commission
CFDU	Conseil français des Urbanistes
CFF	Crédit Foncier de France
CIV	Comité Interministériel des Villes
COS	Coefficient d'Occupation des Sols
CPER	Contrat de Plan État-Région
CU	Communauté Urbaine
DATAR	Délégation à l'Aménagement du Territoire et à l'Action Régionale
DCLG	Department for Communities and Local Government
DDE	Direction Départementale de l'Équipement
DETR	Department of the Environment, Transport and the Regions
DIACT	Délégation Interministérielle à l'Aménagement et la Compétitivité des Territoires
DIV	Délégation Interministérielle à la Ville
DPM	Deputy Prime Minister
DRE	Direction Régionale de l'Équipement
DTA	Directive Territoriale d'Aménagement
EEC	European Economic Community
EIA	Environmental Impact Assessment
EPA	Educational Priority Area
EPCI	Établissements Publics de Coopération Intercommunale
ESDP	European Spatial Development Perspective

EU	European Union
EZ	Enterprise Zone
FBPSG	Franco-British Planning Study Group
GDP	Gross Domestic Product
GLA	Greater London Authority
GMC	Greater Manchester County Council
GONW	Government Office for the North West
GOR	Government Office for the Regions
GPU	Grands Projets Urbains
HLM	Habitations à Loyer Modéré
INSEE	Institut National de la Statistique et des Études Économiques
INTERREG	European Initiative for the Promotion of Regional Cooperation
LA	Local Authority
LDA	London Development Agency
LDF	Local Development Framework
LOADDT	Loi d'Orientation pour l'Aménagement et le Développement Durable du Territoire
LOF	Loi d'Orientation Foncière
LOTI	Loi d'Orientation des Transports Intérieurs
LOV	Loi d'Orientation sur la Ville
LSP	Local Strategic Partnership
LTP	Local Transport Plan
MIIAT	Mission Interministérielle et Interrégionale d'Aménagement
MTI	Market Towns Initiative
NDC	New Deal for Communities
NUTS	Nomenclature des Unités Territoriales Statistiques
NWDA	North West Development Agency
NWRA	North West Regional Assembly
ODPM	Office of the Deputy Prime Minister
ONS	Office for National Statistics
OPQU	Office Professionel de Qualification des Urbanistes
OREAM	Organisation d'Étude et d'Aménagement
PADD	Plan d'Aménagement et de Développement Durable
PADOG	Plan d'Aménagement et d'Orientation Générale
PDU	Plan de Déplacements Urbains
PFI	Private Finance Initiative
PLH	Plan Local de l'Habitat
PLU	Plan Local de l'Urbanisme
POS	Plan d'Occupation des Sols
PPG	Planning Policy Guidance
PPP	Public-Private Partnership

PPS	Planning Policy Statement
PTA	Passenger Transport Authority
PTE	Passenger Transport Executive
PTU	Périmètre des Transports Urbains
RATP	Régie Autonome des Transports Parisiens
RDA	Regional Development Agency
REPC	Regional Economic Planning Council
RES	Regional Economic Strategy
RGU	Règles Générales d'Urbanisme
RPB	Regional Planning Body
RPG	Regional Planning Guidance
RSS	Regional Spatial Strategy
RTPI	Royal Town Planning Institute
RUL	Région Urbaine de Lyon
SCI	Statement of Community Involvement
SCOT	Schéma de Cohérence Territoriale
SD	Schéma Directeur
SDAU	Schéma Directeur d'Aménagement et d'Urbanisme
SE	Scottish Executive
SEM	Société d'Économie Mixte
SGAR	Secrétariat Général à l'Action Régionale
SIVU	Syndicat Intercommunal à Vocation Unique
SNCF	Société Nationale des Chemins de Fer
SPG	Strategic Planning Guidance
SRADT	Schéma Régional d'Aménagement et de Développement du Territoire
SSC	Schéma de Service Collectif
SRB	Single Regeneration Budget
SRT	Schéma Regional de Transport
SRU	Loi relative à la Solidarité et au Renouvellement Urbains
TGV	Train à Grande Vitesse
UDC	Urban Development Corporation
UDP	Unitary Development Plan
UP	Urban Programme
UTF	Urban Task Force
UWP	Urban White Paper
VT	Versement-Transport
WAG	Welsh Assembly Government
WSP	Welsh Spatial Plan
ZAC	Zones d'Aménagement Concerté
ZFU	Zones Franches Urbaines

ZRU	Zones de Redynamisation Urbaine
ZUP	Zone à Urbaniser en Priorité
ZUS	Zones Urbaines Sensibles

Note: there have been sequential changes to the main government department responsible for planning in England, as follows:

1981–1997 DOE: Department of the Environment
1997–2002 DETR: Department of the Environment, Transport and the Regions
2002–2006 ODPM: Office of the Deputy Prime Minister
2006 DCLG: Department of Communities and Local Government

Chapter 1

The purpose and process of comparing British and French planning

Michèle Breuillard and Charles Fraser

Context and objectives

Even if Goethe thought that 'comparing is just an easy way for the ignorant to avoid making decisions', most French and British academics as well as other European colleagues would consider that there is an urgent need for improving mutual knowledge through comparison. Thus although there are apparently comparable problems in both countries and considerable exchange of information about them and the methods of dealing with them in a western democratic environment, there are still continuing debates about their nature and the differing legal and institutional frameworks within which the two societies operate to manage and resolve such problems.

However, the many debates which have occurred, both within the Franco-British Planning Study Group and in a wider policy context, have highlighted the fact that although much is written and spoken about each other there is a dearth of analytical literature *comparing* the two countries, ways of managing their environments and a lack of really detailed analysis of the similarities and differences in practice across a range of aspects of this process. What has been produced to date has been useful and basic, more often than not merely descriptive but in certain areas, particularly the analysis of structures and practices, more fundamental theoretical questions have begun to emerge going beyond the procedures of the system and its contextual frameworks to the social theories (McConnel 1976) which underpin the workings of each. In essence there is a lack of a theoretical framework within which a comparison can be conducted.

There is therefore a need to clarify several issues before plunging into the specific topic comparisons:

- What are the objectives of comparative work generally and what can be achieved by this comparative work in particular?
- What do French and British planners already know about each other? What has been written and when and how well have we used the methodology of comparative analysis to enhance the mutual

comprehension of the two systems and to use this knowledge as a policy and practice enhancement tool?

- What are the main issues for theoretical debate which have emerged from this historic work and how and in what areas can this volume further the process of mutual comprehension of our planning systems and beyond this improve practice and policy efficiency?

The comparative analysis objectives

It would add little to the volume to rehearse the nature of comparative theory and to point to its many difficulties and to its considerable theoretical and practical advantages. These are well documented with respect to planning in Breakell (1975), Masser and Williams (1998) and Couch *et al.* (2003). There is an even more structured and thought-through methodology for comparative work in respect of comparative politics in Ashford (1982) and several other disciplines, such as housing (see Power 1993; Kleinmann 1996). In France comparative method is also a well-used intellectual tool but it has essentially been restricted to the study of law and government and not to more practical areas such as urban planning and policy. The accent has been on using comparison to draw out universal principles which occur in all contexts: 'Comparative law allows one to discover the sense of the Universal in the legal sciences' (Rodière 1972). There is evidence that in recent years a more practically oriented interest has begun to emerge, i.e. Green and Trache's work on public-private partnerships in the UK for the Caisse des Dépôts et Consignations (Green and Trache 2003).

The many problems of comparative work, language and terminology confusions, statistical non-equivalence, incompatibility of structures, competences etc., are familiar to all who attempt comparative work and have been encountered in all the seminars held by the group and by every chapter editor. However, what is more important for this volume is which of the policy objectives of comparison have been addressed by this work and to what extent has any contribution to knowledge been achieved as a result of it. Faludi and Hamnett (1975) identify three basic objectives for comparative work:

- the advancement of theory in planning;
- the improvement of planning practice;
- the harmonisation of planning systems.

These can be placed in any order and their priority is usually defined by the needs and objectives of the researcher. Thus Faludi and Hamnett give precedence to the advancement of theory over the improvement of planning practice and the removal of barriers to the integration of systems. To the technical administrator the second of these objectives might be the more important while to the Eurocrat attempting to harmonise European urban policy, planning or land tenure the last of the three might be the more interesting. Bertinget *et al.* (1979), working in the social sciences, adds two more important uses of comparative research: to explain and interpret social phenomena to assist the understanding of social reality and, through policy evaluation to lead to policy development (an extension of Faludi and Hamnett's, 'improvement of practice'). Implicit in all of these objectives is the almost subliminal product of comparative analysis which is to make the analyst more aware of the nature of their *own* system and to question its practices and values; this is a prerequisite of any attempt to evaluate and improve practice and policy as well as to understand the theoretical frameworks and social theories underpinning the system in any given country. As Robert Burns eloquently puts it:

> O would some power the gift would gie us,
> To see ourselves as others see us

Comparative analysis may provide some of that power.

A final important element in all such comparison is the illumination of the processes which are going on in each country and how the dynamics of not only the social but the economic and political 'reality' in each country are driving the evolution of each system. Are the two becoming more similar in the face of emerging similarity in the challenges of the modern world or less similar as different approaches from these are attempted?

Thus in writing the various chapters of this volume, and in particular bringing their conclusions together, the purpose will be to review where and how the following wider objectives might be met:

- Do we have a better understanding of the nature of 'social reality' in the two countries?
- Can the conclusions assist those attempting to evaluate and improve planning practice or policy development? The question 'Which is best?' might remain unanswered, but a better comprehension of the potential of a different approach might be more clearly articulated.
- Can the work assist, if not in the integration of the two systems, in the development of common approaches to problems which touch both countries?
- Can theoretical analysis and comparative methodology at the various levels, as articulated by McConnel, be advanced by reflection on their structure and purpose?

What do we know about each other?

It could be presumed that the literature available to the student of French planning in the UK or British planning in France is copious and sufficient to provide the basis for mutual comprehension. In effect this is so far, far from the case and although there is a constant series of articles, these are in no way linked in to any cohesive programme of national analysis or comparison.

To begin to build up a comprehensive picture of the French planning system the British reader would find a lack of books in English on the subject and would have to indulge in some eclectic reading to do so. There is almost a dearth of any truly comparative work. Even enormously useful papers such as the analysis of urban policy and the Délégation Interministérielle à la Ville (DIV) by Parkinson and Le Galès (1994) and the South Bank University Occasional Paper by Sebastian Loew (1978), now sadly dated, struggled to answer the comparative questions they posed.

There is thus a rich literature describing the practices in each country for a readership in the other, beginning with the again outdated, *Urban France* by Ian Scargill (1983). The *EU Compendium of Planning Systems* (EU 1999), again out of date, has volumes on each member state in all official languages, thus permitting French readers to acquaint themselves with the principles of British planning in French (Nadin) and for UK readers to similarly find a description of the French system (Marcou). Several British books in the field have chapters on French examples, namely Berry and McGreal have a chapter on the Paris property market; Farthing *et al.* have a chapter on the western regions in both countries in the context of the EU Atlantic Arc; Fraser and Baert have a chapter on the regeneration history of Lille in *Urban Regeneration in Europe*, Couch *et al.* (2003), and Le Galès and Mawson (1994) have produced a study of the Contrat de Ville for the Local Government Management Board.

There is an abundance of articles in British journals, particularly European planning studies, with many different contributors on aspects of French planning, but the professional journal of the RTPI seldom features any work of an international nature, the essay on development control systems by Devereux (2002) being an exception.

Much of the practical comparison has emerged from projects within the framework of the EU Inter-Regional programme, from Ia to IIIb, but these usually have a wider multinational context, e.g. *Living in Towns* (Fraser *et al.*) Urban Regeneration Network (Agence de Développement de Lille Métropole).

There is a considerable literature in the field of housing where the nature of the French system is often compared with that of the UK or good descriptions in English of the French system for British readers can be obtained. The works by Klienmann (1996), Ball *et al.* (1988), McCrone and Stephens (1995) and Power (1993), etc. all give good material which contributes to better understanding of housing management in the French system and how it varies from that of the UK. Wilmott and Murie (1988) provided one of the first real comparative efforts with their study of *Polarisation and Social Housing: The British and French Experience*, a study still of contemporary relevance.

For the French reader there is equally an eclectic collection of essays on various topics. Over the years the Association des Études Foncières (ADEF) in Paris has conducted a series of seminars and published the results of these, as well as other pieces of research, most of which contain some description of British practice and reflection from a French point of view upon it. A major work is that of Vincent Renard and Thierry Vilmin (1990), who examine British land law in the series *Politiques Foncières Comparées – Grande Bretagne*. A further volume on land availability contains a chapter by Barry Redding and Sebastian Loew, on planning gain. A major comparison is that by Le Galès on urban policy (1993) and a recent major work by Breuillard focuses on local administration (2000). Other notable works are by Grive (1998) looking at a specific local planning system in Shepway, Kent and by the Faculty of Law at the University of Dijon (Fromont 1996). A study of the transport system in the UK has also been undertaken by CETUR, the Centre d'Études de Transports Urbains in Paris.

What conclusions have been derived from this considerable body of literature? The recipients of the information can be divided into two camps, those in planning practice and those engaged in academic analysis or some other form of theoretical analysis for its own sake. From the above it can be seen that most of the work is derived from academic study and very little from practitioners seeking new practice or policy initiatives. Only Wilmott and Murie in the housing field had an effect directly into British practice in that their review of the HLM system was a direct contributor to the shift of the housing management model in the UK from 'council' housing to the current mix of housing associations and companies. In France, the analysis of British housing policy is notable by its absence, chapters in twin volumes on the housing systems of the, then, 15 EU member states by Ghékiere (1991) being the outstanding exception.

From this selection it can be seen that the literature relating to planning, as we have tried to define it, is restricted and the reader seeking enlightenment must delve into the fields of law, government, housing and European policy to extend their knowledge. There do not appear to be any resoundingly conclusive works and therefore there remains a great deal still to be examined if useful progress is to be made in furthering mutual comprehension. This work is not therefore the last word in Franco-British comparative studies but in reality the first word as it sets out for the first time to knit together a series of essays which each attempt to *compare* an aspect of the two systems of planning and land management.

Issues to be examined

Many of the authors contributing to this volume have contributed to this body of literature but consider that there is still some way to go if a profound comprehension is to be achieved; other contributors are beginning their careers and need a more defined context within which their work can be fitted if it is to enhance wider understanding and not merely be yet more eclectic articles, theses or book chapters.

The issues discussed in a more profound way in this volume arise from the interests and concerns of the authors and the Franco-British Planning Study Group (FBPSG) in general. As a result of the diversity of that membership and its widespread geographic distribution this makes for a very comprehensive coverage of contemporary concerns. However a major objective of the volume must be to ensure that there is some focus to the work and that it helps establish a framework for further research and analysis and moves beyond being a collection of eclectic essays.

The first question which presents itself is defining what the 'social reality' is in both countries and how the contemporary evolution of society, demographic, social and geographic varies, or does not vary, between the two. The impact of these changes allied to the evolution of the domestic economies of both countries has a profound impact on the objectives and processes of their planning systems as they grapple with new problems from social alienation at a local level to the effects of economic 'globalisation' at the national. Whilst the debates on planning tend in both countries to be urban oriented it is clear that the profound changes in the agricultural sector and in the use and purpose of the 'countryside' pose a grave threat to the rural economy and to rural society and are an equal constituent of the contemporary 'social reality'. The nature of these phenomena in both countries will be explored in Chapter 2 by Stuart Farthing and Jean-Paul Carrière.

A primary point of comparison is the discussion of the legitimacy, the legal justification for public intervention in the rights in land of individuals; the fundamental legal foundation upon which the planning system in both countries is based. The balance of private and public rights is the stuff of planning law debates and a critical comparison is intended to take the reader into the differences between the clearly legal codes of the French judicial system and the more evolutionary pragmatic processes of the UK: in essence to one country where constitutional underpinning is the norm for everything and one where such encoded rigidities are viewed as brakes to social and economic evolution. These issues were debated at one of the group seminars in Lille and the issues raised there are the foundation for Chapter 3 which deals with specific aspects of the two systems by Matthieu Galey and Philip Booth.

Clearly the many changes in the social and economic structures have influenced the two systems and this has been reflected in significant recent amendments to their planning systems. The enactment of the Loi 2000 relative à la Solidarité et au Renouvellement Urbains, SRU 2000 in France is paralleled by the Planning and Compensation Act 2004 in England and Wales. A major debate which has been engendered is whether these developments signal a turning point, in the evolution of planning, taking them in a common direction in both countries. To British readers does this signify that planning is no longer at the crossroads but has at last struck out in a clear new direction from it? The directions in which these changes are taking each country are explored in the chapters which follow.

To develop the comparison of these two pieces of legislation and their effects, the debate proceeds in ensuing chapters to compare the actual administrative frameworks for planning which are now in place, how these are administered and by whom. The frameworks and structures and the actors in the process and their tools form the themes of Chapters 4 and 5. The first theme will be explored by Michèle Breuillard, Richard Stephenson and Stéphane Sadoux. The second will be examined by Philip Booth, Suzy Nelson and Didier Paris.

Having set out and compared the basic structures of the two systems the volume will then proceed to investigate how they operate in practice at various levels in each country, from the supranational to the local. Two contextual themes which will also be discussed in ensuing chapters are the effects of recent reactions in both countries to the need for a more decentralised system and the emergence in recent years of the European Spatial Development Perspective which nests both systems in a wider trans-continental framework. Thus in recent years both countries have evolved from an essentially centralised national, French or UK system, with commonality of practice throughout, to one where there is greater variety in administration and practice, in the various sub-national levels, e.g. Scotland and Wales in the UK and regions and major cities in France. At the same time both countries face challenges at local level and developments in their administrative frameworks to make the planning systems more reactive and accountable to local populations and community groups. The discussion of who are the key actors in the process thus evolves and spills over into discussions of how the administration of planning is changing from being a technocratic exercise to being a process of political management of conflicting demands upon the land of our towns and countryside and how widening participation in this process by individual citizens and community, particularly ethnic minority, groups is being handled.

A general review of spatial planning at the metropolitan level is undertaken by Roelof Verhage, Mark Baker and Paul Boino in Chapter 6, followed by two more specific chapters. Chapter 7 by Olivier Sykes and Alain Motte looks first at the way in which each country engages with the European dimension.

Chapter 8 (Jean-Paul Carrière, Stuart Farthing and Marie Fournier) then looks at the more local level, especially in small and market towns.

Greater involvement of many disparate groups in the process of planning means that there is greater economic, social and cultural pressure on the planning systems and a need to integrate policies for the development of the land and the space in both countries in harmony with and in support of parallel aspatial policies for social development in education, job creation, community development, etc. These tendencies are reflected in France in many of the measures prior to and pursuant to the creation of the Délégation Interministérielle à la Ville (DIV) in 1988 and in the UK by the production of the Rogers Report, 'Towards an Urban Renaissance', and the Urban and Rural Policy White Papers, 'Our Towns and Cities: Their Future' and 'Our Countryside: The Future' in England and Wales. The evaluative review, 'The State of the Cities' (ODPM 2006) has only just been published. There is also the contemporary 'Review of Scotland's Cities' by the Scottish Executive. The integration of disparate policies into a recognisable urban policy has been a feature of government in both countries. The question which will be explored by Gay Fraser and Florence Lerique in Chapter 9 is how this is proceeding and how successful are these developments.

A further set of relationships to be examined, where there is a dichotomy of interaction, is in the relationship of the private business world to the arena of public administration. This is evident in virtually all the discussions, from land rights to economic development, but is especially important in relation to the world of economic and financial planning.

It is emerging as a major point of comparison when one examines the way in which physical planning relates to economic planning and long term financial planning by both governments and the private sector. In France this has been a traditional aspect of the entire system of Aménagement du Territoire linked to the longstanding system of Contrats de Plan. In the UK, however, apart from the ill-fated 'National Plan' of 1965, such links have been tenuous till now, where a growing strategic management over all aspects of social and physical policy by the Treasury has become an accepted fact of policy implementation. These broader aspects of financial management and the ways in which the private and public sectors guide investment in the built environment will be the subject of Chapter 10 by Charles Fraser and Pascal Hoffmann.

The links between private and public agencies has become particularly marked in recent years in the processes of regeneration in urban areas. Here the ways in which financial investment in property development are managed and how they translate into the processes, indeed the very concept of private-public partnership, are contrasted by Hichem Trache, Howard Green and Florence Menez in Chapter 11 who have unrivalled experience of comparing the two systems as a result of several years of cooperation and work on behalf of the French Caisse des Dépôts et Consignations.

As well as being connected together by economic concerns and plans and by the need for integration of spatial and aspatial policy, the various components of the land use pattern are connected physically by the transport systems of both countries. It is here that the ordinary traveller often makes their only meaningful comparison of the two countries by commenting on the efficiency of the Paris metro or how the trains seem to run on time in France and not in the UK. The issue of whether this is true and why the two systems perform differently is explored in Chapter 12 by Reg Harman, Alain l'Hostis and Philippe Ménerault.

This central core of ten chapters will thus link the introductory setting out of the issues and the comparison of the evolution of the basic demography, economy and society of both countries through to a final chapter which will seek to catalogue and analyse the main points emerging from each.

Template for analysis and for drawing conclusions

In setting out the programme for the authors of this series of chapters, it has been necessary to be prescriptive to a certain degree in what they should provide by way of conclusions to enable the volume to end with a final section which does extend our knowledge of the differences and similarities between the two systems and which will provide researchers who are following up our findings to find directions for further study clearly signposted.

The need therefore is for authors to attempt, within reasonable limits of their licence, to each look at the same sets of factors and to pose the same questions about each national experience. This will enable points of similarity in each chapter's conclusions to be identifiable for the construction of more general comparisons and points of difference to be identified and explained.

Thus, first, the conclusions will look for the main points of comparison at the level of implementation and practical operation of the system. Clearly, significant differences in the meaning of terms commonly used in planning and related areas in both countries must be brought out, so that the common error in much comparative work of not comparing like with like can be avoided. The volume must also strive to demonstrate where there are significant similarities and differences between the legislative structures and processes which may have considerable effect on the effectiveness of either system. In the context of the various actors in the process, a fundamental point of comparison to be highlighted is the extent to which the planning system includes as participants other public agencies and thereby sets a wide set of social and economic objectives for the management of the future of any given geographical area; this will be reflected through the extent of participation in policy formulation decision-making and implementation by other government agencies concerned with matters such as unemployment, crime, education and training, etc. The degree of vertical and horizontal cohesion between agencies is a critical factor. Equally as part of this analysis it will be important to establish the ways and the extent to which the system engages with the general public and the way in which they participate in decision-making. Such widening of the participant base of the planning process may also have a profound effect on the speed and efficiency of the system but may also achieve more acceptable results in the long run. In identifying the various actors in the process there are two groups who require identification to show what might be clear distinguishing traits between the two countries: who initiates development and who are considered the main beneficiaries of any development. In the latter case it may be necessary to go beyond simplistic private-public categories to demonstrate the eventual balance of benefit to the community as a whole from either public dominance of a process or private benefit from it. This leads to the question of when the planning process is considered to have ended in both countries and the marking of the point when public authorities cease to have any more responsibility in the process and leave the delivery of the final product to private agencies.

These are indicators of how the system works at the practical level, but the conclusions on how they work and what the differences are between the two countries may illuminate the areas of public policy and general contextual systems which influence how the working of many aspects of the process and the behaviour of the many actors in it determine these outcomes. Since town planning is in its narrowest sense a process of land use management, to what extent do the two land tenure systems and their differing codes of land law affect the way in which public authorities must justify their intervention in the land market and in individuals' rights in land? Equally, since the planning process in both cases is engaged in the improvement of land and its value to the owner and the community, to what extent is the planning process affected by the climate within which investment in land and property and the free movement and remuneration of labour operates? These latter factors can directly affect the prosperity of a region or city and thereby the focus of general development strategies and land use policies. The administrative, legal and philosophical justification for actions either to further economic interests or divert them to other purposes must be made clear.

This leads to the social context for each system which it is hoped each chapter will illuminate, namely why the French and British behave in the way they do. What is their underlying social philosophy and to what extent does it colour the way in which the planning system is used in each country? What is the purpose of the respective planning systems? Is it to create a tidy world? Is it to assist private owners to gain most value from their property? Is it to further a long-term national development process and its ancillary policies? Is it to act as a handmaiden to economic development? Is it to resolve any conflict between private interests and public needs in society at large? Notably there must be some confrontation with the fundamental difference between the two, that one is a republic and the other one of the most traditional monarchies in Europe. How does this affect the nature of the planning system?

Whatever the differences between the two systems there is one undeniable similarity, that they are both engaged in dynamic evolution and are changing quite rapidly. In France the 2000 Loi SRU sets their system off in a new and challenging direction, as does the 2004 Planning and Compensation Act in England and Wales. Devolution of urban affairs in the broadest sense to Scotland, increasingly to Wales and possibly in the longer term to Northern Ireland may see more innovation within the United Kingdom. Of prime interest is the need to identify the directions in which these changes are taking the respective countries and whether there is a degree of convergence in the face of similar social and economic imperatives or whether they remain quite or even more distinct from each other. Thus it is the history of the future that the volume seeks to explore here and each author has been implored not to dwell on past history any more than is necessary to explain and clarify the nature of existing realities.

However, one factor which is common to both countries and will recur as each theme is examined and comparisons made is the nature of the dynamics in each. The direction in which both countries are moving is of great importance. Are they developing common responses to increasingly common problems or are they as distinct as ever? Of equal interest is the question of whether the common European package of policies within which both countries must increasingly work is pushing them closer to a more similar set of procedures, structural contexts and possibly views of how their societies should develop. Here one touches on the realms of planning theory and the apparent contrast of the UK planning system which has changed its justified purpose to accommodate the political and economic objectives of succeeding governments, from the Labour Government of 1945–51 to the long era of Thatcherite Conservatism and the domination of the 'market' with the apparent stability of the technocratic efficiency model of the French Republic. This leads inexorably to a comparison of what appear to be two apparently opposed concepts of the way in which the State should serve society, through liberalism and pragmatism in the UK or as the guardian of the constitutional framework in France.

References

Agence de Développement et d'Urbanisme de Lille Métropole 1999–2002 (2002) *Proceedings of Working Party on Urban Regeneration in Europe*. Lille: Agence de Développement et d'Urbanisme de Lille Métropole.

Ashford, D. (1982) *British Dogmatism and French Pragmatism: Central–Local Policy-Making in the Welfare State*. London: Allen and Unwin.

Ball, M., Harloe, M. and Martens, M. (1988) *Housing and Social Change in Europe and the USA*. London: Routledge.

Berry, J. and McGreal, S. (1995) *European Cities, Planning Systems and Property Markets*. London: Spon.

Berting, J., Gayer, F. and Jurkovich, R. (eds) (1979) *Problems of International Comparative Research in the Social Sciences*. Oxford: Pergamon.

Booth, P. (1993) 'The cultural dimension in comparative research; making sense of French development control', *European Planning Studies*, 1(2): 217–29.

Breakell, M. (1975) *Problems of Comparative Planning*. Oxford: Oxford Polytechnic Working paper no. 21.

Breuillard, M. (2000) *L'Administration Locale en Grande-Bretagne: Entre Centralisation et Régionalisation*. Paris: L'Harmattan.

Centre d'Études des Transports Urbains (CETUR) (1991) *La Loi, l'Espace Public et l'Innovation en Europe. Étude Comparative des Réglementations en Matière de Réaménagement de l'Espace Public aux Pays-Bas, en Allemagne et en Grande-Bretagne*. Paris: Les Dossiers du CETUR, no. 49.

Couch, C., Fraser, C. and Percy, S. (2003) *Urban Regeneration in Europe*. Oxford: Blackwell.

Department of Economic Affairs (1965) *The National Plan*. London: HMSO.

Department of the Environment, Transport and the Regions (2000) *Our Towns and Cities: The Future*. London: The Stationery Office.

Devereux, M. (2002) 'A French revolution', *Planning*, September.

Emms, P. (1990) *Social Housing: A European Dilemma*. Bristol: School for Advanced Urban Studies (SAUS).

Faludi, A. and Hamnett, S. (1975) *The Study of Comparative Planning*. CES Conference papers no. 13. London: CES.

Farthing, S. (2000) *Les Cités Atlantiques: Villes Périphériques ou Métropoles de Demain*. Paris: Éditions Publisud.

Fraser, C. and Baert, T. (2003) 'Lille: from textile giant to tertiary turbine', in C. Couch, C. Fraser and S. Percy (eds) *Urban Regeneration in Europe*. Oxford: Blackwell.

Fraser, C., Le Ny, L. and Redding, B. (2001) *Living in Towns*. Interreg IIc Project Report. London: South Bank University.

Fromont, M. (ed.) (1987) *Les Compétences des Collectivités Territoriales en Matière d'Urbanisme et d'Équipement: Allemagne-Belgique-Espagne-France-Grande-Bretagne-Italie-Suisse*. Faculté de Droit et de Sciences Politique. Institut de Droit Comparé de Dijon. Paris: Litec; Bruxelles: Bruylant.

Fromont, M. (1996) *Compétences Urbaines des Collectivités Locales en Europe*. Paris: Cujas.

Ghékiere, L. (1991a) *Les Politiques du Logement dans l'Europe de Demain*. La Documentation Française, Union Nationale des Fédérations d'Organismes HLM.

Ghékiere, L. (1991b) *Marchés et Politiques du Logement dans la CEE*. La Documentation Française, Union Nationale des Fédérations d'Organismes HLM.

Green, H. and Trache, H. (2003) *Partenariat Public/Privé: L'Intervention des Investisseurs Privés dans les Projets de Renouvellement Urbain*. Paris: Caisse des Dépôts et Consignations.

Grive, A. (1998) *Une Étude du Système de Planification Territoriale en Angleterre: l'Exemple du District de Shepway (Kent)*. Dunkirk: Université du Littoral, Côte d'Opal. Ma.D Geography.

Kleinmann, M. (1996) *Housing, Welfare and the State in Europe: A Comparative Analysis of Britain, France and Germany*. Camberley: Edward Elgar.

Le Galès, P. (1993) *Politiques Urbaines et Développement Local*. Paris: L'Harmattan.

Le Galès, P. and Mawson, J. (1994) *Management Innovations in Urban Policy: Lessons from France*. London: Local Government Management Board.

Le Galès, P. and Parkinson, M. (1994) *Policies for Cities in Britain and France: A Comparative Assessment*. London: The Franco-British Council.

Loew, S. (1978) *Planning in Britain and France*. Occasional Paper. London: South Bank University.

Loew, S. and Redding, B. (1986) 'Les "Planning Gains" en Grande-Bretagne', in *Produire des Terrains à Batir*. Paris: ADEF.

Marcou, G. (1999) 'France', in *The Compendium of Spatial Planning Systems and Policies*. DG XIV. Brussels: European Union.

Masser, I. and Williams, D. (1998) *Learning from Other Countries*. Norwich: Geo Books.

McConnel, R.S. (1976) *Theories for Planning*. Oxford: Pergamon.

McCrone, G. and Stephens, M. (1995) *Housing Policy in Britain and Europe*. London: UCL Press.

Ministry of Agriculture Fisheries and Food, Department of the Environment, Transport and the Regions (2000) *Our Countryside: The Future*. London: The Stationery Office.

Nadin, V. (1999) 'The United Kingdom', in *The Compendium of Spatial Planning Systems and Policies*. DG XIV. Brussels: European Union.

Office of the Deputy Prime Minister (2006) *The State of the Cities*. London: The Stationery Office.

Power, A. (1993) *Hovels to High Rise: State Housing in Europe since 1850*. London: Routledge.

Renard, V. and Vilmin, T. (1990) *Politiques Foncières Comparées: Grande-Bretagne*. Paris: ADEF

Rodière, R. (1979) *Introduction au Droit Comparé*. Paris: Dalloz.

Scargill, I. (1983) *Urban France*. London: Croom Helm.

Scottish Executive (2005) *Review of Scotland's Cities*. Edinburgh: The Stationery Office.

Urban Task Force (1999) *Towards an Urban Renaissance*. London: Spon.

Wilmott, P. and Murie, A. (1988) *Polarisation and Social Housing: The British and French Experience*. London: Policy Studies Institute.

Chapter 2

Contemporary urban and regional changes and policy problems

Stuart Farthing and Jean-Paul Carrière

Introduction

Planning systems in the United Kingdom and France have traditionally been concerned with managing trends in urban and regional growth and with the spatial organisation of urban areas. At the turn of the twenty-first century, key planning policy themes across Europe are economic development and environmental sustainability (CEC 1999) at a time when the 'performance' and competitiveness of cities are seen to be central both to regional and national prosperity. This analysis of urban performance draws on the theory that both cities and societies are in a period of dramatic transition (van Weesep and Dieleman 1993), based on fundamental technological developments – particularly information technology – and, as society changes, it is argued, so the functions of cities have been transformed. The informational economy has produced the 'informational city' (Castells 1989). As a result of these and other trends, Hall (1993) has discerned the emergence of a new kind of urban hierarchy in Europe with global cities like London and Paris concentrating key command and control functions. But this process of change has been both a cause and a consequence of growing competition between European cities and regions (Lever 1993) for investment, population and jobs. Competitiveness has thus become a major policy concern in both countries. This trend and growing environmental concerns have also led to renewed debates about the spatial structure of urban regions. The management of urban sprawl has become a significant challenge. 'Urban renaissance' or 'renouvellement urbain', are the fashionable labels used to express current policy stances to this issue.

This chapter does two things. First, it provides a broad brush description of the nature of urban and regional trends in the UK and France as a context for understanding the way that the common themes of competitiveness and environmental sustainability have been interpreted in each country. The argument developed here is that the context within which they are discussed and the terms of the debate have been shaped by their respective histories of urbanisation and industrialisation, and by some basic facts of geography. Second, it considers the broad policy response to the problems of regional and city region management.

Urban and regional change in the 1980s and 1990s

Regional trends

Both countries share the common experience of having primate cities – the large capital cities of Paris and London – which dominate their respective urban systems, having done so for centuries, and whose growth has been the object of concern of varying nature over recent years. It is clear that in terms of the economy, employment and population these cities and the regions within which they are located represent a large proportion of the population, employment and Gross Domestic Product (GDP).

Two aspects of the regional problem are evident, however, where there are some contrasts between the two countries. The key difference between Britain and France here lies in the industrialisation process of the nineteenth century. This was later in France than the UK, and affected a limited area of the country being concentrated in regions to the north and east of France. Thus the problem of ex-industrial regions has been a less significant component of the French regional problem than it has been in Britain in the 1970s and 1980s. Second, the fact that many have described France as a predominantly rural country until World War II, and given the relatively late urbanisation of the country over the period 1950–70 (discussed below), this means that declining rural regions, experiencing both population loss and the decline of agricultural employment, have been a significant feature of the French regional problem in the postwar period. Areas to the south and west of the country have traditionally been concerned and although this historical legacy was much less significant by the 1990s, it was still important in some regions and departments.

In recent decades, a 'sun belt' pattern of regional growth has been identified both within countries in Europe (Jones 1991; Dunford 1993) and in a broad region of southern Europe from northern Italy through southern and coastal western France to Spain. This trend is moving population away from the traditional core areas of their national territories. In both Britain and France, this pattern has continued in the 1990s. There is a general trend for the highest growth rates and high net in-migration to be in the regions to the south and east of England in the region around London, and areas of decline to be in the north and west, particularly those regions closely linked to the major urban areas or conurbations of Manchester, Liverpool, Birmingham, Glasgow, Tyneside. In France growth has been strongest in the less urbanised regions of western and southern France, and also in Alsace. In general these regions had the highest rates of in-migration in the 1990s (Figures 2.1 to 2.3).

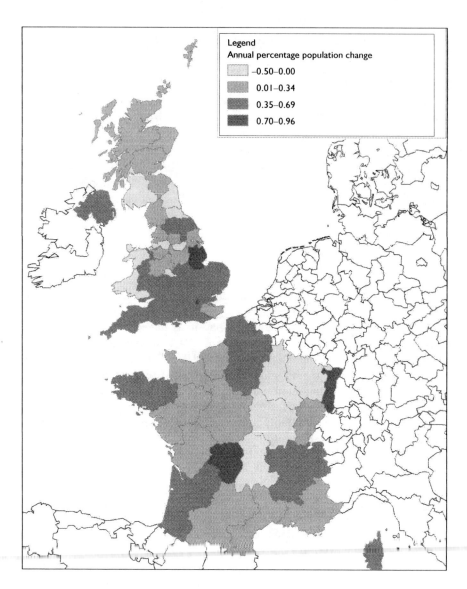

Figure 2.1 Total population change in the 1990s

Source: Mid-year population estimates from ONS; GRO Scotland; NISRA; INSEE.
Note: The data for France are for 1990–1999; data for the UK are for 1991–2001.

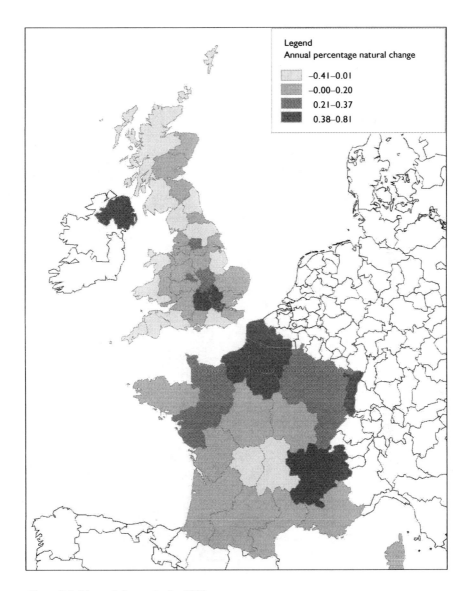

Figure 2.2 Natural change in the 1990s

Source: Mid-year population estimates from ONS; GRO Scotland; NISRA; INSEE.
Note: The data for France are for 1990–1999; data for the UK are for 1991–2001.

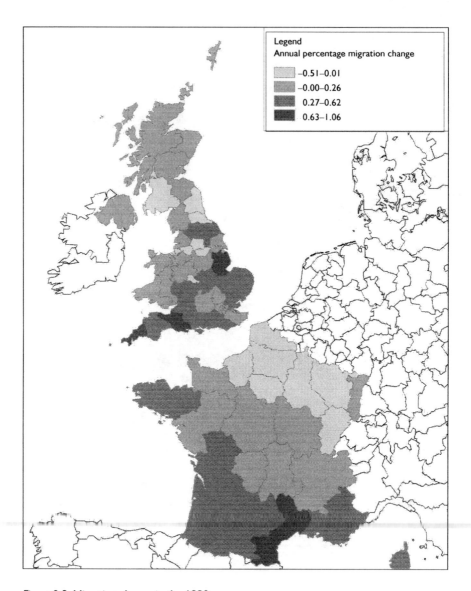

Figure 2.3 Migration change in the 1990s

Source: Mid-year population estimates from ONS; GRO Scotland; NISRA; INSEE.
Note: The data for France are for 1990–1999; data for the UK are for 1991–2001.

Urban trends

In exploring these issues, it is important to understand the urban history of both countries. In Britain, urbanisation and the development of a large number of the main cities in the country were linked with nineteenth-century industrialisation. Manchester, Liverpool, Sheffield, Leeds, Newcastle, Glasgow, and Belfast are notable examples but there are many smaller towns which also expanded under industrialisation. This radically transformed the urban system. In France, urbanisation took place in two cycles. The first in the late nineteenth century was associated with the industrialisation of the country. According to Le Galès (1991: 206), this modified but, in contrast to the British case, did not lead to a complete change in the urban structure. Cities in the north like Lille, Roubaix and Tourcoing, those in Lorraine and in the upper reaches of the Loire (Le Creusot, Saint-Étienne) expanded but Paris maintained its importance within the French urban system. Some cities declined – Le Galès mentions Rennes, Nîmes, Orléans, Besançon, Montpellier – but others like Lyon and Marseille enjoyed continuous growth.

The second period of French urbanisation and industrialisation took place in the period between 1950 and 1970. France was a much less urbanised country than Britain at the end of World War II but by the 1980s, it had achieved levels of urbanisation close to that in Britain. At the beginning of the twenty-first century, as measured by those living in built-up areas, the figure was 76 per cent in France (Pumain 2004) and 80 per cent in the UK. This process of urbanisation was described by Le Galès as the 'revenge of the *ancien régime* cities' – the regional capitals like Bordeaux, Nantes, Rennes, Toulouse, Montpellier – on the industrial cities. Most French cities saw dramatic population growth, some doubling in size in 30 years or so. Three processes were involved: rebuilding of war-damaged cities; national population increase fuelled by high birth rates and international migration from Southern Europe and North Africa; rural–urban migration within France linked to the decline of agricultural employment (Prud'homme and Nicot 2004). The process of dramatic urban growth slowed in the 1970s.

British cities started to show problems of urban decline from the 1960s, in a pattern which affected the largest cities first, then moved down the urban hierarchy to somewhat smaller freestanding cities. Begg *et al.* (1986) show that employment in manufacturing in the core of the largest cities (the conurbations) and in the freestanding cities (250,000+ population) started to decline from the 1950s but service sector growth disguised this decline until the 1960s when service sector growth too declined in the centres of the conurbations. Service sector growth in the freestanding cities in the 1960s postponed the appearance of total employment decline until the 1970s. The largest British cities had been declining in population since the 1950s (Champion and Townsend 1990). So at a time when British cities were showing signs of urban decline, French cities were coming to the end of a period of sustained employment and population growth. At the end of the 1970s too there was in Britain a serious recession which affected manufacturing more than other sectors, particularly in the large conurbations (Fothergill *et al.* 1985 quoted in Turok and Edge 1999).

International migration has been an important urban policy issue in both countries. White (1993) suggests that there have been three waves of international migration affecting postwar Europe: the guest worker or labour migration phenomenon of the 1950s and 1960s which finished with the 1973 oil shock; the subsequent phase of family re-unification, and over the 1980s and 1990s the emergence of a 'post-industrial' pattern which involves a mix of highly skilled workers, clandestine migrants and asylum seekers. In both countries, policy since the 1970s has attempted to stem mass immigration. International migration has continued to be a significant phenomenon in both countries: it has contributed to national population growth at a time of low levels of natural change in the 1980s and 1990s (Champion 1994) and in the case of the UK by the end of the 1990s, it had become the main source of growth (ONS 2005). In consequence there is a large foreign born population in both countries (Table 2.1).

The urban dimension to these trends results from the attraction of immigrant groups predominantly but not exclusively to large urban areas following the growing job opportunities in the post-war period. The re-organisation of European economies from the 1970s, and rising levels of unemployment in the 1980s have impacted strongly on certain immigrant groups (Cross 1996) leading to a situation in the main cities of the UK and France in which ethnically identifiable groups are living in poor environmental conditions with high unemployment rates, prompting a debate about social exclusion (see, for example, Allen *et al.* 1998).

The consequence of these different histories is that in the 1980s and 1990s, the nature of the urban problem was quite different in Britain and France. In France it was not, unlike the case in Britain, a problem of declining large cities; nor was it a problem of industrial decline (though these problems existed in some cities in the North and East of the country); nor was it an 'inner city' problem with falling population but concentrations of ethnic minority groups. In France urban problems were associated above all with the suburbs of towns where housing market processes have led to the segregation of immigrant communities. Such problems also occur in Britain (Power 1998) but with a less distinctive suburban geography.

How do trends in the 1980s and 1990s affect the perception of the urban problem in the early years of the twenty-first century? The performance and competitiveness of cities have become the dominant perspective from which these issues are viewed. In the 1980s Paris out-performed the other cities in France. Table 2.2 suggests that there was a clear relationship between urban size and growth. By the 1990s, the growth rate of Paris had declined relative to the other large cities so that growth was faster in the country's

Table 2.1 Foreign born population in France and the UK, around 1990 and 2000

		Foreign born population	Percentage of national population
France	1990	3,586,000	6.4%
France	1999	3,263,000	5.6%
UK	1991	3,835,400	6.7%
UK	2001	4,896,000	8.3%

Table 2.2 Population and employment: average annual rates of growth by size of city (%)

	1980s		1990s	
	Population	Employment	Population	Employment
Paris	0.83	1.0	0.30	0.0
Large cities	0.67	0.6	0.52	0.6
Other areas	0.22	–0.3	0.25	0.4
France	0.52	0.4	0.37	0.3
London	0.04	–0.9	0.70	1.9
Large cities	–0.26	–0.5	–0.15	1.0
Other areas	0.34	0.7	0.43	1.3
UK	0.18	0.1	0.28	1.3

Source: Estimates based on Turok and Edge (1999); State of the Cities Report; Prud'homme and Nicot (2004); ONS Revised Population Estimates 1982–2000; www.nomisweb.co.uk.

Note: Large cities in France are those with over 100,000 population (1999). Large cities in the UK are those with over 250,000 population (1991). Annual percentage growth rates for the 1980s have been calculated over the period 1982–90 in France and 1981–91 in the UK. For the 1990s, growth rates have been calculated over the period 1990–9 in France and 1991–2001 in the UK.

biggest cities with 11 cities gaining half the total urban population growth. Population growth was fastest in the arc of metropoles furthest from Paris: Toulouse, Montpellier, Nantes, Rennes, Strasbourg. A rather similar picture is found for employment growth rates. Paris out-performed other French cities in the 1980s but experienced a significant downturn in the 1990s recording stable levels of employment between 1990 and 1999. Large cities in France (those with 100,000+ population, excluding Paris) as a group maintained their employment growth rates between the 1980s and the 1990s and, because of the decline in the performance of Paris in the 1990s, have been the best performing places within France, growing at twice the national rate. These trends have confirmed the strength of the regional capitals, and along with the regional trends in population growth suggest that regional inequalities are being addressed. These trends can also be seen as a success of regional policy (Aménagement du Territoire) (see Caro *et al.* 2000), the case of Toulouse being cited as one of the most spectacular successes (Cicholawz 2005), despite new intra-regional imbalances, though accounts of the decline of Paris in the French urban system must be nuanced by a recognition of its strong role in the knowledge economy.

Whilst in the 1980s in France there was a positive association between growth and urban size, the reverse was the case in the UK where, continuing trends dating back over 20 years (Turok and Edge 1999) the smallest cities, towns and more rural areas showed the fastest growth rates and where London and the 20 largest cities (250,000+ population) lost population and jobs. London's population has grown dramatically in the 1990s, under the influence of both strong natural increase and increasingly through international migration, though there is a debate about the numbers involved. The rate of population decline of the other large cities in the UK has slowed. There has been a dramatic change in employment generation in the UK in the 1990s corresponding to a sustained economic upturn in the national economy. London has been by far the most successful of the big cities but the other large cities, though less buoyant, also grew in the 1990s. There are signs of the long awaited 'urban resurgence' in the UK. Parkinson *et al.* (2005) show that there has been a regional dimension to urban performance with places in the south and east of England generating jobs above the national average rate whilst places in the north and west were performing on average below the national average. This report shows that there was something of a U-shaped relationship between urban size and employment growth, with the largest cities growing fast, the slowest rates of growth in middle-sized urban places and the fastest growth in small towns and rural areas.

The key influence shaping perceptions here has been the role of London and its importance to the national economy. Nothing, it is argued, must be done to threaten this. This has had three consequences. First, it has reinforced the view that regional inequalities cannot be addressed by trying to restrain the growth of London and that regional endogenous development will be the key to more competitive regions. Second, there is a growing view that at the heart of competitive regions will be competitive cities: the resurgence of the larger cities is taken as a sign of this. Finally, the shortage and high cost of housing in and around London, a problem widely attributed to the planning system, are seen as a threat to London's and the nation's prosperity.

The spatial organisation of cities

Cities may grow by both population growth within given boundaries but also by spatial expansion and extension of cities into the surrounding areas. The process of suburbanisation was well established in Britain before the end of the nineteenth century and it received a major boost in the inter-war period when the built-up area of London for example doubled in size (Hall 1989). These processes are a more recent phenomenon in France, reflecting France's later urbanisation. Sallez and Burgi (2004) say that suburbanisation began after World War I but accelerated after World War II, as industry moved from dense urban areas to the suburbs. But urban growth has not just been at the edge of the city, taking place by extension of the built-up area. It has also impacted on other settlements in the hinterland of a large city, sometimes some distance from the principal city. Thus rather than the city being defined purely by its built-up area, there is a recognition that there are wider 'city regions' which include these outlying areas. This stage of growth was observable in France in the 1970s.

However, it is much easier to measure these trends in France than in the UK. One reason is that the larger size of France and the relatively small number of large cities means that most cities in France are freestanding, surrounded by rural hinterlands. Another reason is that the French census organisation INSEE measures these city regions in terms of a core urban 'pôle' of 5,000 or more jobs, plus the surrounding communes linked together by journey to work patterns. On the one hand, it is possible to argue that population patterns within urban areas are beginning to show increasingly similar patterns. In the UK losses of population in central cities has been a marked feature of urban change in the postwar period. This phenomenon is beginning to appear in some cities in France. The central commune in the cities of Paris, Lyons and Bordeaux has lost population. On the other hand, in rapidly growing cities – Nantes, Toulouse, Aix, Montpellier, Tours, Poitiers – central areas are still gaining population. Meanwhile, functional urban areas increased their surface area by one-third in the 1990s (Sallez and Burgi 2004) and results of the partial Census of 2005 show that there has been continued very rapid growth at the periphery of these areas (15–25 kms from the urban core).

Two sets of factors are conventionally discussed in relation to the explanation of urban population trends within urban regions: factors affecting the distribution of economic activity (and employment) and factors affecting household locational decisions. Of course these are not independent. In addition there are a range of public policy and institutional factors which have been suggested that shape sprawl. Again, it is not possible to make definitive claims about the impact of different factors in the two countries but merely to point to some possibilities.

Within city regions, there has been an urban–rural shift in all sectors of employment in the UK over a considerable period, but how much of this is employment decentralisation within city regions and how much the greater growth of freestanding but smaller city regions is less clear. The relationship between population change and employment change is also unclear. Recently employment loss in big cities in the UK has been more rapid than population decentralisation, leading to the suggestion that job growth in peripheral areas is beginning to lead rather than follow population decentralisation (Turok and Edge 1999). In France, according to Huriot (2004), the spread of employment from urban cores is more recent and less marked than population. Two major features characterise changes in urban employment in France. First, the concentration of employment within urban agglomerations rose from 1962 until 1990. Thereafter, employment grew more rapidly in the peri-urban fringe leading to a slight decline in concentration within the built-up area (agglomération) by the end of the 1990s. The second feature is the suburbanisation of employment within these urban agglomerations. In general, employment grew faster in the suburbs than in city centres over this period. Prud'homme and Nicot (2004) conclude that urban areas did not grow in the 1990s because firms settled in peripheral areas but because people in outlying areas commuted in larger numbers to the urban centre, implying a significant increase in mobility.

In addition to the changes brought about by natural change and by migration, patterns of household formation have had significant impacts on the changing spatial distribution of population in both countries. Falling average household size (Ogden and Hall 2000) means that the housing stock in cities accommodates a smaller population. Average household sizes are the same in the UK and in France at 2.4. Unless the housing stock of the cities can be expanded by new building and conversions, and this is limited by constraints on space in the major cities, population will overspill into surrounding areas. This process rather than population growth has been a major determinant of rural land conversion within urban regions in both countries.

The shift in policy towards the market in housing provision and towards owner-occupation as a tenure for the majority of households has occurred in both countries but in this trend, the UK has preceded France. In consequence, the level of owner-occupation is higher in the UK at 69 per cent compared with 56 per cent in France, but this has been a strongly growing sector in France and the nature of the owner occupied product 'pavillons' (houses with gardens) in France is land extensive and is likely to have contributed to urban spread.

The structure of local government in the two countries plays a part in explaining recent patterns of population growth. To some degree, the existence of a large number of small communes in France in the periphery of urban areas encourages some competition between communes for development. A growing population, and particularly, a growing employment base increases commune income through local taxes. Communes have thus been willing to zone land for development, to set attractive tax rates for business uses in competition with neighbouring municipalities (especially the urban core municipalities) and through this mechanism there has been some encouragement of urban spread. In the UK larger local government units exist and further urban growth – at least in the form of new housing

– in these areas is less politically acceptable whilst the revenue benefits of increased population are slow to materialise (Barker Report 2004).

Public policies – particularly housing and transport policies – have contributed to but also directed urban sprawl in both countries. It is impossible to assess the effect of recent public policy on urban outcomes but it is possible that the emphasis on the 60 per cent target for re-use of brown field land for housing in the UK has acted to restrain further urban sprawl in the 1990s. In France, housing policies designed to solve housing shortages by building large blocks of flats supported the growth of urban areas without significant sprawl into the 1960s. Subsequently, from 1977 there were changes in the subsidy system for housing which shifted subsidy from organisations building housing to consumers seeking housing. This personal subsidy took the form of loan guarantees for low income households seeking to buy property which in turn encouraged the building of single family dwellings. In both countries transport policies which supported the use of the private car have also facilitated sprawl. The 1980s in the UK was a period in which policy sought to encourage investment in roads to facilitate the use of private cars though this came to a halt in the early 1990s. Pumain (2004) argues that the French state has been particularly active in creating infrastructure favourable to the car, citing motorways and the building of ring roads around cities. Whilst the planning system in the UK has generally aimed to manage and minimise urban sprawl, in France policy has neither explicitly encouraged or discouraged it. However, institutional arrangements have facilitated it. The planning system in the UK has concentrated housing growth whilst in France a more diffuse pattern of urban growth seems to be the consequence.

Rural trends

Urbanisation has been a significant feature of the postwar period in France and the percentage of the population living in urban settlements is now very close to that in the UK. The processes of urban sprawl discussed in the previous section mean that places within commuting distance of the major cities in France are experiencing considerable population growth pressures. And the area of the national territory falling outside 'aires urbaines' is in decline. This has, in consequence, had an impact on the enumerated rural population. Those living outside 'aires urbaines' fell from 13.4 million in 1990 to 10.6 million in 1999, a fall of 2.8 million, the rural population by this measure standing at 18 per cent of French population in 1999 (Sallez and Burgi 2004).

During the postwar period many of France's remote rural regions experienced both a decline of agricultural employment and population loss through net out-migration to the cities and through an excess of deaths over births. This process has nearly come to an end. In the last two decades, some areas have continued to lose population. From 1982–90, 10,227 communes in France lost population, in total amounting to about 400,000 people. In the 1990s, fewer communes lost population (8,966) and aggregate population loss for these rural communes was only around 280,000. 'Deep' rural areas losing population are located in regions in the so-called 'arid diagonal' – the rural central regions located along an axis from South West to North East (see Figure 2.1). Rural regions which are growing by in-migration are in the south and on the coast (Figure 2.3).

The territory of the UK is much smaller than that of France, and population densities in the two countries reflect these differences with 108 persons per km² in France and 247 persons per km² in the UK, and 385 in England, the most populous part of the UK. Similar peri-urban growth pressures are experienced in both countries but because the UK is much smaller, less of the country is remote from large urban areas. For reasons connected with changing definitions over time, and problems with census under-enumeration of the population, the changing rural population cannot easily be measured. The scale at which analysis is conducted also affects the picture obtained. Districts identified after the 1991 census as 'remoter rural areas' are growing as a category, though less rapidly than in the 1980s (Champion 2004) but our analysis of population change (Figure 2.1) at NUTS2 level shows population decline in the 1990s in parts of West Wales and Northern England, though in both cases the results are somewhat distorted by the presence of declining urban areas within their boundaries. These statistical issues and the policy issues raised by the role of small towns in rural areas are discussed in detail by Carrière, Farthing and Fournier (Chapter 8).

Responses to urban and regional change

This section looks, in turn, at the policy response to the issues of regional inequalities and to urban sprawl.

Regional inequalities

In both countries there are regional inequalities in prosperity, employment and population trends. Traditional forms of regional policy in Western Europe associated with the welfare state in which governments sought to direct investment and jobs to particular regions have been undermined by the mobility of transnational companies and of capital flows, as well as fiscal pressures and competition policies. A new regionalist model of development based on the promotion of endogenous growth has developed, coexisting in 'uneasy partnership' with the old but with the new model increasingly supplanting the old (Keating 1998: 73) With a long postwar history in France of a commitment to 'l'Aménagement du Territoire', there has remained a commitment to some balance in development opportunities between regions in order to avoid too great an imbalance between the poorest western and central regions and the more developed Paris and eastern regions. Whilst Cicholawz (2005) describes this form of regional policy as suffering a slow decline from its high point in the 1960s there have remained some attempts to control employment growth in the Paris area and encouragement to the transfer of jobs to the provinces, a multi-scalar concept of planning with agreements called 'Contrats de Plan' (introduced in 1983) between the central State and the regions, which are contracts for both financing and programming public investment and support. As discussed above the strong performance of regional capitals in the 1990s has been taken as evidence that past regional policy has been successful. However, there is some way to go if these cities are to compete with similar cities elsewhere in Europe (Rozenblatt and Cecille 2003). We see the recent announcement of the policy of 'pôles de competitivité' and 'appel à coopération métropolitaine' which aims to support cities seeking to develop their high-level economic functions as signs that territorial competitiveness has now become the key concept behind national policy. The change of name of DATAR to DIACT (Délégation Interministérielle à l'Aménagement et à la Compétitivité des Territoires) is symbolic in this regard.

By contrast in the UK, there is some acknowledgement of the existence of these regional variations, and policy targets have been set which aim to reduce these differences. However at best the resurgence of regional planning in recent years can be seen as an attempt to manage and coordinate growth within regions rather than deal with the balance of development between regions. Much has been made of the Northern Way Growth Strategy which promotes the growth of eight city regions in the north of England as a way of boosting employment and productivity in this broad region and reducing the gap between 'north' and 'south' (ODPM 2004). If these regional targets are achieved, they will be the result of whatever endogenous development opportunities have produced. Efforts to influence the distribution of economic activity more directly are seen to threaten to divert development to other regions of Europe. There are no agreements between central and regional government about regional public investment. Responsibility for development has been devolved to Wales and Scotland. This is a far cry from the regional planning and policy of the 1960s where attempts were made to produce a balance of population and economic activity between regions within the UK. The absence of these national policy goals means that there remains competition between regions for inward investment and the location of national projects (Herschel and Newman 2003: 123). Another notable feature of regional policy in the UK, particularly in England, is the division between regional economic development and regional planning. Here there can be conflicts between economic and planning interpretations of the concept of sustainable development with economic development being associated with economic growth and competitiveness, whilst planning tends to emphasise environmental interpretations (Haughton and Counsell 2004). Though the new spatial planning agenda aims to integrate both regional policy and planning, there are doubts about its ability to overcome this divide.

Urban sprawl

Whilst difficult to measure comparatively, there is some agreement that urban sprawl has been a later phenomenon in France than in the UK, essentially dating from the 1970s. For this reason and because of the greater size and lower density of population in the country, it is not surprising that it has only comparatively recently become a significant issue in France.

How have both countries responded to these trends? Both have responded by adopting 'urban compaction' policies which stress the importance of sustainable development. The approach building on a long-standing tradition of rural protection was adopted in the UK under the umbrella of sustainable development, from the early to mid-1990s onwards and has become increasingly central to planning policy. It was adopted in the late 1990s in France with a series of Acts – la Loi Chevènement, la Loi d'Orientation pour l'Aménagement et le Développement Durable du Territoire (LOADDT), la Loi Relative à la Solidarité et au Renouvellement Urbains (SRU).

'Urban renaissance' or 'renouvellement urbain' is a fashionable ideology in both countries. Having roots in, amongst other things, the EC's Green paper on the Urban Environment (CEC 1990), urban compaction policies involve a range of rather similar and inter-linked policies: the concentration of development within existing urban areas, urban regeneration, higher densities, mixed use, social integration and transport policies which support public transport and attempt to restrict automobile use. This latter approach reflects the view that there should be better integration of urban policies, particularly transport and land use policies. There appear to be some differ-ences in emphasis with a particular focus in the UK on the re-use of previously used urban land.

There have also been institutional changes in both countries to produce more appropriate territorial governance for the management of urban development. The institutional restructuring, too, has different emphases: there is a 'new localism' in French planning, whilst in Britain there is a 'new regionalism'. The French response has involved some rather dramatic changes in institutional structures at the urban level. France has a rather fragmented system of local government with urban areas being composed of large numbers of small communes. There have been various attempts to bring these together for service provision in urban areas but now the groupings of communes created by the Loi Chevènement, 'communautés urbaines' (for the biggest cities), 'communautés d'agglomération' (medium-sized towns) and 'communautés de communes' (smaller communes) has led to the voluntary creation of two-tier city governance with the transfer of responsibilities and fiscal resources previously held at commune level to the new bodies. The new system introduced by LOADDT identified a new local level for planning: the 'pays' or 'agglomération' based on regions defined approximately in terms of travel to work patterns. These areas have considerable advantages over the framework provided by 'communes' and 'départements' in providing the opportunity for integrated urban policies and planning at the city region scale. The new types of policy guidance/ instruments of planning – Schéma de Cohérence Territoriale (SCOT), Plan Local de l'Urbanisme (PLU) – which have been introduced represent a move towards a more strategic, socially and environmentally informed, style of planning with the requirement for public participation close to the British model. There are also clear attempts to integrate various sectoral policies with the new instruments of planning. Transport policies but also housing, economic development, and retailing plans need to be compatible with the SCOT, not just take them into account.

As far as the control of urban sprawl is concerned, the reformed planning system in the UK has been accompanied by modest institutional change, and one which some critics have said will weaken such controls. Responsibility for strategic planning now rests at the regional level with Regional Assemblies. There have been no proposals for the reform of institutional structures at city region level. To understand why this might be, we need to look briefly at the issue of housing supply which has been the dominant planning policy issue in Britain for many years. What has made the issue more important in recent years has been the decline of the mass social housing programme, and what Kleinman (1996) calls the collapse of traditional housing policy. One consequence is that planning policy through its identification of land for housing development and the grant of planning permission has become a significant variable affecting the supply of land for housing and the sensitivity of land supply to housing demand becomes an important issue (Barker 2004). Local authorities in peripheral areas of city regions have adopted, it is widely perceived, a strongly protectionist stance towards development, stressing the environmental costs of further growth under pressure from local residents. There has thus been an under-supply of housing in southern regions of England and the government has responded by identifying four 'growth areas' in and around the South East to address this imbalance in the Sustainable Communities Plan (ODPM 2003). Responsibility vested at the regional level for identifying local housing growth targets, by a body which is not directly elected, is to some degree removed from local political pressure.

New regional spatial plans which are intended to coordinate policy across sectors are being produced with the possibility of sub-regional plans where these are deemed necessary. Structure plans which were produced at county level and which had some capacity to take account of urban-rural linkages have been abolished. Unlike the French system there does not seem to be a clear mechanism by which transport and planning policies will be coordinated at the city region scale except as one critic put it by 'pleading nicely'.

Discussion and conclusions

What conclusions can we draw from this exploration of spatial trends and policy responses in the two countries? There is clearly a degree of convergence of policy themes in both Britain and France. Policy makers here as elsewhere in Europe (see Chapter 7 by Sykes and Motte on the ESDP) are concerned with the twin challenges of competitiveness and environmental sustainability. In both countries the key to regional growth, and the reduction of inequalities between regions, is seen to lie in the promotion of endogenous growth (rather than the redistribution of growth between regions) and in the competitiveness of the large, regional cities. Our analysis suggests that the urban and regional 'success stories' in the 1990s in France and the UK were, respectively, regional capitals and the global city of London. In both countries governments are seeking to build on these successes. In France, the conditions for the formal transition to a more competitive regional and urban policy are favourable in the sense that the trends towards a more balanced distribution of population and economic activity seem to exist, and moreover can be presented as a consequence of past public policy. In the UK, despite the north–south drift and acknowledged regional inequalities, we argue that public policy is shaped first and foremost by the desire to promote the further international success of London and its surrounding region.

Concern about the management of the spatial organisation of urban areas, balancing environmental, social and economic objectives under the banner of sustainable development has been a common trend in both countries. It is difficult to assess the complex relationships between economic, social and policy factors promoting urban sprawl. Inter-communal competition for investment has certainly been a feature of urban development processes in France but it is clear that, here, attitudes to the issue changed in the 1990s. Breuillard, Stephenson and Sadoux discuss the more general evolution of administrative frameworks for planning in Chapter 4. There has been a concern for more effective city region management and the re-scaling of urban governance to pursue policy integration. A cooperative two-tier structure of urban governance is evolving in French city regions. In the UK, or in parts of England at least, there is a perception that the control of urban growth has been too effective. The planning system in peripheral areas of city regions has responded to local opposition to housing growth, which has led to the under-supply of housing in the south of England. The Sustainable Communities Plan (ODPM 2003) has been one response to this. In consequence, institutional restructuring has led to responsibility for strategic planning being vested at regional level, remote from local democratic pressures.

A third common theme has been the adoption of more comprehensive forms of spatial planning which seek to integrate a range of sectoral policies for housing, transport, economic development, environmental management with recognition of the importance of social inclusion in policy development. Later chapters in this book discuss a range of issues connected with the move to new forms of spatial planning (see particularly Chapter 9 by Fraser and Lerique on urban policy, Chapter 6 by Verhage, Baker and Boino on strategic and spatial planning at city region level, and Chapter 12 by Harman, l'Hostis and Ménerault on transport policy).

Whilst there has been some convergence in policy concerns between the two countries, it is also important to recognise that the context within which they are debated is quite different. The different histories of urbanisation and industrialisation have been emphasised in this chapter. There remain important differences between the UK and France rooted in different national institutions and policy cultures, subjects discussed in the following chapters in this section of the book.

References

Allen. J., Carrs, G. and Madani-pour, A. (1998) *Social Exclusion* (London: Kingsley).

Barker, K. (2004) *Review of Housing Supply Final Report – Recommendations* (Norwich: HMSO).

Begg, I., Moore, B. and Rhodes, J. (1986) 'Economic and social change in urban Britain', in V. Hausner (ed.) *Critical Issues in Urban Economic Development*, Volume I (Oxford: Oxford University Press).

Caro, P., Dard, O. and Daumas, J.C. (2002) *La Politique d'aménagement du territoire. Racines, logiques et résultats* (Rennes: PUR).

Castells, M. (1989) *The Informational City: Information Technology, Economic Restructuring, and the Urban-Regional Process* (Oxford: Basil Blackwell).

Champion, A.G. (1994) 'International migration and demographic change in the developed world', *Urban Studies*, 31: 653–77.

Champion, A.G. (2004) 'The quest for "sustainable communities" in the context of Britain's changing population', Paper presented at the Housing Studies Association Autumn Conference on 'Planning and Housing: Policy and Practice', Belfast, 9–10 September.

Champion, A.G. and Townsend, R. (1990) *Contemporary Britain: A Geographical Perspective* (Cheltenham: Edward Elgar).

Cicholawz, P. (2005) 'France and the ESDP in the context of European integration and Mediterranean cooperation', *European Planning Studies*, 13: 285–95.

Commission of the European Community (CEC) (1990) *Green Paper on the Urban Environment* (Brussels: European Commission).

Commission of the European Community (CEC) (1999) *European Spatial Development Perspective: Towards Balanced and Sustainable Development of the*

Territory of the EU (Luxembourg: Office for Official Publications of the European Communities).

Cross, M. (1996) 'Migration, employment and social change in the new Europe', in P. Rees, J. Stilwell, A. Convey and M. Kupiszewski (eds) *Population Migration in the European Union* (Chichester: John Wiley & Sons).

Dunford, M. (1993) 'Regional disparities in the European Community: evidence from the REGIO databank', *Regional Studies*, 27: 727–44.

Fothergill, S., Kitson, M. and Monk, S. (1985) *Urban Industrial Change: The Causes of the Urban–Rural Contrast in Manufacturing Employment Trends* (London: DoE, HMSO).

Hall, P. (1989) *Urban and Regional Planning* (London: Penguin).

Hall, P. (1993) 'Forces shaping urban Europe', *Urban Studies*, 30(6): 883–98.

Haughton, G. and Counsell, D. (2004) *Regions, Spatial Strategies and Sustainable Development* (London: Routledge).

Herschel, T. and Newman, P. (2003) *Governance of Europe's City Regions* (London: Routledge).

Huriot, J.-M. (2004) 'Concentration and dispersal of employment in French cities', in H.W. Richardson and C.-H.C. Bae (eds) *Urban Sprawl in Western Europe and the United States* (Aldershot: Ashgate), pp. 159–84.

Jones, H. (1991) 'The French Census 1990: the southward drift continues', *Geography* 76: 358–61.

Keating, M. (1998) *The New Regionalism in Western Europe* (Cheltenham: Edward Elgar).

Kleinman, M. (1996) *Housing, Welfare and the State in Europe* (Cheltenham: Edward Elgar).

Le Galès, P. (1991) 'Those French inner cities?', in M. Keith and A. Rogers (eds) *Hollow promises? Rhetoric and Reality in the Inner City* (London: Mansell), pp. 202–18.

Lever, W.F. (1993) 'Competition within the European urban system', *Urban Studies*, 30: 935–48.

Office of the Deputy Prime Minister (ODPM) (2003) *Sustainable Communities: Building for the Future* (London: Office of the Deputy Prime Minister).

Office of the Deputy Prime Minister (ODPM) (2004) *Making it Happen. The Northern Way* (London: HMSO).

ONS (2005) 'The UK population at the start of the 21st century', *Population Trends*, 122: 7–17.

Ogden, P.E. and Hall, R. (2000) 'Households, reurbanisation and the rise of living alone in the principal French cities, 1975–1990', *Urban Studies*, 37: 367–90.

Parkinson, M., Hutchinson, M., Champion, A.G., Coombes, M., Dorling, D., Parks, A., Simmie, J. and Turok, I. (2005) *State of the Cities: A Progress Report to the Delivering Sustainable Communities Summit Office of the Deputy Prime Minister* (London: HMSO).

Power, A. (1998) *Cities on the Edge: The Social Consequences of Mass Housing in Northern Europe* (Basingstoke: Macmillan).

Prud'homme, R. and Nicot, B.-H. (2004) 'Urban sprawl in Rennes and 77 urban areas in France, 1982–1999', in H.W. Richardson and C.-H.C. Bae (eds) *Urban Sprawl in Western Europe and the United States* (Aldershot: Ashgate), pp. 93–114.

Pumain, D. (2004) 'Urban sprawl: is there a French case?', in H.W. Richardson and C.-H.C. Bae (eds) *Urban Sprawl in Western Europe and the United States* (Aldershot: Ashgate), pp. 137–57.

Rozenblatt, C. and Cicille, P. (2003) *Les Villes Européenes: Étude comparative* (Paris: La Documentation française).

Sallez, A. and Burgi, J. (2004) 'Urban sprawl in France 1990–1999', in H.W. Richardson and C.-H.C. Bae (eds) *Urban Sprawl in Western Europe and the United States* (Aldershot: Ashgate), pp. 115–35.

Turok, I. and Edge, N. (1999) *The Jobs Gap in Britain's Cities: Employment Loss and Labour Market Adjustment* (Bristol: Policy Press).

Van Weesep, J. and Dieleman, F.M. (1993) 'Evolving urban Europe: editor's introduction to the special issue', *Urban Studies*, 30: 877–82.

White, P. (1993) 'The social geography of immigrants in European cities: the geography of arrival', in R. King (ed.) *The New Geography of European Migrations* (London: Belhaven), pp. 47–66.

Chapter 3

Land law, land markets and planning

Matthieu Galey and Philip Booth

Introduction

One of the purposes of this book is to find explanations for the differences
in the way that the French and the British undertake what is essentially a
similar activity, the management of the use and development of land. It is
characteristically an activity undertaken by public authorities of whatever
kind, who justify their work by reference to a general or public interest,
however that may be defined. In spite of these similarities both the process
and content of planning differs in Britain and France. In this chapter we
argue that one explanation for the differences lies in the fact that planning,
as a public activity, has nevertheless to engage with private property interests.
Indeed the introduction of public control of future land use and development
was a response to the perceived inadequacies of the land market in allocating
land for future development in an equitable fashion. Planning as a sphere
of activity thus finds itself at a crucial interface between public and private
action and of necessity represents an 'interference' in interests in, and rights
to, private property. Some understanding of property in land becomes a
necessary part of an effective public intervention in the way land is used and
developed.

Here, we take the argument further. The understanding of property,
property interests and property rights and their articulation in a body of law
is considerably older than any of the attempts to legislate for public action in
the planning and development of land. Planning, we may argue, is therefore
a response to a well developed system of property very longstanding in both
countries. We may argue further that the planning systems and the law that
underpins them have been substantially influenced by conceptualisations
of property rights and interests. And even a cursory glance at land law in
both countries reveals large differences in the question of property rights,
interests and relations. The State in France and Britain has had to position
itself very differently in each country in order to deal effectively with future
development. That in turn has found its expression in the form that planning
law takes and the nature of planning instruments in both. In this chapter,

we begin by exploring the very different character of the law of property in Britain and France and the nature of interests in property. We continue by looking at the nature of those who exercise property rights and in particular at the way in which the private sector has traditionally allowed for future development to take place. We then move to consider how the State in both countries has rationalised its intervention in private property and how it has developed instruments that respond to the particularities of property in each. The underlying theme is that the influence of administrative and institutional traditions is not a sufficient explanation for the differences that are apparent.

Land ownership and the land market

The way ownership of land is legally conceived and formalised, the types of systems of property that stem from those conceptions, as well as the spatial structure of landed ownership they favour, explain first the way in which the *land problem* emerged in both French and English systems.

Put very approximately, while British land law has evolved from a feudal system that still marks the understanding of property relations, even if the social basis of feudalism has vanished, France jettisoned the feudal system at the Revolution and re-established in the civil code a property system inspired by Roman law. In order to build a bridge between the two legal systems, ownership may be usefully conceived as a set of *relationships* both between the landowner and the land appropriated, and the land and the landowner and others in respect of that land (Krueckerberg 1995). The distinction between the two systems is then well captured by the contrasting typologies of property law that the nineteenth-century American legal theorist, Noyes, presents. The contrast that he makes is between what he describes as lineal or feudal property systems, represented by British property law, and collateral or allodial systems, into which category French property law falls:

> The Roman legal system of property we shall characterize as the allodial, or collateral, system. It is the holding in absolute and original right by independent and coequal units; the character of the interest being the same. The English legal system of property, we shall call (...) the feudal, or lineal, system. It is the holding, except at the apex, in a dependent and perhaps derivative right by successive and ranked units, according to varying degrees of ascendancy; the character of the interest being mutually exclusive.
>
> (Noyes 1936: 222)

This typology has been well developed by Déterville-Papandréou (1996) in the context of French and English law. Within the English derivative and lineal system of property, ownership is partial and contingent on others and the transfer of property rights is rarely, if ever, definitive. On the contrary, in French land law, rights to property must be transferred in their entirety, even if they have been fragmented, such that no control over any part of them can be retained (Déterville-Papandréou 1996). Moreover, the persistence of such a derivative and lineal system of property in common law contexts has led to a conceptualisation within Anglo-American thinking about property as being a bundle of rights (Galey 2006), a phrase that originated with Hohfeld in the early twentieth century (Hohfeld 1913, 1917) and has been regularly invoked since (see Demsetz 1967; Gray and Symes 1981).

The feudal system of property, possibly imposed in England in a purer form than in continental Europe because of the colonisation of the country by the Normans, was founded on the principle that the occupation and enjoyment of land was the reward for service. Landownership was conditional upon service to a feudal superior in a hierarchy in which only the sovereign had absolute ownership of land. Land, therefore, was a mark of social status; but the impact of the system was to ensure that for any one parcel of land there would be several people who might claim an interest simultaneously, and such interests might include the right to future occupation and enjoyment. The twin concepts generated by this system were those of *tenure*, the right to benefit from the land for the time being, as against absolute ownership, and the *estate*, which was a way of giving concrete existence to the nature of the interest that any one person might have in the parcel of land in question (Lawson 1951; Booth 2002).

How long a 'pure' feudal system existed in England is not clear. But already by 1290 with the Act of *Quia Emptores*, which according to legal theorists laid the foundations for modern conveyancing of property rights, the ability to continue creating feudal tenures was replaced the requirement to convey tenure to potential occupiers who would become substitutes for the original occupier. This no doubt hastened what had already become apparent: that service had been commuted into money payments, and that entering into possession of land increasingly became the means of acquiring status, not the result (Gray and Symes 1981).

Such a system of property had significant consequences. One was that given the contingent nature of tenure, the courts were at pains to discover what rights an owner did have, and how conflicting rights to occupation and beneficial enjoyment might be resolved. The result was that the courts increasingly sought to protect the individual who had tenure of a parcel of land from the abuse of power by his or her feudal superiors, and hence to sanction the role of private property in spite of, or rather precisely because of, the absence of absolute rights to the ownership of land. A second consequence was the desire of landowners to protect their land for the benefit of their successors. In the Middle Ages, this was done through the mechanism of the entailed estate, in which only the direct heirs of the original owner could take possession of an estate on the owner's death. In the interest of limiting aristocratic power, the crown outlawed entailment in the sixteenth century, but aristocratic families managed to maintain landholdings through the use of the strict settlement in which land was settled on the second generation and the immediate heir was given only a life interest in the land which he or she was not at liberty to dispose of at will. This inevitably allowed the accumulation of land by the aristocracy but also by the gentry, who collectively came to play a major role in the development of urban Britain (Gordon 1996).

This second consequence does, however, depend on a third, more fundamental, characteristic of English land law. The ability to conceptualise landownership as a question of multiple interests gave English land law very considerable flexibility. It allowed lawyers to distinguish between current and future interests. It facilitated the hierarchical control in which an owner might grant a form of tenure to another without thereby alienating his or her own control over the land. It gave rise to the possibility that someone could hold land in trust for another to enjoy, because ownership, occupation and beneficial enjoyment could all be understood as separate entities (Lawson and Rudden 1982; Booth 2001).

The introduction of leasehold tenure in the later Middle Ages, which was to prove a potent instrument for the promotion of urban development from the seventeenth century onwards, was the direct result of the ability to define and separate concurrent interests in land. It was, too, a way in which the ground landlord could maintain rather closer control over the use that was made of land in that at the end of the lease the land reverted to the landlord, instead of remaining in the possession of the tenant and his or her heirs. It became, therefore, an instrument by which landowners could benefit in the short term from ground rents and in the longer term from the improved capital value of the land at the end of the lease. In urban development the leasehold was used by the landowner to assign the right to build on the land to the lessee. Leasehold tenure was the way in which landowners could overcome the limitations of strict settlement, which made it impossible for them to benefit from the land by selling it outright, and at the same time to transfer some if not all of the risks and responsibilities of development to others. The other aspect of the strictly settled estate was that the landowner whose rights to dispose of the property were severely curtailed, was in effect acting in trust for future generations by granting leases and promoting development. By the nineteenth century that relationship was often formalised and trusts were created to manage what had become an increasingly complicated problem. Guigou (1989) among others has praised this system of leasehold development for its efficiency in allocating land and for the quality of the results that it produced. The realities are rather less clear-cut. The system worked well where landowners demonstrated a will to manage the estate effectively in the hope of longer term gain. Where they did not, the possibilities for close control were lost and the results were disastrous as Clarke and others have shown (Clarke 1992).

This lineal system of property rooted in feudal conceptions of property could hardly be more different from the collateral or allodial system that characterises France. Unlike the English system of land law, there is a clear point of departure with the abolition of feudalism and the liberalisation of the land market that was heralded by the Declaration of Rights in 1789 and the coming into force of the Code civil (Patault 1989; Galey 2004). Within this new context, the right to property was an 'adjunct of freedom' (Malafosse 1979: 336–7) and the right to dispose freely of property without let or hindrance was an integral part of that freedom.

The inspiration for the changes introduced at the Revolution was in part Roman Law, which reduced property in land to its physical attributes, and in part to the study of man and nature, which distinguished between *droit réel* and *droit de créance*, the law of real estate and the law of personal obligation (Patault 1989), a distinction which is foreign to English common law. Behind this was the philosophical approach to property, which had originated with John Locke and was given an important impetus by Rousseau, which saw property in land as a natural right which preceded the State and which could be won by honest labour (Offer 1981). This form of landownership was resumed in the term *dominium*, the absolute control of the material possession, which implied an absence of personal obligation to others. Equally, however, the right to absolute possession did not imply sovereignty. Rousseau recognised the prior right of the sovereign State to land, but the corollary of that right was the duty of the State to protect the rights of the individual landowner. Expressed in legal terms drawn from Roman Law, the power of *dominium* was matched by that of *imperium*, the power of the State to command its citizens. If *dominium* implied that the State had no pre-eminent claim on land, *imperium* nevertheless required citizens to respect restrictions that the State might impose on the way in which land was used for the common good (Halpérin 1995; Galey 1999).

There is then a fundamental difference in conceptualisations of property in the two countries. In France, the collateral system of property gave rise to the concept of absolute right to land, expressed through the term *dominium*. In Britain, the key concept is *tenure* and the right to the occupation and enjoyment of land for the time being. And beyond this contrast is a paradox. In England, the constitutional settlement of 1689 ensured that the monarchy would not rule without the consent of parliament. In practice, parliament, dominated by a landowning elite, was loath to interfere in local affairs. Landowners, whose rights were never absolute, nevertheless had considerable freedom to acquire, use and dispose of their land as they chose and exercised considerable power through their relationship with lessees. The settlement of 1689 reinforced landownership as the means of access to political power and social influence as well as wealth. In France, on the other hand, the State could exert considerable control over the use made of land through the application of the concept of *imperium*, in spite of the constitutional right to absolute ownership of land. The nature of the guarantees provided for landownership by the Declaration of Rights and later, by the Constitution, meant that the accumulation of land was impossible and the role of land in the hierarchy of power much weaker than in England.

These fundamental differences then also had an impact on the nature of what in English is often termed the 'development industry'. The leasehold system encouraged the activities of builders because it enabled them to proceed without having to find capital to finance land purchase. Investment in development was thereby facilitated because risks were shared, and because urban development brought prestige not only to the landowner but to anyone else who had a stake in the process. Throughout the nineteenth century, development was dominated by small investors and the creation of the building societies in mid-century became an important means of channelling funds into the development of housing. At the same time, builders increasingly developed an expertise in what in French would be termed *aménagement* – the whole process of site development – as well as in building construction. After the World War II, the pattern that had been developed long before was used by new sources of capital in the form of insurance companies among others and the major development companies who came to play a major role in commercial development.

The pattern of investment in development was rather different in France. Though there were big developers in nineteenth-century Paris, like the Péreire brothers or Levallois, the activities of site development and construction were generally separate (Roncayolo 1983). Only in the later twentieth century did a structure of investment in land emerge that was comparable to that in Britain but it required legislation to ensure that developers could gain access to the capital necessary to develop. New kinds of contracts were also devised to satisfy demands from developers and also from private households. On the other hand, a tradition of State intervention in urban development from the nineteenth century onwards became essential.

Land ownership and public intervention in the land market

The differences between these two systems of property account for some of the many differences that distinguish the way in which land and urban policies are articulated in French and English law. Our thesis is that the fact of two very different sets of administrative laws, institutions and traditions is not enough to explain some of these differences, which become fully understandable only when one considers the way systems of property are organised in both systems as well as the legal conception of property they rely on. But it becomes clear from the discussion of property that the understanding of property and rights is intimately bound up with conceptualisations of the State (Galey 2004).

For indeed, the ways in which French and English State emerged and set out their power in the face of civil society are very different. In France, the State constituted itself in spite of the initial handicap of a powerless monarchy facing a powerful and oppressive feudality (Esmein 1914), this initial weakness both allowing the fiscal exemption of the French nobility, the underdevelopment as well as the lack of centralisation of the judiciary, and the pluralism of customary laws applying throughout the French kingdom especially in landed matters (Bloch 1936). That is why the historical development of the French State strongly relied, not on a centralised judiciary, but on a powerful and centralised administration, whose necessity was due to the difficulty of collecting scattered fiscal resources. In France, the State developed under the seal of the union of the monarchy, on the one side, and the peasantry and *bourgeoisie*, on the other side, against an aristocracy that was not only relieved of any fiscal duties, but was also the fiscal competitor of the monarchy. The radical legal change that came into force with a Code civil, inspired by Roman Law, was in effect the victory of the *propriété utile* of the peasantry, over the *propriété directe* of the aristocracy,[1] which itself was directly related to the growth of a centralised State built on a strongly integrated administration (Galey 2004).

By contrast, the starting point for institutional evolution in England was a very powerful royal institution, under whose domination feudality was regularly and hierarchically organised (Esmein 1914). Both fiscal duties of the nobility as well as the early emergence of a centralised judiciary, taking over and exercising the judicial power in the name of the king, and enabling the early unification of land law, were the expression of a strong royal power. In this context, the emergence of a doctrine of limited government and the law in the seventeenth century was the union of the nobility and of the middle class against the oppressive power of the State (Timsit 1987).

It is against this background of radically different legal systems for the definition of property and property rights and the significantly different State traditions that we can begin to examine the impact of property law on planning.

Some characteristics of planning in France and Britain

The legal instruments used for implementing policy both in France and in Britain can be classified according to a limited number of categories, whether to do with the control of the use of land, physical development, with land taxation or infrastructure. But these are abstract categorisations which deal only in generalities, and give no understanding of the many particularities that inevitably become apparent in detailed analysis. And these differences are of considerable importance.

In order to control the use and development of land, French law has developed a zoning system whose central feature, since the Loi relative à la solidarité et au renouvellement urbains, has been the plan local d'urbanisme (local plan; PLU). The purpose of the PLU is to define rules for the way in which land may be used which can be opposed by third parties. These rules are given substance by the permis de construire (building permit) whose purpose is above all else to authorise the act of building. English law, on the other hand, has given rise to a planning system which is discretionary and procedural, whose plans have only indicative force. The constraints prescribed for development are arrived at case by case, at the moment at which applications for planning permission are determined. A permission, if granted, may be subject to conditions. Moreover, the requirement to seek planning permission covers far more extensive ground than does the permis de construire since it covers not only physical development but also material change of use.

Unlike the British system, French law has never attempted to collectivise development land. But on the other hand, it has created a series of instruments, much more highly developed than in Britain, that give the administration privileged status in interventions in the land market. These include the early modernisation of procedures for expropriation of land, but also the right of pre-emption that exists in a multiplicity of forms, which is wholly absent in Britain. There are, too, in French law instruments that allow the intervention in the structure of land division which find no parallel in English law. English law, in contrast, is characterised by an under-use of compulsory purchase, viewed as complex and expensive, in spite of attempts to give local authorities a monopoly of development land, most recently in the Community Land Act of 1975.

Finally, recourse to taxation has a long tradition in French law. In the interests of controlling land speculation, French law has also taxed capital gains on the sale of property. And the existence of a series of taxes and fiscal contributions, notably the taxe local d'équipement (local infrastructure tax), has been the means of requiring developers to meet the cost of servicing parcels of land. Britain, after three attempts since World War II, has finally given up any intention to recover betterment value as a result of the grant of planning permission. Nor is there any tradition of using the fiscal system to recover the costs of infrastructure from developers. Instead, the British planning system has relied on contract in the form of planning obligations.

It is these differences that we need now to investigate in more detail.

Property and expropriation

In general terms, France may be characterised by direct interventionism in the land market and the development process, while Britain on the contrary has focused on public regulation of private initiative, with compulsory purchase playing only a secondary role. Nowhere was this difference more apparent than with the Channel Tunnel Rail Link, whose implementation caused major difficulties in England where the French portion was able to rely on a well-oiled legal administrative machine.

In a historical context, this difference appears paradoxical. In France, recourse to expropriation by public authorities only became fully developed after the Revolution and the coming into force of the Code civil (Mestre 1985). England, by contrast had had a tradition of compulsory purchase through the use of private Acts of Parliament that went back several centuries.

The French traditional pattern of interventionism in the land market relied on the public acquisition for the implementation of public works projects, which would thereafter be in the public domain. By this means, the State maintained the public-power strategic leadership in land development, while confining private individuals and companies to a subordinate or executive role, whether through fiscal contributions or the carrying out of projects within the French form of public-private partnership (concession de travaux publics).

This pattern had already operated within a customary law framework, under the Ancien Régime (Blanco 1999). It developed as a consequence of the lack of a mature land market, for want of a unified land law; as well as a consequence of land charges that were both complex and heavy and so hindered the free disposal of land on the market. The paradox is that this interventionism is a consequence of the initial institutional weaknesses of the French monarchy.

The Revolution and the introduction of the Code civil had a double impact. First, it demolished the obstacles to a free market. At the same time, it removed from private law any legal tools able to support a private regulation of the land market, as well as setting up a powerful and dynamic private sector market in land and buildings. In this way, public authorities became able to use the private land market in the realisation of projects in the public interest, without losing an iota of their control over land policy (Galey 2004). Second, both Article 17 of the Declaration of Rights and the coming into force of Articles 537–45 of the Code civil, backed by the case law of the Conseil d'État, enabled the rationalisation of the law relating to public property, to expropriation and to public works. It was through these mechanisms that Haussmann's development of Paris was achieved. Land was expropriated to lay out new streets as the means of stimulating private development, which in turn was rigorously controlled through the imposition of building lines.

Such a system may have been efficient for an essentially rural and agrarian France with limited urban development, but rapidly ran out of steam in the face of the challenges of rapid urbanisation between and after the two world wars. As a result, the legal framework was overhauled and simplified, in order to expand its use. In place of expropriation that could be classified as *organic* in which land was acquired by the State to be integrated into the public domain, a *functional* expropriation was created to further the aims of the development plan in which the land expropriated would be returned to the private sector (Rivalland 1969).

The impressive array of legal instruments available for the appropriation of land by the public sector is thus a reflection of the need to overcome the fragmentation of landownership, whose origins lie in the republican pact between the State and the middle classes and the peasantry against the aristocracy.

In Britain, the comparative weakness of the legal instruments for compulsory purchase is no doubt a reflection of the fact that the need was perceived as being much weaker. A stronger monarchy had long given rise to the use of parliamentary procedures for the redistribution of land, in particular in relation to the enclosures of common land. In the nineteenth century, private Acts of Parliament were the chief means of acquiring land for the construction of canals and then railways. This in turn was codified as the Land Clauses Act of 1845, which has never been fully repealed (Cocks 2002). The first legislation to allow the compulsory purchase of land by local authorities came with the provisions for slum clearance (Wohl 1977) and was gradually extended, most notably by the Town and Country Planning Act 1947. Although considerable use was made of these powers in the 1960s and 1970s there was no attempt to modernise the law in the way that was happening in France, in spite of similar pressures. The result has been that the powers for compulsory purchase are archaic and inadequate in face of the pressures of urban development and redevelopment, as the Urban Task Force Report noted (DETR 1999).

The impact of property law on planning control

Planning by zoning and regulations, supported by an arsenal of mechanisms for public acquisition of land that overrides private law and a well developed system of taxation, acknowledging only a subsidiary role for negotiation and for the use of contract, are the inheritance of strong government, albeit one which is now decentralised. We can see underlying this inheritance an expression of a regime of administrative law, moulded by the jurisprudence of the Conseil d'État[2] as a result of the separation of administrative and judicial authority. In this administrative law regime, the unilateral administrative act has been upheld as the symbol of the power of public authority, whose base in theory is the definition and practice of the intérêt général (general interest), which is without equivalence in English legal doctrine. In this regime also, control by the courts of administrative decision making is as much about the substance of the decision as the procedure (Truchet 1977).

The discretionary, procedural, negotiated planning put in place by English law derives from an administrative tradition that is marked by the absence of formal separation of administration and judiciary, and by the tenet that judicial decision-making has had on administrative decision-making, notably through procedural norms informed by the concept of natural justice (Galey and Girard 2003). The impact of a tradition of autonomous local government in the hands of the justices of the peace, carrying out their responsibilities in a benevolent fashion, treating problems case by case, is clearly present. In this tradition, the emphasis is upon form and not on substance, and the English courts are concerned far more with the procedures than with results.

The fundamental values of English public law mainly focus on the decision-making process. They are concerned with procedural fairness – openness, fairness, impartiality, as the Franks Commission formulated them (Franks Report 1958) – and also with substantive justice in the overall process – legitimate expectation and rationality (Oliver, 1999). In this context, the idea of public interest is in no sense a legal construct, but derives rather from a Benthamite utilitarianism. To that extent, it forms the underpinning for legislation that dealt with sanitation and by extension, building and planning. Never defined by law, it has, as McAuslan writes, formed a competing ideology with that of private property that the courts had long been at pains to uphold in the face of the exercise of arbitrary power. By the beginning of the last century the courts, in McAuslan's words, had 'accepted that adjudication was different to administration [and] that public interest was a legitimate concern for administrators to advance and have regard to' (McAuslan 1980: 4). But they did not attempt to define public interest, except in the face of a decision that was manifestly irrational. Indeed they operated a strict distinction between *law* and *policy*. Development plans in this context become, not legal, but administrative documents whose equivalence would be to the administrative directives of French law.

These differences in property law and the State traditions with which each is bound up begin to offer explanations not only for the nature of plans but also for the way in which the control of development takes place. The introduction of a generalised and uniform system of permis de construire in France dates from 1943, while the generalisation of a system of planning permissions in Britain was introduced in the 1947 Town and Country Planning Act. But the scope and the intention of this formalisation of control occurring at roughly the same moment was radically different.

Quite unlike its French counterpart, planning permission is not the latest expression of a long line of authorisations for building. It is true that in part it was derived from the building controls that had been established first of all in London and then by the end of the nineteenth century throughout the country, but its intentions went well beyond the kind of bylaw regulation of the Public Health Acts. Indeed, its origins lay in the desire to overcome the shortcomings of early planning legislation that had held up, rather than facilitated, the development of new housing. But it was not until 1947 that what had started as an administrative expedient became a central element of the British planning system (Crow 1996; Booth 2003). Until that moment, the leasehold with its restrictive covenants had been the major form of control of urban development and remained the model for what might be done.

In that respect, the Uthwatt report (Uthwatt 1942) is revealing. Uthwatt proposed the nationalisation of all land, for future development, which would then be leased to occupiers, and town planning requirements would then be imposed through restrictive covenants. Though this proposal was not adopted, the reasons why it was not adopted were more pragmatic and economic than to do with the fundamental principle. What was retained, however, was the idea of the nationalisation of development rights through the requirement to obtain consent from the State for development. What Uthwatt envisaged only for 'land lying outside built-up areas', was generalised in the 1947 Town and Country Planning Act to cover all land.

An examination of French law on all these points shows how much influence the conceptualisation and formalisation of property in the law has had on the system of permis de construire. The Conseil Constitutionnel[3] has from time to time pronounced on the incompatibility of both administrative discretion and the control of land use with law of property. One of the explanations for this decision stems from Article 544 of the Code civil which defines property, and we need to note that the exercise of rights to benefit from and dispose of property is limited only by prohibitions prescribed by law or by regulation. This significance of this definition will escape anyone brought up in the tradition of common law because of the distinction made between regulatory orders (actes réglementaires) and individual decisions (décisions individuelles). In this formulation, planning constraints coupled with a zoning plan that identifies their spatial application represent a 'norme générale' whose character is abstract and impersonal. Article 544 allows no restriction on the right of property based upon a discretionary 'décision individuelle'.

It is particularly to be noted in this context that an attempt to introduce in the cities of Paris, Lyon and Marseille a control over the change of use of workshops and commercial premises in order to ensure the diversity of commercial use in neighbourhoods foundered. The Conseil Constitutionnel took the view that the measure was disproportionate to the end to be secured, and cited Article 4 of the Declaration of the Rights 1789 both in terms of the right to property and to the freedom to develop (Schoettl 2001).

Nevertheless, we can note that the decision of the Conseil Constitutionnel did not absolutely exclude the possibility of controlling land use, if the control was not disproportionate to the end to be secured. In this context, we can also note that within the British system the Use Classes Order, secondary legislation that categorises common land uses in order to define what is, and what is not, a *material* change of use, achieves the objective of the Conseil Constitutionnel's judgment, by ensuring that control is indeed not disproportionate to its end. But the nature of French property law does not lend itself to the production of regulatory instruments of the kind that would provide the necessary guarantees.

There is a final point to be made about the effect of property law. In English law, planning permission that is granted is said to 'run with the land' – specifically in the wording of Section 75 of the Town and Country Planning Act 1990, 'planning permission to develop land shall ... enure of the benefit of the land and of all persons for the time being interested in it.' This formulation, whose roots lie in the development of contractual obligations imposed on *private* land transactions in the nineteenth century, seems now to pose no difficulties for the legal profession, so rare is case law commentary. In French law, on the contrary, the rule is not supported by any express legal clause. The fact that the permis de construire is granted for a specific development project and runs with the land, opening up the possibility of its transfer to successors in title, was only finally given formal recognition by a judgment in the Conseil d'État, which itself gave rise to a great deal of doctrinal controversy.

Conclusion

The purpose of this chapter was to demonstrate the imprint that systems of property have left on planning in both Britain and France. What becomes clear from the analysis we present is that the differences to be discerned between planning in both countries is at least in part to be explained by these initial differences in how property was understood, controlled and legislated for. And these differences are not simply ones of legal machinery. They rest upon profound conceptual differences that still make real difficulties of mutual comprehension today. The impact is upon the machinery for planning, but also its content. The objectives of land-use planning and the content of policy can also in part be ascribed to the values and concepts of differing property regimes.

Our remit has been, therefore, one of presenting explanations in order to provide depth to the understanding of the way in which planning systems operate. We believe that developing understanding in that way is in itself a worthwhile objective. But the analysis goes further than that. What becomes apparent is that the weaknesses that are to be detected in British and French planning are in considerable measure due to precisely the way in which systems of property have been structured. The argument is that proposals for reform will fail to be effective if they have not fully assimilated the differences we present here.

Notes

1 *Dominium directum* and *dominium utile* were the words used by continental European medieval scholars in order to describe different forms of ownership competing on the same land within a vertical feudal framework relying on subinfeudation. According to this terminology, the tenant is the owner of *dominium utile*, that is the right to the possession and enjoyment of the land for all practical purposes. His landlord is owner of the *dominium directum*, which empowers him to enforce the conditions upon which the *dominium utile* has been granted to the tenant upon the land.
2 The Conseil d'État functions as the court of highest appeal in France.
3 The Conseil Constitutionnel pronounces on the legality under the Constitution of all laws approved by Parliament.

References

Blanco, C. (1999) 'Historicité et modernité du droit français de l'urbanisme', doctoral thesis (University of Nice-Sophia Antipolis).

Bloch, M. (1960) *Seigneurie française et manoir anglais* (Cahier des Annales, 1936; reprinted Paris: Armand Colin).

Booth, P. (2001) 'Nationalising development rights: the feudal origins of British development control', *Environment and Planning B: Planning and Design*, 29: 129–39.

Booth, P. (2002) 'A desperately slow system? The origins and nature of the current discourse in development control', *Planning Perspectives*, 17: 309–23.

Booth, P. (2003) *Planning by Consent: The Nature and Origins of British Development Control* (London: Routledge).

Clarke, L. (1992, *Building Capitalism: Historical Change and the Labour Process in the Production of the Built Environment* (London: Routledge).

Cocks, R. (2002) *The Expropriation of Rights* 'in rem' *under English Law: An Historical Analysis*, in 'L'expropriation' (Recueil de la société Jean Bodin pour l'histoire comparative des institutions, vol. LXVII, Université de Bruxelles: De Boeck & Larcier), pp. 196–211.

Committee on Administrative Tribunals and Enquiries (Franks Committee) (1957) *Report*, Cmnd 218 (London: HMSO).

Crow, S. (1996) 'Development control: the child that grew up in the cold, *Planning Perspectives*, 11, 399–411.

Demsetz, H. (1967) 'Toward a theory of property rights', *The American Economic Review*, 57(2): 347–59.

Déterville-Papandréou, M.F. (2004) 'Les fondements du droit anglais des biens' doctoral thesis (University of Strasbourg 3, 1996, reprinted in *Bibliothèque des thèses du droit privé*, Paris: Librairie Générale de Droit et de Jurisprudence).

DETR (Department of the Environment, Transport and the Regions) (1999) *Report of the Urban Task Force: Towards an Urban Renaissance* (London: E&FN Spon).

Esmein, A. (1914) *Éléments du droit constitutionnel français comparé* (6th edn) (Paris: Recueil Sirey).

Galey, M. (1999) 'L'indemnisation des restrictions d'urbanisme à la propriété en droit anglais', in *L'indemnisation des servitudes d'urbanisme en Europe*, Colloque international, GRIDAUH, Toulouse, 15–16 October, *Droit et Ville*, 48: 137–88.

Galey, M. (2004) 'Genèse de l'état et droit des sols, l'empreinte de la dynamique institutionnelle sur la formalisation juridique de la propriété (à la lumière d'une comparaison franco-anglaise', *Revue Internationale de Droit Comparé*, 3: 685–99.

Galey, M. (2006) 'La typologie des systèmes de propriété de C.R. Noyes: un outil d'évaluation contextualisée des régimes de propriété privée, publique et collective', conference paper, *Land Law and Natural Resources: Management: Comparative Perspectives*, Facultés Saint-Louis Bruxelles, Government Law College of Pondicherry and French Institute of Pondicherry, Pondicherry, India, 17–19 March (publication forthcoming).

Galey, M. and Girard, C. (2003) 'Le procès équitable dans l'espace normatif anglo-saxon: l'éclairage du droit public anglais', in H. Ruiz-Fabri (ed.) *Procès équitable et enchevêtrement des espaces normatifs* (Paris: Société de Législation Comparée), pp. 53–87.

Gordon, R.W. (1996) 'Paradoxical property', in J. Brewer and S. Staves (eds) *Early Modern Conceptions of Property* (London: Routledge), pp. 95–110.

Gray, K.J. and Symes, P.D. (1981) *Real Property and Real People: Principles of Land Law* (London: Butterworth).

Guigou, J.L. (1991) 'Requiem pour le régime foncier britannique', in J. Comby (ed.) *Un droit inviolable et sacré: la propriété* (Paris: Association des Études Foncières), pp. 324–9.

Halpérin, J.L. (1995) 'Propriété et souveraineté de 1789 à 1804', *Droits, Revue française de théorie juridique*, 22: 67–79.

Hohfeld, W.N. (1913) 'Some fundamental legal conceptions as applied to legal reasoning', *Yale Law Journal*, 23: 1–59.

Hohfeld, W.N. (1917) 'Fundamental legal conceptions as applied in legal reasoning', *Yale Law Journal*, 26: 710–70.

Krueckerberg, D.A. (1995) 'La propriété, un concept difficile', *Études foncières*, 69: 34–41.

Lawson, F.H. (1951) *The Rational Strength of English Law* (London: Stevens).

Lawson, F.H. and Rudden, B. (1982) *The Law of Property* (2nd edn) (Oxford: Clarendon Press).

McAuslan, P. (1980) *The Ideologies of Planning Law* (Oxford: Pergamon).

Malafosse, J. de (1979) 'La propriété, gardienne de la nature', in *Études offertes à Jacques Flour* (Paris: Répertoire du Notariat Défrénois), pp. 335–49.

Mestre, J.L. (1985) 'L'expropriation face à la propriété (du Moyen Age au Code Civil), *Droits, Revue Française de Théorie Juridique*, I: 51.

Noyes, C.R. (1936) *The Institution of Property: A Study of the Development, Substance and Arrangements of the System of Property in Modern Anglo-American Law* (New York and Toronto: Longmans, Green & Co; London: Humphrey Milford).

Offer, A. (1981) *Property and Politics 1870–1914: Landownership, Law and Urban Development in England* (London: Cambridge University Press).

Oliver, D. (1999), *Common Values and the Public–Private Divide* (London: Butterworths).

Patault, A.M. (1989) *Introduction historique au droit des biens* (Paris: Presses Universitaires de France).

Rivalland, J.M. (1969) *Les charges d'urbanisme* (Paris: Librairie Générale de Droit et de Jurisprudence).

Roncayolo, M. (1983) 'La production de la ville', in G. Duby (ed.) *Histoire de la France urbaine*, vol. 4: *La ville de l'âge industriel et le cycle haussmannien* (Paris: Seuil), pp. 77–155.

Schoettl, E. (2001) 'Le Conseil Constitutionnel et la loi relative à la solidarité et au renouvellement urbain', *Actualités Juridiques/Droit Administratif*, pp. 18–26.

Timsit, G. (1987) *Thèmes et systèmes de droit* (Paris: Presses Universitaires de France).

Truchet, D. (1977) *La fonction de l'intérêt général dans la fonction de la jurisprudence administrative* (Paris: Librairie Générale de Droit et de Jurisprudence).

Uthwatt, L.J. (1942) *Expert Committee on Compensation and Betterment: Final Report*, Cmnd. 6386 (London: HMSO).

Wohl, A.S. (1977) *The Eternal Slum: Housing and Social Policy in Victorian London* (London: Edward Arnold).

Chapter 4

Institutional frameworks and planning processes

Michèle Breuillard, Richard Stephenson and Stéphane Sadoux

Introduction

Planning policies are the product of three overlapping elements: the legal system defining national rules, the decision processes which regulate plan making, and administrative procedures that determine the operation of specialised organisations and the bureaucracy in general. Historically, however, French and British traditions have diverged in each one of these three areas, starting with the place of central and local authorities in local politics. Even if various forms of centralisation have appeared across the Channel and despite the French constitutional reform of 2003 that established the principle of a 'decentralised organisation of the indivisible state',[1] this contrast remains evident. 'Even if the Westminster Parliament claims total sovereignty over all the regions of the United Kingdom, it has not chosen to realise this claim through a uniform model of central administration' (Stoker 1998: 230). Thus, spatial planning arises from radically different conceptions and practices: France having chosen to stay unitary and the United Kingdom having become quasi-federal (Hazell 2004) since the devolution of Scotland, Wales and Northern Ireland. Since 2000, Scottish and Welsh local authorities have been subject to the executives (Scottish Executive and Welsh Executive) of the regional assemblies, the Scottish Parliament and the Welsh Assembly, and not the ministry responsible for local government, which must now limit its action to England.

Diverging principles and practices are not, however, explained simply by the political and administrative structures, but also by the geographical organisation of each State's territory. The structures determine the levels of the politico-administrative machinery to which planning powers are attributed. They also determine the political dynamics through which these powers are exercised. Inversely, for the last thirty years the objectives of planning have exerted a major influence on the reforms and the proposed changes in administrative geography: whilst following their own course, planning instruments and procedures are linked to larger questions which touch on the relationship between plans and institutions, as well as the pursuit of the styles and structures best adapted to governing land use change.

The first part of the chapter will present the principal characteristics of the French and British institutional framework. The second will analyse the administrative structures that condition the way planning is conceived and implemented, in the light of local government reorganisation and regionalisation in Britain and the processes of decentralisation and inter-communal working in France.

The institutional contexts: a dual State, a fused State

In Britain, the 'local' is the business of local government: it is everything that is not managed at the national level. There is no real equivalence between British 'central government', encompassing the government, ministers and parliament, and the French concept of the *fonction régalienne*. The 'local' is the consequence of boundaries drawn up by the central power that vary with the philosophy and political priorities of the parliamentary majority, and thus the government. This is the 'dual' State, split between 'high politics', in the elevated spheres of central government, and 'low politics' in the towns and countryside.

In France, the management of local affairs rests as much with the administrative network of the State as with the local authorities, specifically the commune and the region.[2] Article 20 of the French Constitution says that 'the government determines the conduct of national politics. It has at its disposition the administration and the army'. We can speak of 'administration de l'État' meaning central government and 'administration territoriale' (local councils' services and ministry field services).[3] Civil servants, therefore, work in central government's field services under the prefects' supervision, 'l'état territorial' (the 'local State'), within a three-tiered structure (région, département and arrondissement) that parallels the three-tiered structure of local government (région, département, commune). Moreover, since 2004 the staff and functions of the 'local State' have been re-organised into eight *pôles régionaux* that are deemed to be more functional and effective as they cut across the traditional division into central government departments:[4] Education and Training, Public Management and Economic Development, Public Health and Social Cohesion, Agriculture and Rural Affairs, Environment and Sustainable Development, Employment and Work Inclusion, Culture and Fine Arts and finally, Transport, Housing and Planning. All 36,779 communes, whatever their size, exercise the same powers in relation to planning, development and infrastructure. The 26 régions participate in producing and implementing the National Plan, elaborate and approve their own plan within the context of their powers in relation to regional development. They are also responsible for producing a regional transport strategy, for organising passenger transport services outside urban areas, as well as the rail transport of the region. This is the 'fused' State.

In the UK, local authorities play the role of agents of central government for the management of matters of local interest, as expressed in the notion of 'local government'. This excludes the principle of 'free administration' as well as the idea of immutable administrative boundaries which are central to the power and persistence of French *collectivités territoriales*. Whilst the 'regions' of Scotland, Wales, Northern Ireland, and Greater London are run by assemblies that are directly elected, in anticipation of regionalisation in England, they are not 'local authorities'. They constitute a new category of public authority that sits at an intermediary level, a form of 'meso-government', in contrast to French regions, but analogous to the territorial organisation of the major part of our European neighbours (Marcou 2003).

In France the concept of collectivité territoriale, protected by the constitution, brings together communes, départements and régions, with some additional room for manoeuvre in the parts of the French territory located outside the European continent, or outre-mer to use the French term. Other forms of local administration, granted a certain number of powers transferred from communes, were invented at the end of the nineteenth century and subsequently consolidated and improved several times. But successive waves of decentralisation have more or less ignored them (Breuillard 2005). These 'public institutions for inter-communal cooperation' known as EPCI (établissements publics de coopération intercommunale) are particularly potent in terms of the exercise of planning and development policies, but remain subject to the principle of specialisation that gives them only limited powers. Inter-communal working remains founded on the primacy of the commune's unrestricted powers of determination,[5] even if the State supports *intercommunalité* through financial incentives. This doubling up of French local institutions allows the uniform legal position of communes to be maintained and ensures institutional unity and functional diversity, while also easing the inconveniences of dispersion and lack of resources.

Moreover, it should be remembered that collectivités territoriales are strongly represented in the heart of the legislature by the Senate in two ways, direct and indirect. In direct terms, the Constitution gives each senator the mission of representing the nation but also representing his or her constituency, a département. Senators are elected not by the general electorate, but by an electoral college, comprising councillors from communes (95 per cent of electoral college members), départements, and régions, as well as the members of parliament in a département. Moreover, senators can hold multiple elected positions, just as members of parliament can. Thus, the large majority of senators also hold local positions. There are senators who are municipal councillors (77) or mayors (128), councillors in départements (112), regional councillors (29), presidents of départements

(32) or presidents of regional councils (3). Based on the French conception of the operation of institutions of government, the body of senators, coming from very different départements and comparing their local experience, are able to reconcile local and national interests. The work of the Senate and the work in a constituency are two aspects of the same mission: to represent France's local collectivités within the legislature. Those bills concerned with local government are scrutinised by Senators even more than by MPs. The Senate regularly evaluates the progress made in implementing French decentralisation laws and no legislation reforming local government can be voted without its approval. The Senate cannot censure the government but neither can it be dissolved by it, in contrast to the National Assembly.

The British system is far from this uniform but rigid structuring of French local administration: it rests on national democracy and on a complex system of administration, devised according to the different functions to be assured. It is the function and not the space governed which explains the nature of 'local government' and its 'patchwork quilt' appearance (Department of Environment 1996): it is reorganised almost every decade, sometimes by force, offering a great variety of boundaries, powers and structures. Since devolution in 1998 and 1999, Scotland, Northern Ireland (at the time of writing) and Wales have taken full responsibility for the operation of local government simplified and standardised in unitary authorities. Nevertheless, even if English local authorities remain subject to the influence and control of ministers based in London, they are capable, in certain conditions, of rebuffing or delaying the application of the unitary council structure voted through in 1994 (Breuillard 2000). This reform, launched under John Major, is still not completed under the third Blair government. Hence amongst its 468 local authorities, we find on the one hand 296 non-metropolitan districts within 35 non-metropolitan or 'shire' counties in a two-tier structure, and on the other hand 32 London Boroughs and the City of London Corporation along with 45 unitary councils, the latter exercising the complete set of local government powers. According to the Blairite institutional ideal however, the whole of the country should be covered by a still more rationalised and efficient new organisation: 'unitary' councils for the local level and regional councils for the regional level, each one run by an assembly and a leader elected by universal suffrage. But up to now, two thirds of local referenda have already rejected directly elected mayors at the head of unitary councils (Rao 2005) and the North East rejected regional government in a referendum in November 2004. This, however, did not stand in the way of the creation of so-called regional development agencies (RDAs) designed to spearhead economic development. The Regional Development Agencies Act 1998 legitimated RDAs by creating a consultative 'assembly' of local authority, private sector and voluntary sector representatives in all English regions outside London. In the Greater London region a new institutional 'balance' has been struck between 33 local councils and a regional assembly, the Greater London Authority, presided over by mayor Ken Livingstone, both having been re-elected in 2004.

British 'local government' is conceived to ensure the provision of local services, whereas the French vision is that local areas should be managed and developed according to local interests. The French system of local administration is uniform but with a level of dispersion in terms of local government units, the communes, unmatched in Europe, and which seems impossible to modify. Thus, the historic capacity of English local authorities is linked to the nature of British local democracy. Britain's local authorities have the task of providing services for the population, under the direction of the sovereign parliament and under the control of the central administration. 'Rationalisation' is the key argument of British governments. In contrast, the notion of a French collectivité territoriale is established constitutionally in terms of representing local interests, which are different and sometimes in conflict with the interests represented by l'État and the ministry field services. This fundamental divergence can be summarised in two expressions: British functional democracy versus French territorial democracy.

A further divergence concerns the rhythm and the extent of change in the two politico-administrative systems: whilst France may be decentralising, she remains somewhat out of sync with trends elsewhere in Europe and particularly in Britain, where the aim is a simplification of administrative structures. The 'quiet revolution' of the 2003 constitutional reform in France will not alter this feeling of immobility: it does not even acknowledge the existence of the 2,360 EPCI that bring together 30,000 communes and 51 million inhabitants. There are even multiple categories of inter-communal bodies depending on the size and number of the communes concerned: communauté urbaine, communauté d'agglomération, communauté de communes, ... not counting some fine old recipes that still remain in existence after two centuries.

If we want to characterise the French administrative system we can cite four elements: the primacy of the commune and EPCI over intermediary local authorities (the département and the région); the direct election of local institutions (not EPCI); constitutional protection for the concept of 'free administration' of local authorities and the indivisibility of the republic; finally the fused nature of the institutions which means that the State preserves a local administrative network – the State can implement its policies itself, directly, at the local level. As for the collectivités, they have elbow room to exercise their own powers with a significant amount of freedom (Marcou 2004).

On the other side of the Channel, the situation contrasts with France in every respect. First, the submission of local authorities to regional executives in Scotland and Wales is total. This situation however seems unlikely to develop in future English regions. At the local level no other directly elected legal structure exists other than 'local authorities'. 'Joint authorities', notably in the areas covered by the metropolitan county councils abolished in 1985, are not additional institutions but spaces for consultation where local councillors agree actions or strategies that they then implement in their own local authority. Furthermore, the absence of constitutional protection cannot merely be explained by the absence of a written constitution: it is simply impossible since the Westminster Parliament is completely sovereign. Finally, the British State has no administrative network on the ground comparable to the French State and 'déconcentration' is untranslatable into English. The Government Offices for the Regions (GORs), set up in each of the nine English regions do not exercise delegated powers or powers of signature comparable to the préfecture. The GORs group together the personnel of ten ministries that are concerned with the local authorities' responsibilities and administration.[6] They essentially play an interface role, check the correct use of State funds and consult with local authorities and economic actors in their region so as to better inform the government about local situations. Their direct partners are really the Regional Development Agencies.

Hence there is the need to contradict a persistent cliché: French local authorities, particularly the communes, enjoy such liberty as a result of the principle of free administration and the weakness of controls and evaluation, that France is 'one of the most decentralised states in Europe, particularly at the municipal and inter-municipal level' (Marcou 2004: 9).

This judgement leads us to the points that fundamentally separate these two countries: the different relationship that they establish between the pursuit of the right geographical size and the maintenance of the traditional boundaries of each authority. The right size of any British local authority charged with any given responsibility is that which allows the greatest efficiency: in the management of local services provided for the public, or in the drawing up of strategies for social and economic development with the aim of improving the living conditions of residents. For this reason and contrary to the situation in France, which waited until 1983 to decentralise planning and development powers, the United Kingdom has always considered planning to be a matter for local authorities in the same way as all the other duties of service provision or management. The efficient execution of these duties is the very basis for the legitimacy of local government.

Planning and the political and institutional framework in Britain and France – who does what?

Extending the analysis further requires more attention to terminology. 'Urbanisme' and 'aménagement du territoire' are key terms in France, but their distinctive characteristics, which are allied to the role and function of collectivité and État in France, render their translation into English problematic. Equally, to speak of 'town and country planning' and 'regional policy' in Britain is to speak of activities inextricably linked to notions of local and central government, their role, powers and objectives. So, to simplify the semantics, but also emphasise the distinctive nature of terms that share meanings whilst not being perfectly congruent, we shall refer to 'planning' when talking about these concepts in their most general sense but use specific terms in French and English where we wish to highlight the specificity of the 'systems' in each country.

We have already noted the ability of the British system of governance to produce a complex patchwork of areas, powers and structures and create a 'quasi-federal' structure. This is clear in the current reform of its planning systems; the use of the plural here is quite deliberate. While in France one system of law applies across the whole national territory and there is only one legislature, there have always been separate arrangements for England and Wales, for Scotland and for Northern Ireland. This has been further accentuated by devolution, since the Scottish parliament is now empowered to pass its own primary legislation, and is seeking to develop a distinctive Scottish planning system. For simplicity, and because reforms in Scotland and Northern Ireland in particular are still developing at the time of writing we shall focus on England in our discussion, but reference will be made to the other parts of the United Kingdom where there are significant points to be made.

Ministries and planning

The ministry concerned with 'urbanisme' in France at the time of writing is the Ministère des Transports, de l'Équipement, du Tourisme et de la Mer (Ministry for Transport, Planning, Tourism and the Sea). In its various forms this ministry has provided a fairly stable home through the decades for this business of regulating building and land use change. Through its extensive network of field services, the Directions Départementales de l'Équipement (DDE), l'Etat plays a crucial role as a developer (particularly of transport) and regulator of land use, but its role and structure are changing radically with the next stage of decentralisation and creation of eight pôles régionaux. The other main 'planning' activity in France, Aménagement du territoire, has operated in a parallel system with that of 'urbanisme'. The birth of the idea of Aménagement du territoire is strongly associated with Eugène Claudius-Petit, Minister for Reconstruction and Town Planning who first described it at a Cabinet meeting in 1952. The excessive domination of Paris in France's economic and social development was to be counteracted by a deliberate policy to manage economic and demographic growth in such a way as to avoid excessive regional inequalities and reduce those already in existence. The creation of DATAR (Délégation à l'Aménagement du Territoire et à l'Action Régionale) in February 1963 was a key date in French planning history. Originally conceived as a cross-cutting strategic body directed by an inter-ministerial committee chaired by the prime minister, it has, however, been attached to one ministry or another for most of its life. In January 2006 it was re-shaped and renamed as the DIACT (Délégation Interministérielle à l'Aménagement et à la Compétitivité des Territoires) under the direction of the Ministère de l'Intérieur et de l'Aménagement du Territoire. The DATAR's conception was closely linked to France's distinctive system of national economic planning and gave a spatial dimension to the priorities of France's successive national economic plans.

The Department for Communities and Local Government (DCLG) is the English planning ministry and also covers local and regional government, housing, fire and rescue services, and coordinates the GORs. Planning has always been closely linked to local government and spent the period from 1951 to 1970 as part of the Ministry of Housing and Local Government, in contrast to France where the administration of 'collectivités' has essentially been a matter for the Interior ministry. The creation of the Department of the Environment in 1970 did not change this association with local government, but expanded the department to include transport. But despite criticisms of the lack of integration between transport and planning, transport was made a distinct ministry in 1976. The post-1997 experiment of rejoining transport, local government and planning lasted until May 2002 when the Office of the Deputy Prime Minister was created and transport moved to a separate department. The business of 'regional policy' which traces its origins to the 1930s in Britain and was designed to tackle the problem of an over-dominant London and high unemployment in the older industrial regions was essentially seen as an industrial matter and handled by the Board of Trade and its successors. Mention should be made, however, of the cases of Northern Ireland, Scotland and Wales, where the existence of the Northern Ireland, Scottish and Welsh Offices constituted strongly integrated regional administrations outside England. These were an essential precursor to the devolution already outlined above.

'National' planning policy

The meaning of 'national' planning policy is rather different on either side of the Channel. In Britain, the tendency is for central government to guard its sovereignty by carefully limiting the powers of local government. In France, the power of national government to determine policy was traditionally achieved by being the key developer, and with decentralisation, 'collectivités' actually have quite a degree of freedom to produce a plan based on locally determined policies.

The linchpin of the British system of land use controls is the idea of 'material considerations'. Planning permission must be granted taking into account all material considerations, and ministerial guidance constitutes a material consideration in planning decisions. Initially guidance was expressed in an *ad hoc* fashion in circulars and statements by ministers in the Commons. But as the volume and complexity of guidance increased, the most important national policies were formalised into a series of so-called Planning Policy Guidance notes (PPGs). Under the 2004 Act the guidance is now known as Planning Policy Statements in England. There are 25 of these PPGs or PPSs for England. They are regularly updated and hotly debated, particularly for controversial issues such as retailing location and transport. The documents cover the main issues associated with town and country planning in its widest sense, from transport to flood prevention. In the 1990s the system was extended to include Regional Planning Guidance, a form of ministerial guidance regulating the dimensions of land use change in every English region. Ministerial guidance has enormous influence on development control decisions and the content of development plans.

In France, by contrast, the Règles Générales d'Urbanisme (RGU, previously referred to as Règlement National d'Urbanisme) only apply when the local planning document does not address a planning issue. Once a local plan is adopted, it becomes a document with a distinct legal status, which establishes development rights attached to the land within its boundaries. Perhaps partly because of the lack of a mechanism like PPGs in France to assert control over local development policies, the Loi Pasqua (4 February 1995) revived a proposal made three years before: to create a process that would guide the production of Directives Territoriales d'Aménagement. These are elaborated under the responsibility of the State, in partnership with régions, départements, comités de massifs when appropriate as well as the main communes (over 20,000 inhabitants, chefs-lieux d'arrondissements, etc.). They aim to state the main national objectives in terms of Aménagement du Territoire and to ensure a balance between competing objectives.

Regional economic planning

The contrasts between the British dual State and the fused French State are very clear when we consider attempts to create a regional structure for economic planning. In 1964 the Labour government set up the Department of Economic Affairs and advisory Regional Economic Planning Councils in an attempt to create a national economic planning framework with regional structures, but national economic crises throughout the late 1960s and competition with the Treasury made this an abortive experiment long before the department itself disappeared in 1969. In contrast, the regional structures created in France in 1964 based around the 'préfets de région' and the Secrétariat Général pour les Affaires Régionales (SGAR) have survived into the décentralisation era forming an important part of a fused system built around the Contrats de Plans État-Région (CPER) with conseils régionaux on the one hand, and the préfet and SGAR on the other.

Controlling development

A crucial difference between the French and the British planning systems is the nature of land-use control decision. The granting of planning permission in Britain is a classic example of the notion of discretion in local decision-making process. Any land use plan is only one of a number of material considerations that local planning authorities must take into account when reaching their decision. In contrast, a French local plan has legal force, and is *opposable*: it embodies the use rights associated with a piece of land that are confirmed through the granting of the right to build in conformity with building regulations. Thus, if a local plan has been adopted in a French commune, most decisions are administrative in nature. In the UK context, there is a stronger dimension of professional judgement in decisions about planning permission and decades of making those judgements has helped to create a single strongly professionalised corps of planners, virtually all members of the Royal Town Planning Institute, which was founded in 1914. The rationalisation of the size and structure of local government units over the years has reinforced the 'professionalism' of planning and other local government functions. In contrast the professionals employed by national government remained predominant in France even after 'décentralisation'. The DDE has continued to be the primary provider of technical services outside the larger towns, and its advice was offered without charge until 2005.

Plans

In Britain drawing up development plans has, like development control, been a local government activity since the dawn of planning legislation. This was true of 1947 development plans and of subsequent local plans and unitary development plans and is still the case for the local development frameworks put in place by the 2004 Act. Nevertheless local government autonomy has often been constrained: the early development plans and subsequent structure plans required final approval from central government before being adopted, although this requirement was removed in 1991.

It should also be mentioned that the 1968 Act envisaged the *same* planning authority producing both strategic (structure) and local plans, but in the event, local government reorganisation implemented in 1974 split plan-making powers between county councils and district councils. Nevertheless, land use plans remained, almost universally, documents that were drawn up by a single local authority. Local government reorganisation in the 1990s, however, introduced an innovation: joint structure planning arrangements between counties and new unitary authorities in many regions. The situation was particularly complex in Berkshire, Avon, Cleveland, and Humberside where county councils were abolished. This was in parallel with the creation of Regional Planning Guidance (RPG) across England, which required far more cooperation and discussion between neighbouring local authorities than seen in the 1980s (Stephenson and Poxon 2001). In this respect the 2004 Act takes things a stage further: RPG has been replaced by Regional Spatial Strategies (RSS), thus placing regional planning on a firm legislative footing. Until the rise of RPG, and later the RSS in England, structure plans were produced by county councils, and on occasions this has generated conflict with district councils as their local plans can only be adopted when certified as 'in conformity' with the structure plan. What is significant, however, is that with the removal of structure plans from the system, a local authority planning power has effectively been removed and, in a sense, repatriated to the sovereign national government. This illustrates the British functional democratic model presented in the first part of the chapter.

In France the functional needs of plan-making have proved difficult to reconcile with the geography of commune, département and région. The functional urban regions and rural zones of France cross many communal boundaries. As already mentioned, the virtual impossibility of radical reorganisation of administrative areas has taken France in the direction of 'intercommunalité' as a solution to managing services. The issue was partly addressed in 1966 with the creation of 'communautés urbaines' in four of the larger cities: Lille, Lyon, Bordeaux and Strasbourg. A few smaller cities chose to form a communauté urbaine and there were other attempts to promote effective intercommunal working, notably in 1992, but only with the 1999 legislation did the French find a successful formula for inter-communal working that was adopted across the country. The Loi SRU of the following year strengthened the role of 'intercommunalité' in land-use plan-making but conceived the SCOT as a plan for a functional area which could extend beyond the boundaries of the communautés d'agglomération and communautés des communes created under the 1999 legislation. Furthermore, the Loi SRU allows multi-commune local plans, and Lyon, for example, has created a single PLU for the 55 communes of the communauté urbaine.

Plan-making, therefore, involves significant Franco-British contrasts. Many French local plans are adopted by small communes heavily reliant on external advice; and any kind of strategic planning relies on successful cooperation between communes which has often been fraught with difficulties. In Britain, plans have traditionally been drawn up by single, relatively large, local government units with in-house expertise, although that situation has changed recently. In both countries, however, there has been a move towards re-scaling the activity of plan-making, partly through very different systems of joint plan-making, and there has also been a move to the integration of land-use plans with strategies for economic development and transport. In France the focus is on the city and sub-regional scale, through intercommunalité and in Britain the focus is on a move to regions as the most important scale for strategic planning, all essentially a part of the devolution and regionalisation process implemented rapidly after the election of the 1997 Labour government.

Policing planning

Embodied within the concept of regulation is also the right of appeal. In Britain, England and Wales, Scotland, and Ireland currently operate on the same principles: rights of appeal against a planning decision exist only for an applicant. Since plans have no legally binding status, a third party cannot object to a decision on the basis that it is not in conformity with the plan. Appeals are not made to the courts but to a special agency of government, the Planning Inspectorate in England, which operates in a semi-judicial fashion, hearing appeals and issuing recommendations. (Similar arrangements exist in Wales, Scotland and Northern Ireland.) The appeals system essentially considers the merits of the planning decisions taken by local authorities. For example, during the 1980s in Britain the appeal process became an important mechanism for ensuring that national planning policies were respected by local authorities: these policies allowed developers greater freedom to follow market demand, notably for housing and out-of-town retailing and offices, which many local authorities resisted. An increasing number of decisions were overturned at appeal based on the recommendations of the Inspectorate or the decisions of ministers. This is because the ultimate authority to grant or refuse an appeal rests with the minister responsible for planning, since although decision-making power has been delegated to the Inspectorate the minister reserves the power to 'recover' appeals and decide them him or herself. National planning policies have also been established as an important criterion in planning decisions. Third parties can challenge the legality of a planning permission through the courts, but the bases for legal challenges are very narrowly defined. On the other hand, when the courts do allow a challenge, their decision can have considerable impact on future operation of the system.

In France on the other hand, the basis for challenging a planning decision is essentially a question of legality, not the merits of the decision in planning terms. But the legally binding nature of plans offers greater opportunity to third parties as well as developers to challenge the refusal or granting of planning permission. Matters are complicated by the fact that the French legal system is organised into two parallel court systems: the Tribunaux Administratifs (administrative courts) dealing with the actions of public authorities and the Tribunaux Judiciaires (civil courts) looking after actions of private individuals and organisations. In practice however, most appeals related to planning issues go through Tribunaux Administratifs. This is the case if a planning decision is being challenged, a typical example being that of a planning permission (in which case the planning authority is the one being sued, this is referred to as a contentieux administratif). If a person or organisation is in an illegal position regarding a development, this becomes a contentieux pénal: it is the administration that sues the person or organisation. The court in charge is the Tribunal Correctionnel. In the third case, a person or organisation can challenge another on the grounds of a conflict regarding a development. Here, none of the parties are part of the administration.

Technical expertise

A particular feature of British planning over the last 20 years has been the growth of the consultancy sector. This sector traditionally served the needs of private developers but consultancies increasingly serve the needs of local authorities as well. In Britain the role of consultancies is of increasing importance as the number of specialist studies required as part of plan making processes has grown and the specialist resources of local authorities have shrunk. The upshot is a more and more frequent call on specialist consultancies to carry out the necessary research.

In France the technical expertise required to support the policy making of collectivités has been the growth of Agences d'Urbanisme. These organisations were first created under the 1967 Loi d'Orientation Foncière and are non-profit organisations originally created to assist collectivités in the drawing up of studies and plans. The Loi Voynet and Loi SRU reinforced the role and status of the Agences d'Urbanisme and they are now involved in a wide range of policy fields: planning, development, transport, environment, and regeneration. The Agences are sponsored by local government but require national government approval for their creation, and benefit from national government funding. Since 1979 they have operated as part of a national network. Their number has been growing following the Loi SRU. They operate within the same legal framework as associations and private companies that allows, for instance, greater flexibility in recruiting personnel than in collectivités themselves. In many respects these Agences bridge the technical gap between the needs of urban planning and the limited capacities of individual communes and are an increasingly vital part of the implementation of the new Plans d'Urbanisme.

Implementation

Both countries have developed specialist structures for the implementation of planning policy that stand outside the main institutions of central and local government, and both countries have created special agencies and development organisations to tackle particular aspects of land use change and development. The key distinction between France and Britain, however, is the movement in Britain towards the integration of the private sector into partnership arrangements, which often involve a reduction in the role or influence of local authorities, while in France the move is towards decentralisation, privileging collectivités as implementation agents.

The issue of public-private partnerships is dealt with in greater detail in later chapters, but certain basic points should be made here. When faced with the challenges of urban regeneration in the 1980s, the Conservative government identified excessive planning regulation and local authority failure as factors contributing to Britain's urban problems (notably in the White Paper 'Lifting the Burden' in 1985). An experimental solution to the regulative burden was the creation of Simplified Planning Zones: areas with a simplified planning control system and fiscal advantages for developments within the zones. Another new solution was the creation of single-purpose Urban Development Corporations (UDCs) in London and Liverpool, and later in eight other cities, charged with the regeneration of derelict industrial and dockland areas. These UDCs were given planning powers and direct funding from the Treasury, but the board was appointed by the Secretary of State, not elected. Not all major regeneration projects operated within UDCs. Salford Quays in Greater Manchester is a good example of an exception, but UDCs were symbolically important as part of the move towards a more private-sector-led view of planning in a traditionally public-sector-led domain. Local authorities now provide the framework for development and coordinate infrastructure provision, but private developers frequently initiate detailed development proposals.

France also developed an institutional framework for planning that included specialised implementation organisations. The most important of these structures is the Société d'économie mixte or SEM. SEMs are private companies in which collectivités have the majority share of the companies capital. SEMs are a way of ensuring that the *intérêt général*, a concept closest to the idea of public interest in Britain, is taken into account in the decision-making of companies involved in the provision of public services or infrastructure. Although the history of SEMs goes back to the 1950s, their current legal status was established by legislation in 1983, and since the mid-1980s the number of SEMs has grown significantly in parallel with decentralisation and intercommunalité. In 2005 there were an estimated 1,215 SEMs in France and a quarter of these were involved in development activities and a quarter dealt with housing management.[7] Thus, the benefits of single-purpose organisations and a private-sector competitive environment have been pursued in France whilst ensuring that collectivités remain in direct control of development.

Conclusion

The starting point of this chapter was a widely accepted politico-administrative analysis of France and Britain:[8] namely the idea of the British dual polity contrasted with the French fused polity. The ways in which this fundamental difference influences the operation of planning in both countries has been explored above, but an important point is that the systems are not fixed and have undergone significant changes over time, culminating in the recent legislation which is a preoccupation of much of this book. In some respects *décentralisation* has brought France closer to Britain by placing decision-making powers into the hands of 'collectivités' but this still serves to accentuate the differences between the two systems. In Britain, central government directs the system through national policy guidance while France relies on the central State's presence on the ground through the préfets and its field services to influence the process. And while France's 'collectivités' expand their field of action and independence British local government has seen its freedom to act constrained by an increasingly uniform national policy framework.

There are certain trends that are similar, but the evolution of the two systems still reflects the fundamental contrasts in the politico-administrative framework. First, we can observe the development of a more spatialised approach to strategies for regional economic development, stopping short of a national spatial plan. Second, and associated with the first point, there has been a move to link land use policy more closely to sectoral policies, particularly for economic development, regeneration and transport. Third, both countries have developed structures for joint plan-making through 'intercommunalité' in France and joint structure planning and regional planning bodies in England. The political and administrative structures favoured, however, reflect the difference between and paradoxes within both countries.

The French move to decentralisation may appear superficially like a move towards a more British model of local government, but it has been made clear here that the political and administrative framework in France results in a degree of independence in planning and decision making that is absent in Britain. The conception of 'collectivité' representing local interests rather than simply efficiently delivering local services has preserved the territorial structure of 'collectivités' in France, while in Britain territorial reorganisation has gone hand in hand with the so-called modernisation of planning and local government.

While in France greater power has been put in the hands of 'collectivités' the powers and resources of British local government have been curtailed and circumscribed, or even removed as in the case of development corporations. Paradoxically, however, devolution outside England has created the possibility for policies and institutions to diverge from the English model. The fact that planning powers ultimately rest with national government in Britain seems to make the restructuring of local authority planning powers or their exercise by a government appointed body far less problematic than it would be in France. French solutions do show a willingness to use alternative institutional structures such as SEMs or 'associations' but this remains within a strong public sector framework and within the control of 'collectivités'. The role of the private sector in the French system remains far more bounded and controlled than in today's Britain where public-private partnership is key and consultancies play an increasingly important role.

Notes

1 Fifth Republic Constitution, 1958 (Art. 1 modified by the Constitution Reform Act No. 2003-276, 28 March 2003).
2 Loi sur l'Administration territoriale de la République, 2 February 1992.
3 Ibidem, Art.1: 'l'administration territoriale de la République est assurée par les collectivités territoriales et par les services déconcentrés de l'État'.
4 Decree No. 2004-374, 29 April 2004, relating to the powers of préfets, to the organisation and the action of State services in the régions and départements.
5 Code Général des Collectivités Territoriales, Art. L5210-1.
6 These ministries are: Department for Communities and Local Government, Department for Education and Skills, Department of Trade and Industry, Department of the Environment, Food and Rural Affairs, the Home Office, Department of Culture, Media and Sport, Department of Work and Pensions, Department of Transport, Department of Health, the Cabinet Office.
7 Fédération des Sociétés d'Économie Mixte, www.fedsem.fr, site visited March 2006.
8 See, for instance, Newman and Thornley 1996.

References

Breuillard, M. (2000) L'administration locale en Grande-Bretagne, entre centralisation et régionalisation (Paris: l'Harmattan).
Breuillard, M. (2005) 'Searching for relevant areas: a Franco-British comparison of local government reforms', in H. Reynaert, K. Steyvers, P. Dewitt and J.-B. Pilet (eds) Revolution or Renovation? Reforming Local Politics in Europe (Brugge: Vanden Boele Publishers), pp. 559–83.
Department of the Environment (1996) Local Government Reorganization Paper, No. 4 (London: The Stationery Office).
Hazell, R. (2004) 'Conclusion: the unfinished business of devolution', in A. Trench (ed.) Has Devolution Made a Difference?: The State of the Nations (Exeter: Imprint Academic), pp. 255–75.
Marcou, G. (ed.) (2003) 'Les régions entre l'État et les collectivités locales: étude comparative de cinq États européens à autonomie régionale ou à constitution fédérale', Travaux du Centre d'études et de Prévision, no. 6 (Paris: Ministère de l'Intérieur).
Marcou, G. (2004) 'Décentralisation: approfondissement ou nouveau cycle?', Les Cahiers français, no. 318 (Décentralisation, État et Territoires) (Paris: La Documentation française).
Newman, P. and Thornley, A. (1996) Urban Planning in Europe (London: Routledge).
Rao, N. (2005) 'From committees to leaders and cabinets: the British experience', in R. Berg and N. Rao (eds) Transforming Local Political Leadership (Basingstoke: Palgrave Macmillan), pp. 42–58.

Stoker, G. (1998) *Rapport sur la Régionalisation et l'Autonomie Locale – Étude du Royaume-Uni*, Conseil de l'Europe, Comité directeur des autorités locales et régionales (February).

Stephenson, R. and Poxon, J. (2001) 'Regional strategy making and the new structures and processes for regional governance', *Local Government Studies*, 27(1): 109–24.

Chapter 5

Actors and instruments in the planning systems

Philip Booth, Suzy Nelson and Didier Paris

Introduction

Earlier chapters in this book have looked at the conditions within Britain and France which planning – in the widest sense of the word – must address. In this chapter we move forward to consider the instruments that are used in the two countries to articulate and provide for the implementation of spatial policy and the actors who are involved in making plans and policies and implementing them. Specifically, we shall be exploring the nature of the planning systems that have emerged in both countries at the beginning of the twenty-first century as the result of major legislative reform, and be noting the reasons that lie behind the move to reform.

The past 30 years have seen a decisive break with the welfare state model that had prevailed since the end of World War II. In Britain, the break had started in the late 1970s and reached its culmination in the Conservative governments of Margaret Thatcher. In France, the presidency of François Mitterrand, which had begun with a reaffirmation of strong public policy, quickly changed in the period of austerity after 1983. In Britain, the return of the Labour party to power in 1997 did not reverse the trend, and the neo-liberal tendency gained ground in France in the periods of 'cohabitation' (right-wing governments under a left-wing president) and later under the presidency of Jacques Chirac, even if a French social welfare model persisted. Then, too, both countries were experiencing worsening social and economic conditions in the cities. Policies for urban regeneration were put into place, culminating with the Single Regeneration Budget in Britain and the Contrats de Ville and the Grands Projets Urbains programmes in France. The pragmatic approach that is apparent in both countries appears very far removed from the certainties of the 1950s and 1960s.

This, then, is the background for any discussion of the actors and instruments of land-use planning in both countries. Both France and Britain share much in common in terms of the social and economic evolution of the past 30 years. Both countries have grappled with the difficulty of finding appropriate mechanisms for managing the process of change, ensuring progress, and sometimes of assimilating decline, as they affected the location and distribution of activities and development. There is a further similarity that both countries undertook major reforms of their land-use planning systems in the later 1960s and again at the beginning of the new century. There, of course, the similarities end: the nature of the instruments of planning owe much to the administrative and legal frameworks that have been charted in Chapter 4.

Britain from 1968 to 2004: from structure and local plans to integrated spatial planning

In Britain, the problem of land-use planning was seen essentially as the inflexibility and the unresponsiveness to the need for growth of the plans that had been created under the Town and Country Planning Act of 1947. Such was the analysis of the Planning Advisory Group that had been set up to investigate the problem in 1963. The Group's recommendation for a new hierarchy of plans, enacted in 1968, was intended to be a radical departure. Structure plans would provide a strategic context for development at county level and the intention was that the country as a whole would be covered by strategic planning documents. Local plans would then be prepared by the district planning authorities to convert the strategic requirements of the structure plan into detailed policies for land use, but districts were not obliged to prepare such plans, although they were encouraged to do so.

The new system was introduced against a background of a weakening economy. Moreover, the ambitions for the new system proved over-optimistic. Structure plans took many years to complete – coverage of England was not complete until the early 1980s – and released from an obligation to prepare local plans, districts showed themselves reluctant to prepare plans. By the 1980s, too, the policy climate had changed radically. The Conservative government under Margaret Thatcher had little time for strategic planning and generally regarded the planning process as something whose only function was to enable the market to operate effectively.

In practice the approach of the Conservative government resulted in conflict over a series of major developments in the late 1980s. In 1991, an amendment to the law required, first, that district planning authorities had to create plans for the whole of their area and, second, that decisions should be taken in accordance with the development plan, unless material considerations indicated otherwise. Though this wording was ambiguous, the policy intention was clear: ministers referred to the plan as being henceforward the 'first consideration' and to the inauguration of a 'plan-led' system of planning. This did not, however, fundamentally alter the indicative character of plans or the discretionary powers available to decision-makers.

An equally important element of the planning system in Britain has been the policy guidance issued by central government. Originally given in the form of ministerial circulars, in England and Wales, the system of guidance was rationalised from 1988 onwards as the Planning Policy Guidance Notes (PPG), now being reissued as Planning Policy Statements (PPS). At the same time, Regional Planning Guidance was developed for each of the English regions, as a means of adapting national policy to regional conditions. Because of the indicative nature of plans in the British system, this guidance has an important bearing on decisions on planning applications. But PPS also have a role in framing the content of plans themselves.

By the end of the 1990s, the planning system had begun to look inadequate to meet the needs of the circumstances that were very different from the 1960s. Part of the problem was in the nature of the planning instruments themselves: plans that were intended to be flexible and responsive had proved to be neither. Part of the problem had come from incremental change, notably with the abolition of the metropolitan counties in 1986. The inauguration of the plan-led system had had the consequence of increasing the rate of objections to plans in the course of preparation, thus substantially increasing enormously the time that preparation was taking. And finally, the relationship between the classic instruments of land-use planning and newer forms of policy-making that had a spatial impact was not always clear.

France from 1967 to 2000: from the Loi d'Orientation Foncière to the Loi Relative à la Solidarité et au Renouvellement Urbains

Faced at the time with rapid urban growth, France reformed its planning system at the very moment that changes were in train in Britain: the Loi d'Orientation Foncière (LOF) was enacted in 1967. The introduction of the Schéma Directeur d'Aménagement et d'Urbanisme (SDAU), later simply 'schéma directeur', was intended to create documents that fixed main direction for growth at the scale of the urban area as a whole. Originally they were not so much strategic documents as the means of setting a framework for planning for growth. At the level of the commune, the 'plan d'occupation des sols' (POS), which was required to be compatible with the SDAU, controlled land use and the density of development through the use of a plot ratio control, the 'coefficient d'occupation des sols' (COS) for each parcel of land. It was in no sense prospective planning. As for implementation, the tools that had been used before 1967 had suffered from procedural rigidity and were replaced in the new legislation by the 'zone d'aménagement concerté' (ZAC) whose flexibility rapidly ensured its widespread application for major areas of development.

The expectation of growth on which the instruments of the LOF were based faltered in the oil crisis of 1973 and the early SDAU were quickly discredited because of assumptions of high rates of growth which were not realised. But there are two other points to note about the SDAU. One is that they were never intended to cover the whole country, but only urban areas undergoing expansion. The other is that they could not be applied directly to individual development decisions and had to be mediated by the POS to take effect. The possibilities for slippage between the SDAU and the POS were, therefore, considerable (Motte 1995).

Decentralisation of powers in 1983 led to the first significant change to the system. The communes became responsible for taking the initiative in the preparation of POS, determining 'permis de construire' (building permits, roughly equivalent to planning permission), and participating in an intercommunal syndicate for the preparation of an SD, all tasks that had hitherto been the direct responsibility of the State. This decentralisation may have led to certain abuses of power, but it also freed local authorities and allowed them to develop a vision for their areas in a way that had been impossible before.

Moreover, priorities were changing in the 1980s and 1990s, even if the question of controlling urban sprawl remained. The themes of solidarity, social development and the housing crisis came to the forefront of public debate and these were addressed through the development of urban policy, specifically in the Loi d'Orientation sur la Ville (LOV) of 1991, rather than the land-use planning system. But the measures designed to deal with the problem of housing were not much used and quickly showed their limits. The Programme Local de l'Habitat, reintroduced in the LOV, designed to encourage an equitable distribution of social housing, did not fully attain its objective. At the same time, the question of ensuring coherence between the policies of individual communes at the level of the urban area as a whole had been addressed in only a very partial fashion, leaving aside the few 'Communautés Urbaines' created after 1966. The realisation of these problems grew in both political and professional consciousness, particularly on the occasion of the publication of the report produced by the then mayor of Orléans, J.-P. Sueur (Ministère de l'Emploi et de la Solidarité 1998).

Reform eventually arrived at the end of the 1990s in three pieces of legislation that modified both local governance and the instruments of land-use planning. To the Loi Chevènement and the Loi Voynet of 1999 (whose titles in informal usage come from the ministers who were responsible for them), which dealt with intercommunal cooperation and strategic development and local governance respectively, was added in 2000 the Loi relative à la Solidarité et au Renouvellement Urbains (SRU: Urban Renewal and Solidarity Act), which was firmly rooted in the reforms of the two earlier pieces of legislation.

The nature of planning instruments in Britain and France

It is against the background of rapidly changing expectations of land-use planning in both countries that we need to consider the current hierarchy of planning instruments. The system of plans intended to give expression to ideas about the future management of land use and the spatial distribution of activities looks, at least superficially, to have developed on broadly similar lines in Britain and France. In practice there are some fundamental differences in the way in which plans are conceived and used. The tradition of codified administrative law in France led to the development of a planning system in which policy – as it might be expressed in Britain – was expressed as a series of legally binding rules in the Code de l'Urbanisme and then in the zoning plans that the code prescribed. In Britain, on the other hand, with its tradition of case law and of municipal independence, the idea of zoning regulations came to seem too restrictive and flexibility became a key criterion. Plans became, from 1947 onwards, indicative, not binding.

The reform of the planning systems

The current of hierarchy of plans in both countries is the product of reforms that are still very recent. In France the Loi SRU was passed at the end of 2000. In England, the Planning and Compulsory Purchase Act received royal assent in May 2004, although the debate on reform had been initiated in 2001 with the Planning Green Paper. The experience of those reforms is thus very limited.

In France, the underlying rationale for the reform was fourfold: to ensure that urban areas were treated as a whole; to improve the coherence of strategic and operational policy; to promote social balance within urban areas; and to foster local responsibility in the development of planning policy. The concept of sustainable development was introduced for the first time into French planning law, and there was a stated desire to widen the scope of planning from the narrow focus on land-use that characterised the previous system (see Beaurain 2003; Soler-Couteaux 2003). These reforms have to be seen in a wider context of administrative reform already alluded to, however. On the one hand, the reform intended to introduce plans that would be genuinely strategic in their intent. On the other hand, by requiring urban areas to cooperate in plan-making, the new law was intended to cement the intercommunal groupings introduced by the Loi Chevènement. Each of the new Communautés d'Agglomération created under this act were required to prepare a strategic plan.

The planning instruments introduced by the Loi SRU were specifically designed to respond to this rationale: the strategic planning document is now the Schéma de Cohérence Territoriale (SCOT), which is designed to cover the whole of an urban area, specifically the area of the 'communautés d'agglomération'. The detailed planning document is the Plan Local d'Urbanisme (PLU), which is normally prepared for a single commune and carries detailed zoning regulations for every part of the area to which it applies. At the heart of the system is the concept of the 'projet urbain' (urban project) which is essentially a vision for an area's future development expressed in the Projet d'Aménagement et de Développement Durable (PADD; sustainable development document), a requirement for both the SCOT and the PLU. The new planning system of the Loi SRU was intended to be genuinely prospective and strategic, and to allow for a proper articulation between strategy and its application in detail. And the reform of planning was part of the agenda for the modernisation of local government in that communes were obliged to work together in preparing policies for the future of their area (Jacquot and Priet 2004).

The rationale for reform of planning in England in some ways mirrors that for the French reforms. The failure of the previous system to provide a genuinely strategic framework for future development was one element. The desire to broaden the vision of planning, expressed in the term 'spatial planning' that is increasingly being used, was another. But the English reforms also invoked other criticisms, some of which are longstanding: the complexity of planning documents and their lack of flexibility; the failure to engage the 'community' in decision-making; the slowness of procedures. The major output of reform was an entirely remodelled hierarchy of development plans.

Structure plans have been abolished and strategic planning is now to be undertaken at regional level, with Regional Spatial Strategies (RSS) creating a strategic framework for more detailed planning at the local level. Districts are now required to create Local Development Frameworks (LDF) for their areas, which are to be portfolios of documents providing detailed planning advice, though not necessarily for the whole of the local authority area. A major innovation at this level is the requirement for districts to produce a Statement of Community Involvement (SCI) as part of the LDF, in which the local authority must spell out how it intends to allow the public to participate in the production of planning policy. Although public participation in the planning process goes back nearly 40 years to the Skeffington Report of 1967, the SCI gives 'community involvement' a higher formal status than it has ever had before.

This general statement of instruments and themes obscures two essential points about comparison between Britain and France. First, it does not recognise the underlying differences of intention and meaning between the two systems of planning. Second, a focus on plans as the sole expression of the management of future land use in no way reflects the growing diversity of modes of policy making that affect the spatial distribution of activities. Both need to be considered here.

Origins and meanings

Taking the narrow view of the instruments of planning as referring to a hierarchy of plans, it is clear that the reformed planning systems in both countries present many continuities with the systems they replace.

In Britain, there has been a long-standing preoccupation with flexibility and the need for administrative discretion. The revolution of the 1947 Town and Country Planning Act was to make plans an indication of policy to be followed, but not the ultimate authority for decisions on future development. In doing so, it made as its starting point the decision on the particular proposal, to be informed by all *material considerations* in the wording of the Act, of which the development plan might only be one. Such an approach has created some interesting tensions. One is that flexibility also creates uncertainties for developers. The other is that, for all the good intentions, the plans prepared after 1947 all too often were neither sufficiently flexible nor sufficiently detailed as a guide for development (Booth 2003).

The contrast with the French tradition of codified law, the mechanism by which the exercise of discretionary power could be limited, is stark. The Code de l'Urbanisme sets out in detail how responsibilities of decision-makers are to be exercised and what the State requires of individuals. Zoning with regulations was the natural expression of a concern to define rights and obligations in a way that minimised chance and the abuse of power. Two difficulties were apparent in such a system. One had to do with the difficulty of making changes in a legitimate fashion. The other was the problem of making and implementing truly strategic plans.

These differences account for the significant differences of emphasis in the debate on reform. Where in France a desire to overcome the rigidity of the regulations is matched by a fear that to do so undermines the legitimacy of the system as whole, the British have struggled to maintain the integrity of the system while at the same time as preserving the flexibility of the plans.

Other forms of spatial policy making

To limit this discussion of planning instruments to the hierarchy of land-use plans identified by town planning legislation in France and Britain is of course to ignore a great deal that might reasonably be called planning. Other spatialised policies have been developed, including discrete area policy making. These have led to contractual and negotiated policy-making that is directly concerned with the spatial distribution of development. It includes, finally, policy-making that is not specifically spatial, but which nevertheless has an important incidence on places. These categories are, moreover, not self-contained.

Discrete-area planning was given a particular boost in the 1980s when Enterprise Zones were introduced, the purpose of which was to stimulate economic development by freeing industries from regulatory control and, more importantly, from local taxes. The paradox is that an instrument which was specifically intended to free wealth-generating enterprise from the need for planning control can in fact be seen as a planning instrument. Also in the 1980s, the creation of the Urban Development Corporations (UDC) led to powers to control development being taken from local authorities in designated areas and vested in UDCs. The introduction, in 2000, of the Community Development Strategies that local authorities are now required to produce has led to the emergence of a policy document that, while not specifically an instrument of land-use planning, nevertheless will almost inevitably have a bearing on spatial policy.

Finally, no account of the nature of British planning instruments would be complete without reference to the long-standing use of agreements (since legislative change in 1991, referred to as planning obligations) between developers and local authorities. These have been used to secure benefits, often in the form of improvements to infrastructure, in the context of applications for planning permission. These planning obligations undertaken by developers confirm the importance of negotiation in the planning process, but have been criticised for the way in which they may distort decision-making (Campbell *et al.* 2000).

France also has a tradition of discrete-area planning, which it can be argued is in any case a logical extension of a zoning system. The ZAC discussed above, is the obvious example of this. Until the reforms of the Loi SRU, ZAC were regarded both as an essential means of promoting and controlling development and as a potential danger to approved POSs because of the way in which they could depart substantially from the plan. The Loi SRU remedies this defect by requiring the detailed regulations for a ZAC to feature in the PLU itself.

In parallel to these instruments of land-use planning, in both France and Britain other forms of policy-making designed to deal with urban problems more generally were also beginning to have an impact on the way in which development took place. These are dealt with in detail in Chapter 9. For the purposes of this chapter, the point about all these forms of policy-making in both countries is that, although they may be primarily about the allocation of funding, developing partnership arrangements between levels of government or involving the community, they all have a significant impact on the spatial distribution of activities. In that sense, they are also planning documents which run in parallel to the core instruments of land-use planning. It was of course a key objective of the recent reforms in both countries that land-use plans should incorporate policy made in other arenas. It remains an open question as to how far that objective will be met in practice. But they raise another question about the nature of those involved in policy-making, and it is to the actors within the systems in both countries to whom we must now turn.

Actors in the planning system

Central government and national politicians

One of the important impacts of the French decentralisation reforms of the 1980s was the way in which the State began to use contracts as a major means of maintaining working relationships with newly empowered local governments. These contracts commit the State to making financial contributions to programmes of work carried out by different tiers of government, even if the contracts are not always honoured. First used to implement specific policy initiatives, such as the Politique de Villes Moyennes in the 1970s, they have since decentralisation become widespread. At the same time, the Ministère de l'Équipement continues to be actively involved in preparing plans and processing applications for permission for small communes that lack the technical resources to do so themselves. However, the recent reinforcement of intercommunal cooperation by the Loi Chevènement has allowed for a strengthening of technical services at the level of the intercommunal grouping.

In Britain central government has continued to be more actively involved in the administration of localities. During the 1980s, Conservative governments intervened in local government administration both to reduce spending and involve the private sector in public service provision and to promote private sector development. Since 1997 Labour governments have advocated the modernisation of local government, which in practice means an emphasis on cost effectiveness and on customer satisfaction with service provision, and the encouragement of effective local political leadership and more active engagement of citizens. Central government in Britain is in a strong position to set the agenda for local government, because it provides the majority of the funds for local government services from general taxation. The Labour government has continued to follow the policy, originally initiated by the Conservatives, of promoting more efficient local planning services by setting target times for making decisions on planning applications and by rewarding local authorities that meet them with additional resources.

Although central government in Britain intervenes in the administration of local government, the worlds of local and national politics are more distinct than in France. Some national politicians may have begun their political careers in local government. However, once elected to parliament, they invariably resign as local councillors, although there is no legal requirement to do so. Whilst parliamentary backbenchers may champion the interests of their locality, it would be seen as improper for the holders of government office to use their position to obtain preferential treatment for the locality which they represent.

In France national and local politics are much more closely integrated. National politicians are strongly linked to their localities through the system of 'cumul des mandats' (accumulation of public office) which involves politicians simultaneously holding a number of elected offices. A mayor is frequently also a deputy or a senator in the national parliament and perhaps the president of a Communauté d'Agglomération or Communauté Urbaine as well. The holders of local political office thus frequently have direct access to national government and are able to use this to the advantage of their localities.

Local authorities working in partnership

In both countries local authorities are now the central actors in the planning process. As changes in the structure and competences of local authorities are discussed in Chapter 4, we limit the discussion here to the growth of their involvement in partnership working (and the changes in the structure of political leadership within local authorities).

In France, the process of contractualisation that marks central-local relations is becoming increasingly used to define relations between local and regional government, too. The Contrats d'Agglomération that have become a key instrument of defining the spatial distribution of activities as the basis for funding involves regions negotiating with Communautés d'Agglomération or indeed with intercommunal syndicates which group such communautés into larger groupings for the purposes of policy-making.

In Britain, the focus of recent change has been the formalisation of partnerships within, rather than between, local authorities. After several decades of *ad hoc* experimentation, latterly in the context of the Single Regeneration Budget programme, the Labour government in 2000 introduced Local Strategic Partnerships (LSP), which local authorities are responsible for initiating. They are intended to promote policy coordination between public sector organisations, such as health trusts, housing associations and the police, and typically involve representatives of the voluntary sector as well as local business and local communities. They have a specific responsibility for preparing the community strategy.

The professions

Professions have evolved very differently in the French and British contexts (Campagnac and Winch 1997). In the context of the more market-orientated system of development in Britain, professional organisations are important in defining and regulating the role of technical experts. In the context of the greater State-led system of development in France, the systems of State administration and, since decentralisation, local administration perform these functions. Thus in Britain the Royal Town Planning Institute plays a key role in determining what planners do, much more important than that of the Conseil Français des Urbanistes (CFDU) even if the profession has made moves to organise itself, notably through the creation of the Office Professionnel de Qualification des Urbanistes (OPQU).

In Britain there is continuing debate about the role of the planning profession and questioning of how professional planners should relate to contemporary policy agenda (see for example Evans 1993; Royal Town Planning Institute 2001). In the last two decades, regeneration and sustainability have emerged as new important policy fields, but planning departments do not generally lead on these issues in local authorities and many, possibly most, of those involved in policy development and implementation in these fields are not planners. The Royal Town Planning Institute has acknowledged that planning overlaps with a number of other policy fields and has responded by setting up networks focused on various themes including regeneration and sustainability open to other professionals.

The recent reform of the planning system in England and Wales is likely to change the roles played by planners working within local authorities. If the Government's intentions are realised, there will more emphasis on the plan-making stage. This may challenge the long established division of labour within local authority planning departments, which usually have separate teams responsible for plan preparation and development control. Planners will now need to set planning policy within the context of the Community Development Strategy and to become more active in involving the community in the plan-making process. This is likely to result in a change in the expertise of planning professionals and also for planners to work more alongside others with some overlapping and some different skills (Tewdwr-Jones 2004).

Development agencies

In both France and Britain, development agencies play an important role in the development and the implementation of planning policy. In the UK, central government is responsible for the creation of these agencies, where as in France local government plays the key role in their creation. In both countries such agencies operate with a degree of autonomy and their activities are less directly subject to public scrutiny. In the UK agencies have been set up to promote regeneration in targeted areas and are expected to complete this work in a fixed time period, whereas in France agencies are a more established part of the local institutional networks. In the UK development agencies are involved both in the planning and implementation of development, but in France there are two types of organisations involved at different stages of the development process.

In France, Agences d'Urbanisme, grouped together in the Fédération Nationale des Agences d'Urbanisme, are set up to provide technical services to a number of different local authorities. They are public sector partnerships, involving the central State and local authorities, but are outside the main system of local administration. They usually operate at the level of an agglomération and are managed by a board presided over by an elected member of a leading commune. They tend to concentrate on studies relating to future plans and projects, and the collection of data about the localities they serve. They also play an important monitoring role in the area that they serve. The renewed emphasis on intercommunality since the introduction of the Loi Chevènement has led to the creation of new agencies. However, there are sometimes rivalries between Agences d'Urbanisme and the technical services of local authorities.

Sociétés d'Économie Mixte (SEMs) are widely used by French local authorities to implement development such as urban renewal programmes and business parks. Some are linked to a single commune, whilst others are linked to several communes or to regions and departments. Although SEMs involve private sector partners, they are generally non-profit making. However, they allow local authorities to operate effectively in the commercial environment of development, as they are regulated by private sector law. The Société Centrale d'Équipement du Territoire provides advice to SEMs and services a network of 200 SEMs, which provides the opportunity for professional staff to move from one organisation to another.

The UK Labour government has set up both national and local organisations to deal with the problems of urban renewal and economic development. Within England, a series of Regional Development Agencies (RDA) were put in place after 1997 specifically to promote the economic development of the regions. At a national level, English Partnerships was set up as regeneration agency, designed to offer support to local authorities. In 2000, central government created a new type of organisation, Urban Regeneration Companies, to implement development. The purpose of the Urban Regeneration Companies is 'to redevelop and bring back into use the worst areas in our towns and cities' (DETR 2000). They are intended to provide a focus for regeneration activity within defined areas and aim to provide a high quality urban environment, attract private sector investment and deliver projects which will enhance economic prosperity. URCs in many ways resemble the earlier UDCs, but they are more firmly based on a partnership model. They are largely funded by the RDAs, local authorities and English Partnerships, but tax relief is available to businesses who wish to contribute to their running costs. The chair of the board, as for UDCs, is drawn from the private sector and it is the express intention of the government that they should be 'business friendly'.

It was widely assumed that the creation of UDCs had ended under the Conservative government in 1992. However, in 2003 the government announced the creation of three Urban Development Corporations in areas designated for growth in its plan for Sustainable Communities. The reason for this is that UDCs have greater powers than URCs; they are able to compulsorily purchase land and make decisions on development control. The new UDCs will be given powers to approve strategic planning applications, whilst the local authorities will continue to deal with applications for small-scale development. It is hoped that the new UDCs will work in close collaboration with local authorities and LSPs (Raco 2005). However, there are concerns that there may be tensions with existing local communities, which will have to absorb large new populations.

Developers

In the UK developers, particularly housebuilders, have had a big impact on the planning system in recent decades. The House Builders Federation is a very effective lobbying organisation and they have over a period of several decades argued for a planning system which makes more land available for housing development, and which offers more certainty and quicker decision-making (Ball 1983; Hull 1997). These demands correspond very closely with the objectives of the recent planning reforms.

At a local level in Britain, those with interests in potential development sites have usually been actively involved in local plan preparation, because the plan is likely to determine what they can build, and hence the profit to be made from development. Central government has actively encouraged developers to become involved in pre-application discussions with the local planning authority as a means of ensuring a speedier process and a more certain outcome. In this way, developers have been actively involved in the planning process at the local level.

In France the development industry does not exert the same kind of influence on the plan-making process, because developers are generally smaller and are not as powerful a lobbying group as in the UK, and because plan-making procedures are more bureaucratic there. In France nearly half of dwellings in 2001 were built by individual owner developers (Ball 2003). Much of this type of development is approved through the 'lotissement' (subdivision) procedure used for development of plots of land on greenfield sites, usually previously used for agriculture. However, there is some evidence that large French construction firms are moving into housebuilding as part of a strategy of diversification of their activities (Ball 2003), so they may begin to exert an influence on the plan-making process. Indeed, the Fédération Nationale des Promoteurs-Constructeurs, which subsumed the Association des Constructeurs des Maisons Individuelles, is becoming an increasingly important player.

Conclusions

There is within this discussion of actors and instruments in British and French planning a certain symmetry. Both countries have faced broadly similar pressures over 30 years. Both have perceived weaknesses in their instruments of planning and have sought to reform their planning systems to respond to the new exigencies of the early twenty-first century. It is particularly in the recent reforms that both the similarities and the striking differences between the two countries become apparent.

First and foremost, there is a distinction that must be drawn between the rhetoric and the reality of reform in both countries. Elements of the rhetoric are shared: the insistence on promoting sustainable development, the need to develop prospective planning; the need for strategic planning as well as informative local guidance. In other things, the rhetoric is highly specific to each country. The emphasis on flexibility in the reforms in England is part of a long established way of thinking, just as the greater emphasis on certainty is characteristic of French discourse on planning over many years. But it is important to note, too, that in both France and Britain, reform has attempted to recognise some of the inherent weaknesses. In Britain, reform was intended to reduce the uncertainty that was an essential concomitant of an indicative system of planning. In France, the emphasis upon rights and legal certainty militated against plans that were really prospective, a fault the Loi SRU was designed to address.

The implementation of reform suggests that in both countries the change is less radical than announced. In neither country has reform fundamentally changed the character of the system, and there are many continuities between old and new. The practical differences between the old POS and the new PLU are slight and are not so much in the form of the plan itself as the requirement to produce a PADD. The extent to which the LDF will differ from the predecessor local plans is not at all clear. On the other hand, the SCOT in France and the RSS in Britain are indeed innovations, though what their impact will really be remains to be seen.

There are other aspects of the instruments and actors of planning that offer similarities and contrasts. The first is that planning reform has been closely allied to administrative reform in both countries. This link is far more substantial in France, where reform of the planning system is intended to reinforce the intercommunal cooperation that was the subject of the Loi Voynet and the Loi Chevènement that immediately preceded it. Changing governance informs planning reform in Britain too. The move to forms of deliberative democracy represented by partnership arrangements is now felt within the plan-making process and in the specialist agencies that are being developed to implement change.

The second is the way in which, in both France and Britain, there has been a growth in the ways in which spatial policy is being prepared. Land-use planning has run the risk in both countries of being marginalised in the face of new forms of policy document – particularly the Projets d'Agglomération in France and the Community Development Strategies in Britain. In both countries, therefore, there has been pressure to rediscover the integrative capacity of land-use planning.

The third is the parallel growth in the range of actors involved in planning. In France, it has been very largely a matter of developing new forms of public sector agency, but with an increasing emphasis on local responsibility. In Britain, again following an already well developed track, it is the further involvement of the private sector that is most characteristic of recent changes. As important as the emergence of new actors has been the development of relationships between actors. In France, these new relationships are characterised by the use of contracts; for the British, it is partnership in its various guises that has become the key term.

In spite, therefore, of the similarity of the pressures that both countries have faced, the forms of planning instrument and the nature of actors has remained substantially marked by national characteristics. The experience of the past 30 years may have been shared, but the responses have been mediated by the political, administrative and legal traditions of each country. Indeed, the whole interest of comparisons such as these comes from the interplay of generalised problems and specific circumstances.

References

Bailey, N. (2003) 'Local strategic partnerships in England: the continuing search for collaborative advantage, leadership and strategy in urban governance', *Planning Theory and Practice*, 4(4): 443–57.

Ball, M. (1983) *Housing Policy and Economic Power*, London: Methuen.

Ball, M. (2003) 'Markets and the structure of the housebuilding industry: an international perspective', *Urban Studies*, 40(5–6): 897–916.

Beaurain, C. (2003) 'Économie et développement durable dans le discours de la production territoriale', *Mots*, 72: 45–9.

Booth, P. (2003) *Planning by Consent: The Origins and Nature of British Development Control*, London: Routledge.

Campagnac, E. and Winch, G. (1997) 'The social regulation of technical expertise: the corps and the profession in France and Britain', in R. Whitley and P.H. Kristensen (eds) *In Governance at Work: The Social Regulation of Economic Relations*, Oxford: Oxford University Press.

Campbell, H., Ellis, H., Gladwell, C. and Henneberry, J. (2000) 'Planning obligations, planning practice and land use', *Environment and Planning B: Planning and Design*, 27: 759–75.

Department of the Environment, Transport and the Regions (DETR) (2000) *Our Towns and Cities: Delivering an Urban Renaissance*, London: HMSO.

Evans, B. (1993) 'Why we no longer need a town planning profession', *Planning Practice and Research*, 8(1) 9–15.

Hull, A. (1997) 'Restructuring the debate on allocating land for housing growth', *Housing Studies*, 12(3): 367–8.

Jacquot, H. and Priet F. (2004) *Droit de l'Urbanisme*, 5th edn, Paris: Dalloz.

Jégouzo, Y. (2001) 'La loi solidarité et renouvellement urbains', *Actualité Juridique Droit Administratif*, 1, 20 January: 9–17.

Local Government Association (2002) *Probity in Planning (update): The Role of Councillors and Officers*, London: Local Government Association.

Ministère de l'Emploi et de la Solidarité (1998) *Demain la Ville*. Report to the Ministre de l'Emploi et de la Solidarité, Paris: La Documentation française, 2 vols.

Motte, A (1995) 'Un renouvellement du mode de gestion des espaces urbanisés français? Hypothèses exploratoires', in A. Motte (ed.) *Schéma Directeur et Projet d'Agglomération*, Lyon: Editions Juris Services, pp. 15–32.

Raco, M. (2005) 'A step change or a step back? The Thames Gateway and the re-birth of the Urban Development Corporations', *Local Economy*, 20(2): 141–53.

Royal Town Planning Institute (2001) *A New Vision for Planning: Delivering Sustainable Communities, Settlements and Places*, London: Royal Town Planning Institute.

Soler-Couteaux, P. (2003) 'L'ardente obligation du schéma de cohérence territoriale', *Actualité Juridique Droit Administratif*, 8 September: 1528–34.

Tewdwr-Jones, M. (2004) 'Spatial planning: principles, practices and cultures', *Journal of Planning and Environment Law*, 57(5): 560–9.

Zetter, R., Darke, R. and Mason, R. (1997) *The Role of Elected Members in Plan Making and Development Control*, London: Royal Town Planning Institute.

Chapter 6

Strategic spatial planning at the metropolitan level

The cases of Manchester and Lyon

Roelof Verhage, Mark Baker and Paul Boino

Introduction

Throughout Europe, cities are developing strategic policies for their future development. Thus, they become the driving force behind a new type of strategic planning, through the elaboration of 'metropolitan development strategies' aimed at social, economic, or cultural development in a context of both competition and co-operation between cities or city regions in Europe. These strategies involve choices that do not primarily have a spatial character, but that have consequences for territorial development. Cities in France and in England are no exception. At the same time, efforts are being made in these two countries to reinvigorate statutory spatial planning (Loi SRU of 2000 in France, Planning and Compulsory Purchase Act of 2004 in England), through comprehensive spatial plans that should produce coherence between different public policies. The relation between these spatial plans and the emerging development strategies of the cities becomes an issue. Numerous questions impose themselves, such as: do comprehensive spatial plans correspond to the needs of a globalised, networked society? Can the actors of the new strategic planning and the procedures of the traditional land-use planning be brought in line? How do the different forms of spatial planning relate to sectoral policies?

A renewed preoccupation with strategic spatial planning can be observed both in France and England. In France, the Loi d'Orientation Foncière of 1967 introduced a hierarchy of planning documents that – primarily through the Plan d'occupation des sols (POS) – allowed detailed control of the urban fabric. Yet it was widely seen as having failed to produce an adequate framework for strategic thinking at the metropolitan level. The Schéma Directeur was too rigidly focused on land use, and not sufficiently aimed at implementation, to be effective. The Loi SRU has attempted to reintroduce a strategic dimension to urban planning, with its emphasis on *cohérence*, creating direct linkages between land-use planning, transport and housing. In England, there has been increasing concern over the failure of existing planning instruments to grapple with the metropolitan dimension in development. As with the Schéma Directeur, the 'structure plan' has failed to live up to its promise, and in any case was much weakened by the abolition of the metropolitan counties, where Unitary Development Plans were introduced to perform both a strategic, and a detailed, land-use allocation role. As with the Loi SRU, the Planning and Compulsory Purchase Act 2004 was partly designed to recast the hierarchy of planning documents in order to strengthen strategic spatial planning at the level of the conurbation.

What becomes clear from any investigation of the changes taking place in France and England is that a discussion of instruments necessarily begs questions about *agencies* and *actors*. The effective implementation of land-use planning is intimately bound up with the nature of local governance, which itself has been undergoing radical change in both countries. A disjointed analysis of local decision-making processes on the one side, and the legal framework on the other, is artificial. A well-wrought analysis of the strategies of the actors, and the resulting evolutions in local governance, is required to understand the consequences of new legal initiatives concerning spatial planning and, more generally, to capture the evolution of spatial planning.

As Salet *et al.* (2003) argue, the evolution of spatial planning in Europe takes place in a context of tension between decentralisation and co-operation at the metropolitan level. Decentralisation increases the competition between local authorities. At the same time, co-operation at the metropolitan level is more than ever necessary to assert the attractiveness of an area in a globalised economy. Spatial planning, which has always aimed at creating coherence between different sectoral policies, operates in this field of tension between endogenous dynamics (local actors, local identity, local development) and the diffusion of globalised models in the form of best practices. Metropolitan development strategies and new practices of negotiation take place at the hinge between spatial planning and urban government. As such, they offer a good entry to study the way in which spatial planning and urban government are articulated, the way in which this articulation is structured in the decision-making processes and the extent to which it responds to the needs of European cities.

The French situation

Institutional and legal situation

The Loi Relative à la Solidarité et au Renouvellement Urbains (SRU), as of 13 December 2000, aims at reinvigorating spatial planning by a revision of the existing regulatory tools. As has been described in Chapter 5 of this book, the Loi d'Orientation Foncière (LOF) of 1967 had a similar objective, but did not result in an increased attention for strategic spatial planning, as was the aim of the introduction of the strategic plan Schéma Directeur. Most of the *communes* drew up a local land use plan (POS) in the decades following the law. The Schéma Directeur, on the contrary, quickly fell into disuse.

In the absence of a comprehensive spatial planning document at the local level, the legislator preferred to support throughout the 1980s and 1990s sectoral planning procedures. In 2000, the Loi SRU was introduced in order to bring coherence into the proliferation of sectoral planning documents which had resulted, and to reinvigorate strategic spatial planning at the local level. To that aim, the law introduces a new strategic planning document, the Schéma de Cohérence Territoriale (SCOT). The SCOT was supposed to be comprehensive, integrating all the dimensions of the functioning of cities. To allow the field of spatial planning to be enlarged in this way, the Loi SRU introduced the notion of the Projet d'aménagement et de Développement Durable (PADD). Through the PADD, each agglomération is supposed to present a comprehensive 'project' for its future development, which was the basis for its planning efforts.

The ambitions of the Loi SRU in the field of metropolitan planning are clear from the changes in the planning system that it advocates. However, the capacity of the SCOT to actually relaunch strategic spatial planning at the metropolitan level can be questioned (Boino and Verhage, forthcoming).

The areas covered by the SCOT do not necessarily correspond to any institutional entity. They are designated by the *préfet*, who bases his decision on propositions of co-operating communes, and are supposed to cover the catchment areas of agglomérations. In practice, this turns out to be difficult to realise. Furthermore, the adjustment of different types of plans and procedures pose problems. The sectoral plans that were mentioned above, and between which the SCOT is assumed to create coherence, have in most cases been elaborated before the SCOT. Moreover, the areas they cover and, as a consequence, the institutions that are in charge of their elaboration are not always the same. This compromises the possibilities of creating coherence. The SCOT is more easily considered as a new plan procedure besides all the others. As a result, the efficiency of the new system of plans introduced by the Loi SRU can be questioned. Finally, a large part of the policies that determine the development of urban areas are insufficiently, or sometimes not at all, articulated to the procedures of spatial planning. Economic policies, cultural policies, marketing strategies, etc., which are important elements of current metropolitan development strategies, are not incorporated into the plan system.

Metropolitan planning in practice: the example of Lyon metropolitan area

The metropolitan area of Lyon covers an area of 4,500 square kilometres and has around 2.3 million inhabitants. It is structured around the urban centres of Lyon and Saint-Étienne, situated at some 60 kilometres south-west of Lyon (préfecture de Région Rhône-Alpes, 2004). However, the city of Lyon is, in many ways (demographically, economically, culturally) the central city of the area. The institutional structure of the area is complex and multi-layered. The agencies involved in strategic planning in the area have differing statutes and competencies, reaching from directly elected local governments to 'negotiation scenes' without any legal status.

The first strategic planning effort that concerned an area close to what is now considered as the metropolitan area of Lyon was the Plan d'Aménagement et d'Orientation Générale (PADOG), launched in 1962 and completed in 1965. The Ministère de la Construction determined the elaboration of PADOG for the 'Métropoles d'Équilibre' that were appointed in 1963, but some local partners were associated to its elaboration in working groups co-ordinated by the central State. The PADOG was a real strategic document in the sense that there was no implementation strategy attached to it. The ideas that were developed here (realisation of a 'green belt' around Lyon, direct urban growth towards secondary centres beyond the green belt) have, however, had their effects for the territorial development of the Lyon metropolitan area because of its influence on the first real strategic spatial document for the area, the Schéma Directeur d'Aménagement for metropolitan areas.

In 1966, an Organisation d'Étude et d'Aménagement (OREAM) was created for the region around Lyon and Saint-Étienne, which was later to be expanded to Grenoble. The objective of this organisation was to elaborate spatial planning at the city-regional level. The studies of OREAM were in line with the orientations of PADOG. What is new is the proposal to create two new towns to the east of the agglomération of Lyon, and to designate important areas (10,000 hectares) in large entities around the agglomération for industrial activities.

With the reorganisation of the planning system in the Loi d'Orientation Foncière of 1967, the Schéma Directeur d'Aménagement et d'Urbanisme (SDAU) became the strategic spatial plan. The State, which still had the competency of spatial planning, prescribed the elaboration of spatial plans, but there was a shift in scale from the level of the metropolitan area to the level of the agglomérations. The communes, regrouped in intermunicipal co-operation structures, were to play an important role in the elaboration of the SDAU. Even in the agglomération of Lyon, where a culture of intermunicipal co-operation existed, this was not simple and it took ten years to elaborate the SDAU which was approved only in 1978. Other parts of the metropolitan area did not produce a SDAU at all. So, after the 1967 law, strategic spatial planning at the level of the metropolitan area more or less disappeared. The central role of the State since the early days of strategic spatial planning had evolved over time. The communes had become important actors in this field. This was reinforced by the decentralisation laws of 1982–3. The SRU law is an attempt to relaunch strategic planning in a situation where the communes and their co-operating structures are the central actors.

The competency for spatial planning lies with the communes. However, these are often considered too small an entity to effectively develop and implement spatial planning. Therefore, these tasks are often transferred to intermunicipal co-operation structures, which exist in various forms. What they have in common is that they are not directly elected bodies to which the communes can delegate parts of their competencies. The most far reaching form is the Communauté Urbaine (CU). The CU Grand Lyon regroups 55 communes, of which the commune of Lyon with some 440,000 inhabitants is the largest, and a total of about 1.2 million inhabitants. The CU has far reaching competencies in the field of urban planning: it both elaborated the PLU for all the communes in the Greater Lyon area, and it is in charge of elaborating a SCOT for the same area.

The CU Grand Lyon does not cover the whole metropolitan area of Lyon. This means that the SCOT that is being elaborated by the CU Grand Lyon covers only part of the metropolitan area of Lyon. No less than nine other SCOTs are at least partly situated within the Lyon metropolitan area. This situation compromises the objective of the SCOT of bringing coherence into sectoral policies. This has been acknowledged by the different actors in the Lyon metropolitan area and it has encouraged them to start the so-called 'Interscot' procedure (Agence d'Urbanisme de Lyon 2003). Through this procedure, coherence between the different SCOTs is pursued. However, the Interscot procedure has no official status and participation in it is entirely free.

Another governance structure for the metropolitan area of Lyon is the Région Urbaine de Lyon (RUL). This is an associative structure in which the région Rhône-Alpes, the départements Rhône, Ain, Loire and Isère and a number of intermunicipal co-operation structures (among which the CU Grand Lyon) are represented. With a total of 2.6 million persons, the area covered by this entity, which includes the agglomération of Saint-Étienne, comes closest to the metropolitan area of Lyon on the basis of 'objective' data (as defined by INSEE). It is also close to the area covered by the DTA (under project) for the Lyon metropolitan area, elaborated by the central State. However, the RUL has no official competencies in the domain of spatial planning. The RUL was founded in response to the growing inconsistency between official administrative boundaries and the level at which the issues of metropolitan development are to be addressed. It is a unique construction in France, with the stated objective to transcend the boundaries of official administrative structures in order to propose a coherent and shared vision for the development of the metropolitan area.

We can note that the notion of territorial coherence is common to the objectives of both the SCOT and the RUL. Creating coherence in a territory with the fragmented institutional structure that we have depicted above is not a simple task (cf. Préfecture de Région Rhône-Alpes, 2004). The question we want to address here is the extent to which the SCOT can be considered as being capable of realising this task. Elements of an answer to this question can be found by analysing the metropolitan development strategy launched in 1997 by 'Grand Lyon' under the name of Millénaire 3 and its follow-up; its consequences for the spatial development of the metropolitan area of Lyon; and its articulation with statutory strategic spatial planning expressed, especially in the procedure of the SCOT.

Millénaire 3 was realised by a department of 'Grand Lyon'. The procedure resulted among others in the Plan de Mandat for 2001–7 of the current mayor of Lyon and president of Grand Lyon, Gérard Collomb. Since the appearance of this document, the procedure continues, but more in the background, even though a follow-up in the form of Lyon 2020 has been launched in 2004. The strategic choices in Millénaire 3 revolve around five key axes (urban ecology and quality of life; the organisation of urban development – towards a new strategic plan; territories – competencies – governance; social cohesion; Lyon's position in a globalised economy). The work in these five axes has resulted in 21 priorities. The elaboration of a SCOT in order to realise a better organisation of the urban development is one of these 21 priorities. Others are, for example, the development of a selected number of 'poles of excellence' in order to play a part in the global economy, a dialogue with neighbouring governance structures (such as the RUL and the intercommunal co-operation structure in Saint-Étienne), and the creation of an accessible and welcoming city. The choices in Millénaire 3 are the issue of a real effort of co-production of development strategies, for which new participative structures with both the private and the civil sector have been created and used. The objectives in which the effort has resulted mainly concern a change of the image of the city through a renewal of activities. Concrete actions concern the support of bio-technologies and ICT, and also the reinforcement of tourism.

Millénaire 3 is a product of 'Grand Lyon' and, as such, strongly coloured by the influence of the central city of Lyon. The position it reserves for the SCOT (the elaboration of which is one of the 21 objectives) is already a sign that the central position of this document among different levels of spatial and sectoral policies is not entirely recognised. The practice of the elaboration of the SCOT reinforces this impression. For the time being, the Greater Lyon Authority does not seem particularly motivated to elaborate a SCOT. This can probably also be explained by the fact that the Greater Lyon Authority only recently elaborated its new PLU, which covers its entire territory. Even though this document does not have the same statute, nor the same objectives, as the SCOT, the local politicians do not seem to have any urgency to engage in yet another plan-making procedure for the same territory.

Strategic spatial planning through a metropolitan development strategy in Lyon

The description of the objectives of the Loi SRU concerning a re-launch of strategic spatial planning at the metropolitan level, and the specific experiences in the Lyon metropolitan area, lead us to two observations. On the one hand, a re-launch of strategic planning initiatives can be observed. The Millénaire 3 procedure and its follow-up clearly bear characteristics of strategic planning with spatial implications. On the other hand, the Loi SRU, and more explicitly the SCOT, is not the vehicle that carries this re-launch of strategic spatial planning. It might serve as a document that fixes objectives and strategies developed elsewhere, but for the moment even that limited function is not certain.

The strategic spatial planning that is thus developed is not necessarily articulated with other levels of spatial planning or with sectoral planning as was intended with the SCOT. Spatial planning at the metropolitan level appears to be necessary from the point of view of the city of Lyon, but not in the quality of a comprehensive strategic spatial plan that acts as the 'great integrator'.

Millénaire 3 has resulted in clear policy objectives and actions, especially through the intermediary of the Plan de Mandat of the mayor of Lyon. These have partly been incorporated in the PLU for Grand Lyon, a document which the city feels the urgency to establish because it fixes, in the continental European tradition, the rights that are attached to land and, as a consequence, the use that can be made of it. Such a sense of urgency seems to be lacking where the SCOT is concerned. This seems to be experienced as yet another procedure which does not add anything new to what is already there. Strategic planning, in the tradition as it has been introduced by the LOV law in 1967, seems to be reincarnated in the Loi SRU. This type of planning does not seem to be suited to the current needs of metropolitan development in the city region of Lyon (see also Castel 2002).

The English situation

Institutional and legal situation

There is currently a movement in the UK towards 'spatial planning'. The new Planning and Compulsory Purchase Act 2004, which covers England and Wales, incorporates this phrase and requires the production of regional (sometimes possibly sub-regional) spatial strategies and local development documents with a spatial planning approach. Planners are still trying to understand what 'spatial planning' means in terms of the new Act, but there seems to be a real tendency away from 'land-use planning' to 'spatial planning' and, as a consequence, towards greater coherence in spatial activity.

At the regional level in England, new forms of Regional Spatial Strategy (RSS) are also being introduced to replace earlier forms of Regional Planning Guidance (RPG) (ODPM 2004a). These embrace the concept of spatial planning as well as gaining enhanced statutory status in planning decisions. The RSS may also include sub-regional spatial strategies where appropriate. Such documents are ultimately issued (for the most part) by central government (except London) although the process begins with the preparation of guidance on the content of RSS by the relevant Regional Assembly. This is submitted to the Secretary of State and is subject to a public examination process before the final RSS is issued.

At the metropolitan level, there is no mandatory requirement for the provision of a spatial plan (except in London) but such areas are incorporated in the wider RSS; instead such areas will form the basis of a sub-regional strategy.

At the local level of government, 'spatial planning' is intended to be manifested in the form of a Local Development Framework (LDF), where a strong emphasis is to be placed on integration of all policy which has spatial implications across different sectors (economic development, transport, housing, health, etc.) and on stakeholder and community involvement in policy development (ODPM 2004b) (see also Chapter 5). Unlike the previous development plan system where the whole plan was reviewed or modified from time to time, individual elements or documents making up the LDF will be updated as necessary. Planning policy preparation is thus seen as more of a continuous process and, in some respects, planners will be expected to act rather more as project managers whose task it is to bring together the resources and agencies required to tackle some of the big issues facing the cities. This is one view of spatial planning.

Metropolitan planning in practice: the example of Greater Manchester

As with the metropolitan area of Lyon, Greater Manchester is an assemblage of a multitude of separate units of local governance. The city of Manchester lies at the heart of a sprawling conurbation of around 2.6 million people within an area of some 500 square miles that has its origins in the industrial revolution and the coalescence of a number of originally freestanding industrial towns including Bolton, Rochdale, Wigan, Stockport and Oldham. There has thus been a long history of institutional fragmentation across a complex, polycentric, conurbation with discussions over the need for closer collaboration between authorities on issues relating to infrastructure provision and a more strategic approach to urban development dating back to at least the 1920s (Williams 1999: 112). However, rivalries and conflicts of interest between both the urban authorities and the neighbouring shire counties of Cheshire and Lancashire meant that little in the way of formal joint working, or the joint implementation of such visions, took place until well into the latter half of the twentieth century.

As part of a major reform of local government throughout England and Wales in the 1970s, parts of no fewer than 72 elected authorities were transformed into a two-tier structure consisting of a metropolitan county council and ten metropolitan district councils (Williams and Smith 2003: 5). Greater Manchester is thus the name of the former 'Greater Manchester Metropolitan County Council' (GMC) which was established in 1974. Under this two-tier structure of elected authorities, and its associated division of powers and responsibilities, the GMC took responsibility for matters such as education, transport and strategic planning whilst the districts had a more local responsibility for, for example, domestic waste collection and local planning matters. Thus, the GMC took on responsibility for strategic planning matters within the conurbation, preparing a strategic land use plan – the Greater Manchester Structure Plan – in 1981 and a subsequent review of this document just prior to the county's abolition in 1986. The key themes of the structure plan focused on urban concentration and the provision and efficient use of urban infrastructure. A significant problem that emerged was that the tightly drawn boundaries of Greater Manchester did not fully reflect changing demographic and socio-economic conditions, commuting patterns and housing market areas, with the 'functional' hinterland of Greater Manchester expanding ever further beyond GM boundaries.

This two-tier local government framework lasted for 12 years, before the Conservative central government under the leadership of Margaret Thatcher decided to abolish all the metropolitan county councils along with the Greater London Council in 1986. Thus, institutionally, the Greater Manchester area was left from this time as a collection of the 10 neighbouring elected metropolitan district authorities. Each of these now had unitary status, although there remained a number of attempts to preserve a degree of joint collaboration in terms of policy development and service delivery, most notably through the formation of the Association of Greater Manchester Authorities (AGMA). Strategic planning in the metropolitan areas in the late 1980s and early 1990s was subject to widespread criticism. Its main expression was through Strategic Planning Guidance (SPG) for Greater Manchester (DoE 1989); a very slim and anodyne document issued by central government following the submission of advice on its content by AGMA. It was seen to represent a weak and vague framework coupling 'lowest common denominator' compromises to get an agreed framework through all 10 districts whilst also meeting prevailing national planning policy which, at that time, placed an emphasis on freeing up developers from unnecessary planning restrictions.

Since the current Labour government first came to power in the late 1990s and, most significantly, the reforms to the planning system instituted by this government following its re-election in 2001 which resulted in the introduction of the Planning and Compensation Act 2004, the role and position of strategic spatial planning has changed. In fact, a degree of change was already evident before the 1997 Labour election landslide. The post-Thatcher Conservative administrations had already become less hostile to planning and, in the early 1990s, emphasis was placed on the introduction of a more 'plan-led' system, with the existing UDPs and new forms of mandatory district-wide local plans across the shire areas of England and Wales given enhanced status in planning decisions. At the metropolitan scale, the SPG approach to setting a framework for strategic planning in the metropolitan areas proved to be something of a one-off as attention increasingly shifted to a wider regional focus. The procedural mechanisms established by the SPG initiative prevailed, however, with new forms of 'Regional Planning Guidance' (RPG) prepared along similar lines – in the North West, a newly established regional association of local authorities (NWRA) took on the AGMA role in preparing advice to the Secretary of State. Later, this body transformed into the North West Regional Assembly (NWRA) and has become one of the three key regional players in the North West alongside the relatively recently established North West Regional Development Agency (NWRDA), responsible for the preparation of an economic strategy for the region and related economic development and regeneration activities, and the Government Office for the North West (GONW), essentially the arm of central government departments at the regional level.

As explained elsewhere, the Planning and Compensation Act heralded wide-ranging reforms to the existing statutory planning system in England (and Wales), both in terms of procedural change and in wider aspects of scope, purpose and underlying philosophy. This includes emphasis on the need for a 'cultural change' in the attitudes and working practices of those associated with planning – both planners and developers – and the focus on 'spatial planning', which clearly is intended to embrace a broader, more integrative approach than the narrow physical land-use definitions of planning that prevailed in a statutory sense during the 1980s and 1990s. These more conceptual shifts were accompanied by a new emphasis on the regional and sub-regional levels through the replacement of RPG via the new, statutory, RSS, and the introduction of LDFs at the local level.

Thus, of most immediate significance from a strategic planning perspective in the North West has been the work undertaken by NWRA in preparing a new RSS for the North West region and, in particular, the emerging sub-regional elements of this strategy. This work is itself being widely influenced by recent government initiatives linked to a 'Sustainable Communities' banner (ODPM 2003). For the North West, this has manifested itself via the government's Northern Way Growth Strategy (ODPM 2004) and the resulting emphasis placed on the role of defined city-regions – including the Manchester City Region – within the three northern English regions of the North West, the North East and Yorkshire and the Humber. Furthermore, the government primarily sees the RSS as a vehicle for the further elaboration of the Northern Way agenda (Northern Way Steering Group 2004: 55).

Accordingly, the interim revisions to the RSS for the North West (NWRA 2005), published by NWRA for consultation purposes in October 2005, include a vision and spatial development framework for the Manchester City Region, broadly defined by the ten GM districts but further extended to the south and west into neighbouring local authorities within northern Cheshire together with Warrington and parts of the High Peak, thus going some way to address earlier difficulties with the tightly drawn boundaries of GM itself. This vision draws on earlier work by AGMA in preparing a 2003 Strategy for Greater Manchester: Sharing a Vision, which places emphasis on developing Greater Manchester in a global context and of transforming it into a globally significant city-region. Interestingly, in the context of this chapter, the reference points to other global city-regions included that of Lyon as well as the likes of Milan, Munich, Amsterdam, Barcelona, Vancouver and Boston (AGMA 2003: 10). Through such initiatives, AGMA itself has been seen to have significantly changed its primary focus from coordinating service delivery to a more forward, long-term, strategic approach (Deas 2005; Marvin *et al.* 2002). Moving beyond traditional land-use planning, there have also been interesting moves towards the development of a Knowledge Capital Partnership centred on the city-region, linked to the role of local universities, technology transfer, cultural industries and digital technologies.

Strategic spatial planning at various levels in the Manchester city region

Coalition and consensus building between traditional local authorities, other actors particularly in the economic development arena, and the regional players such as the GONW, NWRA and NWDA, have thus characterised recent strategic planning initiatives within Greater Manchester. In many ways, the current situation can be seen as more complex than ever, as a multitude of interests and players – operating at different spatial scales – have been brought together by a shared vision of a globally vibrant and successful city-region. But the history of collaborative ventures in Greater Manchester (and indeed the wider region, which has often been described as one of the most fragmented of all UK regions, notably because of traditional rivalries between the two main urban cores of Greater Manchester and Liverpool) has more often been one where the rhetoric has been more in evidence than the reality. Under such conditions, either the quest for agreement amongst a diversity of partners has led to weak and vague strategy development, or the rivalries and tensions between erstwhile collaborators have prevented successful implementation.

One clear potential advantage of the new system is that, through the sub-regional elements of the RSS, it offers a potential mechanism to prepare a strategy for the city-region as a whole which will have statutory weight in subsequent local planning policy development and decision-making. However, although it is still too early to reliably make predictions over the likely success or failure of the new RSS/LDF processes, there are already danger signs from anecdotal evidence of increasing tensions between the city of Manchester and the remaining authorities over the extent to which Manchester takes a prominent position in the development of the city-region, and also between the city-region authorities and the more rural constituencies in terms of wider North West strategy development.

Meanwhile, there remain a plethora of initiatives, organisations and interests at different spatial scales that are operating within Greater Manchester and have implications for its future planning and development. As well as the Knowledge Capital initiative mentioned above, these include a wide range of sectoral and area-based initiatives such as Housing Market Renewal Areas and a development company and a new deal for communities (NDC) area in East Manchester. These involve a complex mix of different national, regional, sub-regional, local and community-based organisations whose territories or areas of interest overlap with each other and cut across local government boundaries. It thus also remains to be seen whether the new emphasis on integrative approaches under the recent planning reforms can get to grips with this, or whether the new forms of spatial planning will eventually be forced to retreat back towards a narrower, regulatory, physical land-use focus.

Conflict and complementarity between strategies at the metropolitan level

The experiences in the metropolitan areas of Lyon and Manchester show that conflicts between statutory spatial planning and metropolitan development strategies occur at several levels. At the same time, they illustrate how statutory spatial planning and the elaboration of metropolitan development strategies are intimately linked and how they could mutually reinforce themselves.

Relationship between development strategies and statutory spatial planning

Although it is not completely absent, metropolitan scale is certainly not at the centre of the newly introduced spatial planning system in England. The relations between the elaboration of metropolitan development strategies and the statutory planning system are therefore necessarily different from those in France where the idea that spatial planning, through the intermediary of the SCOT, can play an integrating role in policies at the level of metropolitan areas is central. This seems to be a fundamental difference between the planning system introduced by the SRU law in

France, and that introduced by the Planning and Compulsory Purchase Act in England.

In France, since the SRU law, strategic spatial planning is assumed to be best realised at the level of what could be called 'functional areas'. Thus, strategic spatial plans are in direct competition with other types of metropolitan strategies because they concern the same, or in any case very similar, territories. Strategic spatial plans could hence be used by metropolitan planning authorities to give an official statutory legitimisation to their development strategies. However, in the case of Lyon, it is rather the opposite that happens: the mechanisms to elaborate metropolitan development strategies being in place, there seems to be little sense of urgency for the realisation of the statutory planning document of the SCOT. Given the situation at hand, it is difficult to see any real complementarity, from the point of view of the metropolitan area, between the official planning document and any other strategic endeavours.

In England, the statutory strategic spatial plan is now elaborated at the regional level. It seems to be rather widely acknowledged that the English regions do not correspond to what could be termed a 'functional area'. For that reason, it can be expected that there is less competition between the official strategic planning documents (the RSS) and the metropolitan development strategies. Complementarity between the two types of strategic thinking does not seem to be excluded. However, the concern for the cities might be to find a way to make sure that the RSS does not interfere too much with their metropolitan development strategies. Indeed, it seems that the sub-regional strategies might be used as an 'emergency exit', enabling the metropolitan area to give an official status to its already developed strategic endeavours.

Relationship between statutory spatial planning and project planning

Instead of regulating urban development, local planning authorities aim more and more at stimulating such development. This leads to a type of spatial planning which can be described as 'project-led'. At the same time, it also leads local planning authorities to elaborate territorial development strategies in order to attract inward investment. This gives rise to a potential tension between statutory spatial planning on the one hand, and a project-led type of development strategy on the other. Furthermore, the logic underlying both types of activity can be very different, with spatial planning primarily aiming at redistributing wealth by sustaining 'weak' parts of the territory whilst 'project-led' development strategies aim in the first instance at creating wealth by exploiting localised potentialities. Through a 'trickle down' effect, this is assumed to benefit the wealth of the entire territory.

The existence of such a tension seems to be confirmed by the Manchester situation. The Greater Manchester Council and, in particular, the city of Manchester has pursued throughout the 1990s an active policy of urban regeneration. Large investment projects have changed the face of the city and continue to change its image. In this policy, large urban projects more or less replace more strategic spatial reflections at the scale of the conurbation. This policy has been very successful in recent years. As a result, the city council does not feel the urgency to develop a more embracing overall development strategy.

In Lyon, the development of the city through a limited number of large-scale urban projects also takes an important place. Even though the city uses these projects to a lesser extent than Manchester to profile itself, they do play a key role in urban policies. As a result, they have to be incorporated into any type of strategic reflection concerning the territorial development of the city. So in Lyon too, large urban projects partly replace the effort of strategic spatial planning at the scale of the whole territory. However, for both Manchester and Lyon, these large urban projects strongly focus on the central city, which is one of the elements that gives rise to the last type of tensions that we want to describe.

Relationship between different levels of spatial planning

The coexistence of different territorial levels of planning gives rise to two types of tensions. The first one concerns the predominantly urbanised part of the territory as opposed to the predominantly rural part. As a result of the emphasis that is given to the cities as 'growth engines' in the North West's RSS, the document is perceived by the rural counties of the region as largely dominated by the cities. A similar tension is at the basis of the division of the metropolitan area of Lyon into 10 different SCOTs, some of which seem to have as a central theme the way in which the pressure from the Lyon agglomération on the territory can be encapsulated.

A second type of tension concerns the central city and the other cities in the metropolitan territory. This tension is more explicit in the case of Manchester because of its more polycentric character, with a number of relatively important cities, most notably Liverpool, in proximity. As we mentioned above, the city of Manchester is pursuing a development strategy based on the regeneration of parts of the city through large urban projects. This policy has allowed the city of Manchester to relaunch its local economy which was in crisis after the quasi-disappearance of manufacturing activities in the 1970s to 1980s. This approach is generally seen as successful. As a result, the city of Manchester feels strong and independent. This can give rise to tensions with other cities in the metropolitan area, even though the city of Manchester acknowledges that it is a part of a greater whole, and that its economic attractiveness is based on the whole, rather than on the city of Manchester alone.

These tensions are in line with earlier observations, in which we mentioned the contrast between the absence of an official spatial planning strategy for England as a whole and, in contrast, the central place that is being accorded to it in the French planning system. Both situations have their inconveniences. In France, the idea of elaborating a strategic spatial planning document at the level of the metropolitan area exists on paper but the Lyon case illustrates how, in reality, this idea clashes with existing institutional structures and established planning practices. In England, the proposed subdivision of RSS into sub-regional strategies illustrates the continuing need to have some mechanism to act below the level of the region, and closer to the metropolitan scale.

References

Agence d'Urbanisme de Lyon (2003) *Vers un Aménagement Coordonné de la Région Lyonnaise*, Lyon: Agence d'Urbanisme.

Association of Greater Manchester Authorities (AGMA) (2003) *Sharing the Vision: A Strategy for Greater Manchester*, Wigan: AGMA Policy Unit.

Boino P. (unpublished) *Poids et Rôles de l'Action Publique sur le Développement de Lyon: Aménagement, Planification et Croissance Urbaine*, working paper, Lyon: Institut d'Urbanisme de Lyon – Université Lumière Lyon 2.

Boino, P. and Verhage, R (forthcoming) *La Planification territoriale au niveau des aires metropolitaines en France et au Royaume-Uni*, Paris: L'Harmattan.

Castel, J.S. (2002) *La SRU: Nouvel Ordre Urbain ou Ultime Avatar des Années Soixante?*, Contribution au séminaire planification urbaine METL-ENPC 2001–2002.

Deas, I. (2005) 'Reinventing the metropolitan region: experiences of scalar conflict in Manchester and North West England', Paper presented to the Urban Affairs Association 35th Annual Meeting, Salt Lake City, Utah, 14 April.

Department of the Environment (DoE) (1989) *RPG4: Strategic Planning Guidance for Greater Manchester*, London: HMSO.

Jouve, B. and Lefèvre, C. (1999) *Villes, Métropoles: Les Nouveaux Territoires du Politique*, Collection Villes, Paris: Antrophos.

Marvin, S., May, T., Perry, B. and Puglisi, M. (2002) *Evaluating Urban Futures: Enhancing Quality and Improving Effectiveness*, Manchester: Centre for Sustainable Urban and Regional Futures (SURF).

Northern Way Steering Group (2004) *Moving Forward: The Northern Way – First Growth Strategy Report*, Newcastle: Northern Way Steering Group.

North West Regional Assembly (NWRA) (2005) *The North West Plan: Interim Draft Revisions to the Regional Spatial Strategy for the North West of England*, Wigan: NWRA.

Office of the Deputy Prime Minister (ODPM) (2003) *Sustainable Communities: Building for the Future*, London: ODPM.

Office of the Deputy Prime Minister (ODPM) (2004a) *Planning Policy Statement 11: Regional Spatial Strategies*, London: ODPM.

Office of the Deputy Prime Minister (ODPM) (2004b) *Planning Policy Statement 12: Local Development Frameworks*, London: ODPM.

Office of the Deputy Prime Minister (ODPM) (2004c) *Making it Happen: The Northern Way*, London: ODPM.

Pelletier, J. and Delfante, C. (2004) *Atlas historique du Grand Lyon: Formes Urbaines et Paysages au fil du Temps*, Seysinnet-Pariset: Xavier Lejeune – Libris.

Préfecture de Région Rhône-Alpes (2004) *Directive Territoriale d'Aménagement de l'Aire Métropolitaine Lyonnaise*, project.

Salet, W., Thornley, A. and Kreukels, A. (eds) (2003) *Metropolitan Governance and Spatial Planning: Comparative Case Studies of European City-Regions*, London: SPON Press.

Verhage, R. and Boino, P. (forthcoming) *La planification territoriale au niveau des aires metropolitaines en France et au Royaume-Uni*, actes du colloque IFRESI 'logiques métropolitaines', Lille, 2–3 June 2005.

Williams, G. (1999) 'Greater Manchester', in P. Roberts, K. Thomas and G. Williams (eds) *Metropolitan Planning in Britain: A Comparative Study*, London: Jessica Kingsley and Regional Studies Association.

Williams, G. and Smith, A. (2003) 'Regional agendas and the governance of city regions: the Manchester conurbation', Paper presented to the Regional Studies International Conference 'Reinventing Regions in the Global Economy', Pisa, Italy, 12–15 April.

Chapter 7

Examining the relationship between transnational and national spatial planning

French and British spatial planning and the European spatial development perspective

Olivier Sykes in collaboration with Alain Motte

Introduction

This chapter explores the relationship between the emergence of transnational spatial planning within the European Union (EU) and spatial planning in the UK and France in the context of reform of spatial planning systems and policies. In order to provide a sufficiently 'discrete focus' (Williams 1983) for comparative investigation, the main emphasis is on how spatial planning in the two countries is related to, and has interacted with, the European Spatial Development Perspective (ESDP).[1] This transnational spatial planning document was agreed by European Ministers for spatial planning and regional policy at Potsdam, Germany, in 1999 as an indicative framework to guide spatially significant public policy making in the EU. It is a non-binding policy statement, which seeks to guide institutions in the exercise of existing competences, which influence spatial development. The ESDP promotes three overarching spatial development guidelines for territorial development in Europe: first, the development of a balanced and polycentric urban system and a new urban–rural relationship; second, securing parity of access to infrastructure and knowledge; and third, sustainable development, prudent management and the protection of the natural and cultural heritage (Commission of the European Communities (CEC) 1999). These principles are supported by 60 policy options, which propose more concrete measures which can contribute to the achievement of the overarching spatial development guidelines. The application of the ESDP is achieved through voluntary co-operation based on the principle of subsidiarity and by a reorientation of national spatial development policies and community sectoral policies, at three levels of spatial co-operation; the community level; the transnational/national level; the regional/local level. In addition to the need for 'vertical' co-operation between the different levels of government, in order to achieve integrated spatial development, the ESDP also calls for 'horizontal' co-operation between the authorities responsible for sectoral and spatial policies at each administrative level. Given the non-binding status of the ESDP and the territorial, administrative, and cultural diversity in Europe, both between and within EU member states, the potential for differentiated application of the ESDP by member states is strong (Tewdwr-Jones 2001a). This is underlined by the fact that different conceptions of planning and national spatial planning systems and traditions within EU member states played a very significant role in shaping debates during the formulation of the ESDP (Faludi and Waterhout 2002; Faludi 2005). Different member states brought different dimensions to the development of the ESDP which reflected both their conceptions of the role, purpose and practice of spatial planning, and their substantive concerns in relation to spatial development issues (Guigou 2001). In light of this, it is important to undertake comparative studies of the influence of the ESDP in different national contexts, particularly of the relationships between the ESDP and spatial planning systems which have been identified as belonging to different European 'planning families' or 'spatial planning traditions' (Newman and Thornley 1996; Commission of the European Communities (CEC) 1997). Recognising the contextual issues discussed above, this chapter contributes to the comparative study of the influence of transnational spatial planning on planning in member states by investigating the application of the ESDP in two member states of the European Union representative of different European 'spatial planning traditions': the United Kingdom and France. The investigation of relationships between the ESDP and French and British spatial planning takes into account the wider 'receiving context' within which the ESDP is applied in the two countries (Sykes 2004) and is informed by themes in wider 'Europeanisation' research (Börzel 2005). The literature on 'Europeanisation' stresses that this process is not simply a 'one-way street', but that EU member states contribute to the making of European policy as well as having to subsequently apply it in domestic contexts (Bulmer and Radaelli 2005). The degree to which member states shape policy, for example, by 'exporting' domestic policy models to the European level can influence the degree of 'misfit' between subsequent European policy requirements and national approaches and the amount of adaptation of domestic policy which is necessary. It is therefore important here to consider both the role of France and the UK in the emergence of transnational spatial planning in the EU and the development of the ESDP, and the relationship, or degree of 'fit', between the spatial planning model promoted by this document and the existing spatial planning 'tradition' and approach of the two countries. Reflecting this, the discussions below consider two key issues:

- The role which the UK and France played in the emergence of transnational European spatial planning;
- How the ESDP's model of 'spatial' planning relates to the spatial planning tradition and approach in the two countries.

These two 'axes of comparison' are developed in the following sections.

The emergence of transnational European spatial planning

France: a pioneer and a driving force

The role that France and French thinking on spatial planning and regional development played alongside that of certain other member states, notably the Netherlands and Germany, in the initiation and evolution of the field of European spatial planning is widely acknowledged (Faludi and Waterhout 2002; Faludi and Peyrony 2001; Faludi 2003a, 2003c). Essentially, the historic concern of Aménagement du Territoire (AT) with achieving balanced spatial development of France's national territory, which underpinned the emergence and prosecution of this policy during its formative years, and continues to be a theme to this day, has been recast in the wider spatial context of the European territory (Faludi and Peyrony 2001). Indeed, the growing recognition of the impact of European integration on the spatial development of the national territory was one of the factors which contributed to a revival of interest in AT in France from the mid-1980s onwards. Aside from the effects of European integration on territorial dynamics and the relative position of places in European space, in the 1980s the European level took an increasing interest in reducing development disparities and enhancing cohesion between the different regions of the EEC member states. The accession of new member states such as Greece (1981), Portugal and Spain (1986) led to an increase in the level of development disparities across the regions of the member states of the EEC, and contributed to an increased community interest in regional policy. The anticipated effects of the creation of the SEM after 1992 led to the formalisation of regional policy as a European competence and the reform of the structural funds in 1989 which meant that Europe emerged as a key partner in the design and implementation of the policy of AT (Lacour et al. 2003). Against this backdrop the French national spatial planning agency DATAR was required to play a key role in negotiating the eligibility of different French regions for structural fund support and undertook to consider the wider spatial position of France in European space (Faludi and Peyrony 2001; DATAR 2003; Jacquet 2003b).

In 1986 a report entitled 'Propositions pour l'aménagement du territoire' produced by Olivier Guichard considered the changed context in which AT now operated, following decentralisation in France, and the continuing process of European integration and growth in transnational interdependencies (Mazet 2000). This was followed in May 1989 by the publication of the RECLUS report 'Les villes européennes' (Brunet et al. 1989) that contributed to significantly raising the profile of AT and the attention given to spatial development policy in France and across Europe. The spatial representation of the concentration of spatial development in a 'dorsale' stretching from England to Lombardy, which became known as the 'blue banana', has become one of the most enduring and debated images of European spatial planning representing a centre-periphery interpretation of the organisation of European space (Lacour *et al.* 2003; Faludi and Waterhout 2002; Jensen 2002).

The fact that large sectors of national territory were identified as being outside this putative 'core' of Europe, and that France was presented as having a less-developed urban structure of cities of European standing than certain other member states resulted in a great deal of debate which caused AT to rise once more on the governmental agenda (Mazet 2000). In response, DATAR undertook to consider the wider spatial position of France in European space in the preparation of the second generation of 'Contrat de Plan État-région' (CPER) which ran from 1989 until 1993 (Faludi and Peyrony 2001) and in November 1989 the French organised the first informal meeting of the European ministers responsible for spatial planning and regional policy at Nantes, with the President of the European Commission Jacques Delors in attendance (Faludi and Waterhout 2002). Thus began the process by which DATAR sought to 'export' the AT model to Brussels, and which culminated with the agreement of the ESDP ten years later. Therefore France can be characterised as having played a 'pioneering role' in relation to the emergence of European spatial planning and the promotion of the territorial approach to European integration and policy development (Faludi and Peyrony 2001). In a similar way, it seems that the renewed form of AT which has evolved in the 1990s have also contributed to the emergence of the 'territorial cohesion' agenda (Faludi 2003c; Jacquet 2003). Given this perspective it might be expected that the ESDP has been applied with vigour in the French spatial planning system.

The UK: a late but enthusiastic convert

The evolving relationship between planning in Britain and EU policies such as environment and transport policy has been well documented and discussed since the mid-1990s (Davies 1993; Bishop *et al.* 2000; DETR 1999; Jordan 2002). An overarching theme in the literature is that until 1997 when Tony Blair's first 'New' Labour government came to power, Conservative governments attempted to keep the influence of Europe 'at arms length' and even where the impacts of EU legislative actions were clear and direct, attempted to minimise the acknowledgement of the European origins of certain changes (Davies *et al.* 1994; Tewdwr-Jones and Williams 2001: 57). Such attitudes reflected longer standing trends in the relations between the UK and the emerging field of European environmental policy and in the 1980s 'Ministerial attitudes towards environmentalism and European integration remained at best ambivalent and at worst completely negative' (Jordan 2000: 26). Tewdwr-Jones *et al.* (2000) discuss the relationship between British planning and Europe and identifies the influence of broader forms of 'Euroscepticism' on this. Tewdwr-Jones and Williams (2001: 19) note that 'despite the policy vacuum at the national level of government, aspects of European policy have nevertheless been present as an important context in the formulation and development of planning strategies at the local and regional levels'. At the level of local authorities, statutory development plans and other strategic planning documents have been shaped by European influences in three main ways:

- providing a context for preparation of development plans;
- influencing the formulation of individual policies;
- requiring the identification of critical areas (Wilkinson *et al.* 1998; Bishop *et al.* 2000; Tewdwr-Jones and Williams 2001).

National level planning policy documents such as Planning Policy Guidance Notes (PPGs), increasingly, although to a varying degree, confirmed the need for local authorities to ensure that their decisions complied with European directives, and planning procedures were sometimes altered to meet the needs of EU directives as in the case of the Environmental Impact Assessment (EIA) Directive. However, Tewdwr-Jones and Williams (2001: 160) conclude that 'in the later 1980s and for most of the 1990s local government leapfrogged central government in responding (and being prepared to respond) to a European context for British planning' (2001: 76). On the political front, whilst the hostility of the Thatcher period New Right governments towards planning began to mellow during 1990s (Tewdwr-Jones 2002), Europe continued to be a very divisive issue and contributed perhaps more than any other issue to the unravelling of the premiership of John Major. Given this political context, it is unsurprising that when discussions began at the European level about a form of spatial development framework for the EU territory the UK government was less than enthusiastic. The conjunction of 'Europe' and 'planning' was hardly calculated to appeal to a Conservative government intellectually wedded to a neo-liberal view of society and economy and the all pervasive discourse of national sovereignty. Therefore whereas planning gradually regained its position during the 1990s, in part due to the inherent 'growth v. conservation' contradictions of the New Right coalition and new international obligations relating to sustainable development, a significant shift in the UK's level of engagement with, and commitment to, the emerging European spatial planning agenda had to wait for a more fundamental regime change with the election of 'New' Labour in 1997.

After this date the UK's engagement with the European dimension of planning and the ESDP process changed fundamentally (Tewdwr-Jones *et al.* 2000; Tewdwr-Jones and Williams 2001; Zetter 2001). Faludi and Waterhout, for example, describe the UK's henceforth 'unambiguously enthusiastic' attitude towards the ESDP (Faludi and Waterhout 2002: 15). At the Noordwijk meeting of European Spatial Planning Ministers in

1997, the new UK Minister for the Regions, Regeneration and Planning, Richard Caborn announced his intention of completing the ESDP under the forthcoming UK Presidency of the EU and the first complete draft was duly presented at Glasgow in the following year. Also in 1998, a policy statement on planning reform entitled 'Modernising Planning' (DETR 1998: 6) stated that 'The European context for planning has largely been missing from the planning system in England' and that 'we fully recognise therefore that there needs to be a significant European dimension to our planning system'.

A significant indicator of the new congruence between British thinking and the rationale behind the development of the ESDP was the acknowledgement that 'spatial development issues do not respect national boundaries', and that 'for too long, there has been a tendency to ignore cross-border and transnational planning issues' (DETR 1998: 6). Thus the idea in the ESDP that an insular approach to planning at regional or national scale is no longer possible was now clearly accepted and transposed into British policy. In stating that 'there needs to be a significant European dimension to our planning system', 'Modernising Planning' added national-level political commitment to existing professional and local-level awareness of the European context, and participation in transnational planning.

Summary

To employ the terminology of the 'Europeanisation' literature, from the discussions above France emerges as one of the EU member states which proactively sought to 'upload' or export a domestic model of spatial planning to the European level through the process of developing a transnational European spatial planning framework. In contrast, the UK was at first a reticent participant in this process reflecting domestic political conditions during the initial period of the ESDP's development. Following the political change at the national level in 1997 however, this attitude changed fundamentally and the UK was one of the states which helped to drive the ESDP process to its conclusion.

The following section develops the second axis of comparison and considers the relationship between the ESDP's spatial planning model and the planning traditions and approaches characteristic of France and the UK.

Domestic spatial planning traditions and approaches and the ESDP

France: assimilation and evolution

In France, the AT approach has been characterised by the 'European Compendium of Spatial Planning Systems and Policies' (the Compendium) as belonging to the 'regional economic planning' tradition of spatial planning in which 'spatial planning has a very broad meaning relating to the pursuit of wide social and economic objectives, especially in relation to disparities in wealth, employment, and social conditions between different regions of the country's territory' (CEC 1997: 36). The Compendium also notes that the French system of spatial planning incorporates the 'urbanism' tradition 'which has a strong architectural flavour and concern with urban design, townscape and building control' and is characteristic of southern European member states of the EU. It is therefore more appropriate perhaps to talk of French spatial planning 'traditions'. Stephenson (2002, 2003) describes how achieving coordination between the two strands of the spatial planning system has been a longstanding issue, and how one of the aims of recent reforms is to secure a better articulation between these in terms of the relationship between the land-use planning instruments of the urbanisme system and the development 'projets' (projects) funded for different territories through the contract-based AT system. In keeping with trends across Europe, there has also been a sustained period of reflection and policy change in France over recent years in relation to key dimensions of spatial planning including land-use management and transport (CEC 1997; Booth 2003). On the legislative front, two key laws have reformed and set the context for the pursuit of AT. The Loi d'Orientation pour l'Aménagement et le Développement du Territoire (LOADT) (Pasqua law) of 4 February 1995 and the Loi d'Orientation pour l'Aménagement et le Développement Durable du Territoire (LOADDT) (Voynet law) of 25 June 1999, reflect the shift in the policy of AT from a centrally driven redistributive model to a more bottom-up approach based on empowering lower levels and supporting the endogenous development capacities of particular territories (Josserand 2002; Comité Stratégique de la DATAR 2003), referred to in Chapter 5.

For Josserand (2002: 3) the Pasqua law and the Voynet law represented a 'return to a more strategic future-oriented approach to regional policy and a 're-launch' of spatial planning'. The Pasqua law also re-emphasised the role of the regions in AT by requiring these to produce a Schéma Régional d'Aménagement et de Développement Durable du Territoire (SRADT) (regional spatial development strategy – OS) which were to take into account the policy orientations of the national level. In 1999, a new planning law, the Loi Relative à la Solidarité et au Renouvellement Urbains (law on urban solidarity and renewal – loi SRU) (Booth 2003) was passed alongside re-energised provisions for transport planning (plans de déplacements urbains) (PDUs) and new legislation on the organisation of territorial governance at the local level in the form of the 'loi Chevènement' which simplifies and strengthens the arrangements for intercommunal working. Peyrony (2002) suggests that recent reforms of the system of 'urbanisme' like the SRU which are designed to strengthen strategic-level spatial planning for urban and rural areas also form part of the legislative framework in which the ESDP is applied in France.

As explained above, France was one of the initiators or 'pioneers' of the ESDP process and consequently the genealogy of the ESDP is closely related to the French AT approach to strategic spatial planning which is undertaken primarily at the national and regional levels. This relationship is related to the fact that in discussing and applying the ESDP domestically in France, an immediate contrast with the UK situation is that in France the term 'AT' continues to be used to describe the developments in spatial planning *for* Europe such as the ESDP. Peyrony (2002: 3–12), for example, notes how 'Aménagement du Territoire' is not a competence of the European Union; that EU regional and cohesion policy constitutes an implicit Aménagement du Territoire; and entitles a section of his book 'The birth of the ESDP or the emergence of European cooperation in the field of Aménagement du Territoire'. Therefore unlike the UK where the emergence of a European spatial planning discourse and initiatives have contributed to a linguistic and, arguably, a conceptual modification in the way in which planning is described and conceived (see below), in France such developments appear to have been more closely equated with, and assimilated to, the national practice of AT. Notwithstanding this, there have been changes to the formulation of AT in the 1990s with the Pasqua law (1995) adding 'développement' (development) to the title of this policy and the Voynet law (1999) 'durable' (sustainable). The full official title of AT is thus now 'Aménagement et développement durable du territoire'. Faludi and Peyrony (2001) suggest that the French learnt much in relation to the concept of sustainable development from their northern European neighbours, and this was confirmed by an interview with a DATAR representative (see Sykes 2004) which suggested that sustainability has been a particularly important ESDP policy message in France. Therefore the evidence suggests that, in France, exposure to the process, initiatives, and discourse of spatial planning *for* Europe, including the ESDP, has had an effect on the re-specification of the national policy of AT. It is clear however, that domestic political changes have also had an impact on this development, for example, the arrival of Dominique Voynet of the Green Party as 'Ministre de l'Environnement et de l'Aménagement du Territoire' at the Environment Ministry after the Socialists returned to power in 1997.

Another area in which the policy messages of the ESDP appear to have had an influence in France is in relation to the need for horizontal and vertical coordination in spatial development policy. The rationale behind the creation of DATAR in the 1960s was the realisation that all governmental decisions influence the location of activities, and its role within the State apparatus was to adopt a 'transversale' (horizontal) outlook on governmental activities and to incite different government departments to think spatially rather than simply sectorally about the impact of their different policies and actions (DATAR 2003). Yet in an interview, a DATAR representative (see Sykes 2004), suggested that the importance of 'horizontal and vertical' cooperation and coordination was one ESDP message which has been important in France. In addition, evidence from case studies of selected French regions (Sykes 2004) suggests that the ESDP had played at least some role in promoting the importance of horizontal cooperation, even if this was a theme which already featured in national and regional policy reflection during the 1990s.

The interrelationship between the ESDP's model of spatial planning and its policy concerns and those of the French spatial planning system also has more substantive dimensions. In the context of post-war economic growth DATAR's core policy orientation was the promotion of more balanced development of French territory, for example, through the policy of designating 'Métropoles d'équilibre' (Josserand 2002). Reflecting this heritage, work on ESDP themes such as polycentricity continued in France after the adoption of the ESDP, with Faludi (2003b: 125) noting that the French 'effortlessly combine this with the advancement of their own ideas'. There is much evidence that the recent reforms and renewal of the policy and practice of AT are coherent with the spatial development policy approach and substantive policy messages of the ESDP. Interviews at national and regional levels in France pointed to an implicit, rather than explicit, application of the ESDP, and suggested that the degree of coherence partly reflects the fact that the ESDP's principles echo the 'big consensual ideas of the time', and the fact that the French model of AT has both shaped, and been shaped by, the ESDP during the course of its elaboration (Sykes 2004).

The importance of planning traditions in conditioning the response to the ESDP is also reflected by the iteration of the ESDP principles at the member state level in France which contrasts with the reluctance of the UK government to develop a national spatial framework for either the UK or England which might provide a vehicle for the explicit iteration of such principles. The French, and DATAR in particular, are familiar with such exercises and the development of prospective scenarios of the development of the national territory, and with an approach to regional policy which is more explicitly framed by spatial objectives. Furthermore, in countries such as France where the 'regional economic approach' to spatial planning is dominant, central government has historically often played an important role in managing development pressures across the country, and in undertaking public sector investment (CEC 1997). Significantly, the strongest evidence of a direct influence of the ESDP in France is to be found in State-led initiatives such as the France 2020 report, the 'Schémas de services collectifs' (SSCs) (strategies which give spatial expression to the planning and delivery of public services in nine key areas) and reports for interregional macro-regions (the 'MIIAT' reports), through which there has been an iteration of how the principles of the ESDP might apply to France. The France 2020 report produced by DATAR provides an assessment of the current condition of the national territory and alternative spatial visions of its future development opting for the scenario of 'networked polycentrism'. The rationale provided for the adoption of this is that it responds to the imperatives of sustainable development; builds on existing territorial dynamics; and is also in accordance with the ESDP. The argument for the choice of networked polycentrism thus reflects the interaction of the territorial dynamics which are affecting the national territory, and policy objectives derived from the international and European spheres including the ESDP.

The UK: re-conceptualisation and rediscovery

During the 1980s, planning's characteristic as a regulatory intervention in the development process made it sit uncomfortably with New Right thinking. One way in which the planning system was affected was in the restriction of its scope to a narrow land-use regulation remit. This is reflected in the EU Compendium's identification of the UK planning system as being the main example of the 'land use management tradition' of planning in Europe, in which planning's role, at least at the statutory level, is primarily related to the regulation of the change of use of land (CEC 1997). Although in practice and in policy terms, the planning system has been called upon to adopt a wider scope and contribute to the delivery of a range of social, economic and environmental objectives (Tewdwr-Jones and Williams 2001), the integrated approach to spatial development promoted by the ESDP has been seen as suggesting a more wide-ranging and explicitly integrative approach to planning than that represented by the traditional statutory definition of planning. Indeed, since the later 1990s the 'Euro English' term 'spatial planning' has become a term of 'good currency in British English' (Faludi 2002: 4), with an early mention of the term in official government policy discourse being in 'Modernising Planning' (DETR 1998). The 'spatial' planning approach is also emphasised in subsequent national policy documents. 'Planning Policy Guidance Note 11 – Regional planning' (PPG 11) (DETR 2000), for example, stated explicitly that 'Widening the spatial planning scope of RPG is in keeping with trends elsewhere in Europe' and that 'both the European Spatial Development Perspective (ESDP) and the Community Initiative on Transnational Co-operation on Spatial Planning – INTERREG II C and INTERREG III B – programmes will provide a European context for the preparation of RPG'. PPG 11 also referred to planning being concerned with the 'range of public policies that will manage the future distribution of activities in the region' (DETR 2000) a form of words similar to the EU Compendium's (CEC 1997: 24) definition of spatial planning as 'the methods used largely by the public sector to influence the future distribution of activities in space'. This rapprochement of concepts is also reflected in 'Planning Policy Statement 11: Regional Spatial Strategies' (RSS) which states that these documents should not 'be restricted to policies that can be implemented through the grant or refusal of planning permission' (ODPM 2004a: 13). More recently, Planning Policy Statement 1 (PPS 1) which sets the fundamental parameters and principles for the planning system in England, for example makes the distinction between past approaches and 'spatial planning' clearly noting that 'Spatial planning goes beyond traditional land-use planning to bring together and integrate policies for the development and use of land with other policies and programmes which influence the nature of places and how they function' (ODPM 2005: 13). The genealogy of the term 'spatial planning' in the discourse of European spatial planning and the ESDP has been noted by a number of authors (Tewdwr-Jones and Williams 2001). Similarly, the draft 'Wales Spatial Plan' published in 2003 explicitly noted that 'The concept of spatial planning gained momentum from the publication of the European Spatial Development Perspective (ESDP) in 1999' (Welsh Assembly Government (WAG) 2003: 3).

It seems therefore, that in the UK, the model of integrative 'spatial planning' promoted by the ESDP which considers interdependencies and the horizontal and vertical coordination, and therefore 'coherence' of policy interventions affecting a particular territory, has been perceived in a number of quarters as offering a different approach to planning than that traditionally legislated for and practised in the UK. There is also variation however in the extent to which the spatial planning concept is seen as representing a new approach to planning. Official policy documentation produced by central government makes clear the association between the 'spatial' approach and European developments. Recent case-studies of regional planning in the English regions however, revealed diversity in the extent to which horizontal/sectoral coordination was perceived as being a key message of the ESDP (Sykes 2004). The ESDP's substantive spatial development policy aims seem to have been the policy messages most widely recognised, and when questioned on the issue of sectoral coordination and any contribution the ESDP has made to promoting such thinking and practice, in a number of cases policymakers responded that 'we were doing it anyway'. This is not surprising in many respects as the notion of integrating land-use planning more effectively with other sectors has been a key theme in for example in relation to transport and land-use planning integration since the mid-1990s and was increasingly emphasised by the new Labour government after 1997 (DETR 1998).

Despite the emphasis on integration however, it is arguable that the plethora of regional initiatives which have developed in the English regions in recent years, and issues surrounding inter-agency working and inter-strategy coordination, create a complex institutional and policy framework, which is un-conducive to the effective realisation of the kind of integrated spatial development strategy promoted by the ESDP. The issue of the relationships between regional strategies is an issue which is addressed in PPS 11 on RSSs with the East Midlands region's approach of first adopting an Integrated

Regional Strategy to frame the preparation of other regional strategies often being cited as a good practice example (ODPM 2003a).

Also on relating to the issue of horizontal coordination, it is interesting to note that the UK's engagement with the ESDP elaboration process and its steps to apply the document since its agreement have been handled by the planning focused DETR and its successor departments. At the regional level the task of having regard to the ESDP has similarly been handed to the traditionally land-use focused Regional Planning Bodies. The delivery of an ESDP style horizontally integrated approach to spatial development is therefore dependent on coordination between the land-use planning focused RPG instrument and the Regional Economic Strategy (RES) produced by the economic development focused Regional Development Agency (RDA). This provides a striking example of how the 'receiving' context for the application of the ESDP in a member state is conditioned by established traditions and practices of spatial planning, in this case reflecting the traditional dichotomy between regional land use and economic planning in the UK. Reflecting the new popularity of the concept of spatial planning described above, the Planning and Compulsory Purchase Act (2004) introduces RSSs which are intended to have a wider spatial remit and may address issues of inter-strategy coordination and provide a more robust instrument for the delivery of the kind of integrated spatial development approach promoted by the ESDP.

Therefore the evidence suggests that in the UK the ESDP and the discourse of European spatial planning more generally have contributed to the promulgation of the notion of 'spatial planning', which has been perceived by many in government and academia as representing a new more integrative approach to planning than that pursued by the traditional 'land-use management' tradition which has characterised UK practice in recent decades. There is however, also evidence from the case-studies of the practice of spatial planning at the sub-national level that the extent to which the 'spatial' approach is regarded as new or a departure from existing practice or as being a key message of the ESDP varies. For some the ESDP and political change at the national level have enabled a 'rediscovery' of the art and science of spatial planning at strategic territorial scales rather than invented a completely new approach to planning.

Yet whilst the later 1990s have seen a more positive engagement on the part of the UK with the European spatial planning agenda, both from a political and intellectual perspective, it is arguable that, by essentially handing the task of interpreting and applying the ESDP over to sub-State levels of territorial government, the UK national government has effectively side-stepped an explicit consideration of how substantive ESDP principles such as balanced and sustainable polycentric development might relate to the wider national territory. In England national planning policy continues to be expressed through Planning Policy Statements (PPS), which, although nationally applicable and expressing national land use and development policy, are essentially aspatial in character. The development of spatialised strategic planning policy in England proceeds in a bottom-up manner and each region interprets national planning policy guidance (and the ESDP), in terms of their relevance to the regional context.

This piecemeal approach is perhaps surprising given the longstanding imbalances of spatial development in the UK which have preoccupied successive governments and commentators since the 1920s (Hennessy 1992); the continuing concentration of economic activity in certain regions with the attendant pressure on the environment, infrastructure and inflation of living costs and house prices; and moves towards the decentralisation of power (Alden 2002). The lack of an overall spatial framework has been cited as a hindrance in effectively tackling certain interregional issues and imbalances of the national territory (Wong 2002; Tomaney *et al.* 2003). However, despite recent calls from the English RDAs and England's 'Core Cities',[2] this does not form part of the government's agenda for the reform of the planning system. (ODPM 2003b: 14). Despite this, initiatives such as the Communities Plan (ODPM 2003c) or the 'Northern Way' growth strategy for the Northern English regions (ODPM 2004b; Northern Way Steering Group 2004) are essentially spatially defined programmes of investment, which target resources at certain areas within a national context. They therefore perhaps approach the kind of spatial strategy which Faludi and Waterhout (2002) distinguish from regulatory conceptions of planning or the French model of AT which does not require a hierarchical system of statutorily defined and binding plans. It should also be noted that, following the devolution of responsibility for spatial planning policy, different approaches to strategic spatial planning are being pursued in the different constituent parts of the United Kingdom (Roberts and Beresford 2003). Wales and Scotland for example, have produced national spatial planning frameworks whilst no such framework exists at the UK scale (Scottish Executive 2004; WAG 2004).

Summary

The discussions above illustrate how differences in planning tradition and approach in the two countries and wider political contexts and trends have conditioned the interaction between domestic approaches to spatial planning and the transnational ESDP. In France the spatial planning approach promoted by the ESDP seems to have been more closely assimilated with the existing model of AT although this is not to say that this model has not evolved significantly in the 1990s (partly as a result of exposure to other European models and planning debates). In the UK, the ESDP's approach has been seen as representing a more significant shift in the understanding and practice of planning, implying a more spatially integrative approach than a narrow definition of planning limited to land-use management (although the extent to which this is approach is seen as being novel or as a return to earlier more strategic and spatial planning approaches varies). This shift in thinking is reflected in the widespread use of the term 'spatial planning' in policy and professional discourses. The tradition and structures of domestic planning are also reflected in the levels and sectors which have responded to the ESDP in the two countries. In France the primary explicit response to the ESDP has occurred at the member state level, with the national spatial planning agency DATAR leading a long-term reflection on the future spatial development of France (France 2020), and different public policy sectors developing spatialised planning schemes in response to this. In the UK, in England the ESDP has been primarily handled by the land-use planning focused ministry (the DETR and successor departments) and the government has eschewed the development of a national spatial report or framework to reflect on what the ESDP principles might mean at the UK or all-England level. The UK government has instead opted to allow the English regions to interpret and apply the ESDP in terms of its perceived regional relevance. Similarly, following devolution, responsibility for spatial planning and hence for responding to the ESDP is vested in the administrations of the devolved territories (e.g. Wales and Scotland).

Conclusion: the importance of 'receiving contexts' in conditioning interactions between transnational and domestic spatial planning

The discussions above of the interaction between the ESDP and French and British spatial planning tend to confirm the arguments in the introduction. The role played by different countries in developing European policies and different domestic 'receiving contexts' do seem to contribute to shaping the interactions between transnational and domestic spatial planning. Characteristics such as the member state spatial planning tradition; variations in the institutional and policy frameworks for spatial planning; political shifts and evolving policy agendas; the activism of institutions and individual policy makers; all play a role in conditioning the manner in which the ESDP and its policy themes are applied.

The importance of 'departure points' in different national and sub-national contexts in relation to the emerging discourses of transnational spatial planning emerges strongly. For example, the fact that France was one of the initiators or pioneers of the emergence of spatial planning *for* Europe, and can be considered to have 'exported' or 'uploaded' AT to the European level, is one reason why in France the ESDP's approach is generally assimilated with the model and practices of AT. Similar trends are observable in other member states which played a similar role in the emergence of transnational spatial planning, for example in Germany where a study of planning in the Hanover region found that 'The European spatial planning discourse was of little direct relevance, since this itself was already strongly shaped by established German concepts' (Albrechts *et al.* 2003: 120).

The discussions of the relationships between the ESDP and spatial planning in France and the UK also serve to emphasise the importance of different traditions and experiences of spatial planning in conditioning how this transnational planning framework is applied. The impact of the ESDP's integrative model of spatial development in contributing to the evolving nature of 'spatial' planning, for example, appears to have been greater in the UK case where planning's role, particularly since the New Right governments of the 1980s, tended to be more tightly circumscribed and limited to land-use issues, and there has traditionally been a cleavage between economic and land-use planning. In France, as already noted, the ESDP's spatial development model has tended to be equated with the existing regional economic approach of 'Aménagement du Territoire', although this concept has also been evolving in recent years and its scope extended to encompass more sustainability issues in the new formulation of 'Aménagement et Développement Durable du Territoire' (partly due to the impact of European exchange and mutual learning through initiatives such as the ideas of the ESDP). The French and British cases therefore point to the complex interaction of the ESDP's policy discourse and ideas with the planning approaches and spatial development conditions of different territories. Experiences at the sub-state scale in English and French regions also point to the importance of the 'receiving context' in conditioning the manner in which the ESDP's discourse and European spatial planning concepts are more generally interpreted and applied (Sykes 2004). This pattern of interaction also emerges from other studies which have considered the relationship between transnational European spatial planning discourses and the practices and processes of strategic spatial planning and regional governance in EU member states (Shaw and Sykes 2001, 2004). Albrechts *et al.* (2003: 126) for example, highlight 'the importance of the value given to a regional territorial development approach by key local actors and the role strategic spatial concepts within it, rather than the formulaic translation of general concepts into local arenas'. This conclusion accords well with the application view of how strategic frameworks such as the ESDP exert an influence, and the evidence here, which suggests that the 'receiving context', in the different national and sub-national contexts where the ESDP is applied, conditions the manner of its application. For this reason it is important to nuance research into effects of the ESDP and other transnational spatial planning strategies which articulate policy ideas in relation to 'European space' (Jensen and Richardson 2004), with a recognition that in practice different territories and localities provide differentiated receiving contexts for their application which have an effect in conditioning processes of interaction and adaptation.

In summary, the discussions above serve to emphasise the importance of considering the particular planning culture and traditions of member states and the role that particular states have played in the development of European level spatial planning frameworks such as the ESDP. As noted by Böhme (2002) there is an iterative and ongoing relationship between the emergence of 'planning *for* Europe' (transnational and European-level spatial planning) and established and evolving forms of 'planning *in* Europe' (the planning traditions and approaches existing in different countries). This investigation of the interplay between the ESDP and spatial planning in France and the UK reflects this, and demonstrates the continued role which *comparative* perspectives can play within the wider study of European spatial planning, by providing nuanced and contextualised pictures of how emerging forms of transnational spatial planning interact with domestic spatial planning traditions, systems and policies.

Notes

1 The chapter is primarily based on ESRC-funded PhD research completed between 2000 and 2004 which considered the influence of European spatial development policy on the process of strategic regional spatial planning in EU member states.
2 The 'Core Cities' is a grouping of eight major English regional cities established in 1995, by the city councils of eight major English regional cities: Birmingham, Bristol, Leeds, Liverpool, Manchester, Newcastle, Nottingham and Sheffield. The cities have worked to set out a vision of the role that big cities play in national and regional life in the UK in the new century. The group's motivation is to 'ensure that the profile and prosperity of our cities in the 21st century compares favourably with the best regional cities in our competitor countries – particularly in other parts of the European Union' (www.corecities.com).

References

Albrechts, L., Alden, J. and da Rosa Pires, A. (2001) *The Changing Institutional Landscape of Planning*, Aldershot: Ashgate.
Albrechts, L., Healey, P. and Kunzmann, K. (2003) 'Strategic spatial planning and regional governance in Europe', *Journal of the American Planning Association*, 69(2), Spring: 113–29.
Alden, J. (2002), 'Scenarios for the future of regional planning within UK/EU spatial planning', in T. Marshall, J. Glasson and P. Headicar (eds) *Contemporary Issues in Regional Planning*, Aldershot: Ashgate, pp. 35–53.
Bailly, A. and Fremont, A. (2001) *Europe and its States: A Geography*, Paris: La Documentation française.
Bishop, K., Tewdwr-Jones, M. and Wilkinson, D. (2000) 'From spatial to local: the impact of the EU on local authority planning in Britain', *Journal of Environmental Planning and Management*, 43(3): 309–34.
Böhme, K. (2002) *Nordic Echoes of European Spatial Planning: Discursive Integration in Practice*, Stockholm: Nordregio.

Booth, P. (ed.) (1983) *Design and Implementation of Cross-National Research Projects, Department of Town and Regional Planning Working Paper – 44*, Sheffield: University of Sheffield.

Booth, P. (2003) 'Promoting radical change: the Loi relative à la Solidarité et au Renouvellement Urbains in France', *European Planning Studies*, 11(8): 949–63.

Börzel, T. (2005) 'Europeanisation: how the European Union interacts with its member states', in S. Bulmer and C. Lequesne (eds) *The Member States of the European Union*, Oxford: Oxford University Press, pp. 45–69.

Brunet, R., Boyer, J.-C. and RECLUS (1989) *Les villes 'européennes': Rapport pour la DATAR*, Paris: Groupement d'Intérêt Public RECLUS and La Documentation française.

Bulmer, S. and Radaelli, C. (2005) 'The Europeanisation of national policy', in S. Bulmer and C. Lequesne (eds) *The Member State of the European Union*, Oxford: Oxford University Press

Commission of the European Communities (CEC) (1997) *The EU Compendium of Spatial Planning Systems and Policies, Regional Development Studies No. 28*, Luxembourg: Office for Official Publications of the European Communities.

Commission of the European Communities (CEC) (1999) *European Spatial Development Perspective: Towards a Balanced and Sustainable Development of the Territory of the European Union*, Luxembourg: Office for Official Publications of the European Communities.

Comité Stratégique de la DATAR (2003) *Une Nouvelle Politique de Développement des Territoires Pour la France*, Paris: La Documentation française.

Davies, H.W.E. (1993) 'Europe and the future of planning', *Town Planning Review*, 64(3): 235–49.

Davies, H.W.E., Gosling, J.A. and Hsia, M.T. (1994) *The Impact of the European Community on Land Use Planning in the UK*, London: RTPI.

Délégation à l'Aménagement du Territoire et à l'Action Régionale (2002a) *Aménager la France de 2020: Mettre les Territoires en Mouvement*, Paris: Délégation à l'Aménagement du Territoire et à l'Action Régionale.

Délégation à l'Aménagement du Territoire et à l'Action Régionale and Jacquet, N. (2003) *40 Ans d'Aménagement du Territoire: Supplément à la Lettre de la DATAR, no. 176, janvier 2003*, Paris: Délégation à l'Aménagement du Territoire et à l'Action Régionale.

Department for Regional Development (2001) *Shaping Our Future: Regional Development Strategy for Northern Ireland 2025*, Belfast: Corporate Document Services.

Department of the Environment, Transport and the Regions (DETR) (1998) *Modernising Planning: A Policy Statement by the Minister for the Regions, Regeneration and Planning. January 1998*, London: Her Majesty's Stationery Office.

Department of the Environment, Transport and the Regions (DETR) (1999) *Subsidiarity and Proportionality in Spatial Planning Activities in the European Union*, London: Her Majesty's Stationery Office.

Department of the Environment, Transport and the Regions (DETR) (2000) *Planning Policy Guidance Note 11: Regional Planning*, Norwich: Her Majesty's Stationery Office.

Faludi, A. (ed.) (2001) 'Regulatory competition and co-operation in European spatial planning', special issue, *Built Environment*, 27(4).

Faludi, A. (ed.) (2002) *European Spatial Planning*, Cambridge, MA: Lincoln Institute of Land Policy.

Faludi, A. (2003a) 'The application of the European spatial development perspective: introduction to the special issue', *Town Planning Review*, 74(1): 1–9.

Faludi, A. (2003b) 'Unfinished business: European spatial planning in the 2000s', *Town Planning Review*, 74(1): 121–40.

Faludi, A. (2003c) 'Territorial cohesion: old (French) wine in new bottles?', paper presented at the Joint Congress of the Association of Collegiate Schools of Planning and the Association of European Schools of Planning, Leuven, Belgium, 8–12 July.

Faludi, A. (2004) 'Spatial planning traditions in Europe: their role in the ESDP process', *International Planning Studies*, 9(2–3): 155–72.

Faludi, A. and Peyrony, J. (2001) 'The French pioneering role' in A. Faludi (ed.) 'Regulatory competition and co-operation in European spatial planning', special edition, *Built Environment*, 27(4): 253–62.

Faludi, A. and Waterhout, B. (2002) *The Making of the ESDP: No Master Plan*, RTPI Library Series – 3, London: Routledge.

Guichard, O. (1986) *Propositions pour l'Aménagement du Territoire*, Paris: DATAR.

Guigou, J.L. (2001) 'Europe and territorial planning', in A. Bailly and A. Fremont (eds) *Europe and its States: A Geography*, Paris: La Documentation française, pp. 3–4.

Hennessy, P. (1992) *Never Again: Britain 1945–1951*, London: Jonathan Cape.

Hooghe, L. and Marks, G. (2001) *Multi-Level Governance and European Integration*, Lanham, MD, Boulder, CO, New York and Oxford: Rowman and Littlefield.

Jacquet, N. (2003) 'The new financial framework: challenging EU road for the future', Contribution to *Bridging the Gaps: The Contribution of EU Cohesion and other Policies to Competitiveness and Territorial Cohesion*, Helsinki, Finland, 27 February 2003.

Jensen, O.B. (2002) 'Imagining European identity: discourses underlying the ESDP', in A. Faludi (ed.) *European Spatial Planning*, Cambridge, MA: Lincoln Institute of Land Policy, pp. 105–20.

Jensen, O.B. and Richardson, T. (2004) *Making European Space: Mobility, Power and Territorial Identity*, London: Routledge.

Jordan, A.J. (2000) 'The Europeanisation of UK environmental policy, 1970–2000: a departmental perspective', *ESRC One Europe or Several? Project: Working Paper 11/00*. Available http://www.one-europe.ac.uk/pdf/W11Jordan.PDF (accessed 18 May 2006).

Jordan, A.J. (2002) *The Europeanization of British Environmental Policy: A Departmental Perspective*, Basingstoke: Palgrave.

Josserand, F. (2002) *The Spatial and Urban Dimensions in the 2000–06 Objective 2 Programmes – France*, Glasgow: European Policies Research Centre Region, University of Strathclyde.

Lacour, C., Delamarre, A. and Thoin, M. (2003) *40 Ans d'Aménagement du Territoire*, Paris: DATAR and La Documentation française.

Mazet, P. (2000) *Aménagement du Territoire*, Paris: Armand Colin.

Newman, P. and Thornley, A. (1996) *Urban Planning in Europe*, London: Routledge.

Northern Way Steering Group (2004) *Moving Forward: The Northern Way*, North West Regional Development Agency, One North East, Yorkshire Forward.

Office of the Deputy Prime Minister (ODPM) (2003a) *Draft Planning Policy Statement 11: Regional Spatial Strategies*, London: ODPM.

Office of the Deputy Prime Minister (ODPM) (2003b) *Cities, Regions and Competitiveness: Second Report from the Working Group of Government Departments, The Core Cities, and the Regional Development Agencies*, London: ODPM.

Office of the Deputy Prime Minister (ODPM) (2003c) *Sustainable Communities: Building for the Future*, London: ODPM.

Office of the Deputy Prime Minister (ODPM) (2004a) *Planning Policy Statement 11: Regional Spatial Strategies*, London: The Stationery Office.

Office of the Deputy Prime Minister (ODPM) (2004b) *Making it Happen the Northern Way*, London: ODPM.

Office of the Deputy Prime Minster (ODPM) (2005) *Planning Policy Statement 1: Delivering Sustainable Development*, London: The Stationery Office.

Peyrony, J. (2002) *Le Schéma de Développement de l'Espace Communautaire*, Paris: DATAR and La Documentation française.

Roberts, P. and Beresford, A. (2003) 'European Union spatial planning and development policy: implications for strategic planning in the UK', *Journal of Planning and Environment Law*, Occasional Papers No. 31, pp.15–26.

Scottish Executive (2004) *National Planning Framework for Scotland*, Edinburgh: Scottish Executive.

Shaw, D. and Sykes, O. (2001) *Report of the Planning Officers Society Delivering the ESDP Project*, Policy Evaluation and Research Laboratory, Liverpool. Available http://www.liv.ac.uk/civdes/POSReport.pdf.

Shaw, D. and Sykes, O. (2004) 'The concept of polycentricity in European spatial planning: reflections on its interpretation and application in the practice of spatial planning', *International Planning Studies*, 9(4): 283–306.

Stephenson, R. (2002) 'The pursuit of wider involvement in French urban and regional planning', paper presented at the XVI AESOP Congress, Volos, Greece, 10–15 July.

Stephenson, R. (2003) 'Regional strategies in England and France: new tools for policy coherence, territorial cohesion, and democratic legitimacy?', Paper presented at the Third Joint Congress of the Association of European Schools of Planning and the Association of Collegiate Schools of Planning, Leuven, Belgium, 8–12 July.

Sykes, O. (2004) 'Diversity and context dependency in European spatial planning: investigating the application of the European spatial development perspective', unpublished PhD thesis, Liverpool.

Tewdwr-Jones, M. (2001a) 'Complexity and interdependency in a kaleidoscopic spatial planning landscape for Europe', in L. Albrechts, J. Alden and A. da Rosa Pires (eds) *The Changing Institutional Landscape of Planning*, Aldershot: Ashgate, pp. 8–33.

Tewdwr-Jones, M. (2002) *The Planning Polity: Planning, Government and the Policy Process*, RTPI Library Series – 4, London: Routledge.

Tewdwr-Jones, M. and Williams, R. (2001) *The European Dimension of British Planning*, London: Spon.

Tewdwr-Jones, M., Bishop, K. and Wilkinson, D. (2000) '"Euroscepticism", political agendas and spatial planning: British national and regional planning policy in uncertain times', *European Planning Studies*, 8(5), October: 651–68.

Tomaney, J., Pike, A. and Benneworth, P. (2003) 'Reducing regional disparities through public policy', *Town and Country Planning*, 72(4), May: 126–9.

Welsh Assembly Government (WAG) (2003) *People, Places, Futures: The Wales Spatial Plan – Consultation Draft*, Cardiff: Welsh Assembly Government.

Welsh Assembly Government (WAG) (2004) *People, Places, Futures: The Wales Spatial Plan*, Cardiff: Welsh Assembly Government.

Wilkinson D., Bishop, K. and Tewdwr-Jones, M. (1998) *The Impact of the EU on the UK Planning System*, London: DETR.

Williams, R.H. (1983) 'Translating theory into practice', in P. Booth (ed.) *Design and Implementation of Cross-national Research Projects – TRP 44*, Sheffield: University of Sheffield, Department of Town and Regional Planning, pp. 28–46.

Wong, C. (2002) 'Is there a need for a fully integrated spatial planning framework for the United Kingdom?', *Planning Theory and Practice*, 3(3): 277–300.

Zetter, J. (2001) 'The British perspective on the ESDP Process', in A. Faludi (ed.) 'Regulatory competition and co-operation in European spatial planning', special issue, *Built Environment*, 27(4): 287–94.

Chapter 8

Policy for small towns in rural areas

Jean-Paul Carrière, Stuart Farthing and Marie Fournier

Introduction

Any chapter dealing with recent policy in England and France for small towns in rural areas has to recognise that there are different concepts of the 'rural' in these countries linked to their social, economic and cultural histories (Lowe and Buller 1990) and there are thus distinctive national contexts for the appreciation of rural issues. The context, as Lowe and Buller (1990: 5) put it, 'for one is a densely packed and decidedly urbanised nation, and for the other is a nation which covers more territory and was until recently predominantly rural and agrarian'. Quoting Bodiguel (1986) they argue that 'French civilisation remains still, at heart, a rural one' (Lowe and Buller 1990: 5). Whether such a bold claim about French national identity can still be justified, it remains true that rural issues have a greater salience in French political life.

Together these contrasting national contexts have shaped the approach to the issue of small towns in rural areas in a number of inter-related ways. First, in comparison with Britain (and more particularly England), most of France has a rural appearance and a landscape on which a network of widely spaced small towns and villages has developed. Small towns, then, are significant features in the rural landscape and share in the wider significance of the rural in social and political life in France. By contrast the key symbolic component of the rural landscape in England is the village with its village green. Towns, even small towns, fit uncomfortably into the imagined rural landscape. Second, the approach to the issue of small towns in rural areas reflects the distinctive rural ideologies in both countries which in turn have been shaped by distinctive socio-political forces – the 'peasantist' movement in France, and the 'preservation' movement in Britain (Lowe and Buller 1990). These ideologies are expressed in terms of a desire to protect the countryside from physical development in Britain and to protect agriculture and the farmer in rural France. Third, the divergent concepts of the rural and the differing salience of rural issues in national politics has shaped national approaches to the definition of small towns in rural areas in national statistics and the conceptual framework within which much research has been conducted. Hence, as we shall see, despite the later onset of the urban–rural shift in France discussed in Chapter 2, and the perception that small towns and rural areas are undergoing broadly similar processes of change (Buller and Lowe 1990: 33), systematic comparisons of the performance of small towns, and the nature of the problems they face in the two countries are difficult to present.

Finally, there are distinctive approaches to policy for small towns in both countries reflecting their different policy regimes. Policy in England, unlike France, has been largely framed within the context of the aims and purposes of the town and country planning system, and the protection of the countryside from physical development. But there have also been some interesting changes in the culture and mechanisms of government in both countries in recent years. A notable feature of both French and British policy has been the appearance of new institutional forms which operate at new scales of government in rural areas (Edwards *et al.* 2001). In France, these new institutional forms seem typically to be the result of the joint working of communes whilst in England a strong theme in the Market Towns Initiative (MTI) has been the development of partnerships in and around small towns with an attempt by the State to involve a broader range of institutions and individuals in the allocative/policy process. One crucial contextual condition needs, of course, to be recognised here, that is the general decentralisation of more responsibilities and resources to local government in France for policy and service delivery whilst local authorities in England are seen to be facing a diminution in their capacities to act.

Changing rural governance

According to Little (2001: 97) in a review of recent rural research, understanding why new forms of governance have emerged in countries like Britain and France has been

> located theoretically within broader debates about regulation. The shift from a Fordist to post-Fordist mode of accumulation has resulted, it has been argued, in the transformation of regulatory processes in advanced capitalist societies ... Put very simply it has been argued that changes in the cultures and mechanisms of government have occurred as a response to (and as part of) shifts within the social mode of regulation. The adoption of the terminology of rural governance itself suggests a new role for the state – in particular its retreat from a welfarist position as a provider of support to one of a coordinator and manager of the various participants in the process of governance.

> (Little 2001: 98)

The attempt to involve a broader range of institutions and individuals in the policy process through the mechanism of market town partnerships would seem to point to some significant differences in the emerging 'geometry of power' between England and France in relation to policy for small towns in rural areas. However, previous writers have raised questions about the degree to which a new rural governance is developing in Britain (Little 2001). Similarly, Edwards et al. (2001) having investigated the 'geometry of power' being constructed through a range of rural partnerships, concluded that partnerships tended 'to shift power between existing state institutions rather than dispersing power beyond the state' (p. 303); and that State actors remained dominant actors within rural partnerships.

The socio-political process of creating new institutional forms is also simultaneously a process involving the social construction of the geographic scale at which governance is to operate. Hence the scale at which the State operates is not fixed but is the outcome of political processes. Scales are socially constructed but once fixed themselves become part of social and political processes. Any particular 'scalar fix' is thus associated with particular institutions, regulatory mechanisms and processes and will be influenced by policy discourses about the nature of rural areas. Existing institutions become involved in future 'contestations over the meaning and representation of any given scale' (MacLeod and Goodwin 1999). Hence Edwards et al. (2001) argue that the creation of new forms of governance takes place against a background of the existing territorial division of the State. These divisions may be reinforced by the creation of new institutions or they may be called into question. In relation to the rescaling of governance, there are three aspects which are of particular interest: the direction of rescaling; the relationship of new spatial scales of activity to existing levels of governance; and the setting of boundaries. The case of France and England show some interesting contrasts in evolution in recent years.

In the following sections we explore national approaches to the definition of small towns, assess the difference significance attached to the issue of small towns in rural areas, and present some analysis of small towns' 'problems'. Finally, we explore the changing culture of rural governance, the new institutional forms which have developed and the question of the rescaling of governance for small towns in rural areas.

Small towns in rural areas in a national context

Defining rural areas and small towns

We should begin with definitions. In both England and France there has been debate about what rural means. Rural areas are defined as those which are 'not urban'. In France, the basic building block for defining the French territory as urban or rural is the commune. Nearly half (49.4 per cent) of all communes are defined as being in 'urban space'. This can be sub-divided into three categories. First, there are communes which are part of large employment centres (pôles urbains) with more than 5,000 jobs in 1999. Then there are communes which are linked to these employment centres (communes périurbaines). At least 40 per cent of economically active residents of a commune must work in the pôle urbain or in one of the communes which meet the 40 per cent threshold. Together these communes are counted as part of a city region of 'aire urbaine'. In 1999 there were 354 aires urbaines. These contained 77 per cent of the French population. Finally there are communes which by the 40 per cent criterion are linked to two aires urbaines (communes multipolarisées). Rural areas are, therefore, composed of communes which do not fall into the categories above. These cover some 70 per cent of the land area of France.

In a separate statistical process, towns (unités urbaines) are defined by the land use characteristics of the communes. Those which are partially or totally covered by buildings (there must not be a larger gap between dwellings than 200 metres) and in which the population is 2,000 or more are counted as urban. Of these, 354 are pôles urbains but this means that there are large number of towns (1,641, 82 per cent of all French towns) which are either part of an 'aire urbaine' and accessible to a large urban employment centre or are situated in more remote rural areas.

This then leads us to consider on what basis small towns are distinguished from others. Three criteria are conventionally used: the extent of the urbanised area, discussed above; the population; and the extent to which they act as service centres for a surrounding population. Demographic weight is obviously important in most analyses. For INSEE small towns are towns whose population is between 5,000 and 20,000 inhabitants. The Association des Petites Villes de France (APVF) uses the range of 3,000–20,000 population. The employment role is also considered to be an important characteristic. Within rural France, for example, there are 525 rural small towns (pôles d'emplois de l'espace rurale) where there are between 1,500 and 5,000 jobs. Finally, there is the service role based on the range of market and non-market service provision situated in the town. Settlements are classified as: 'village-centre'; 'bourg-centre'; 'centre urbain' (INSEE/INRA 1998). A final category should be noted: the 'bassin de vie'. This is defined as the area within which the residents have access both to services and to employment. France, outside the large towns, has been divided into 1,745 bassins de vie des bourgs et des petites villes, and with an average population of 12,000 they accommodate 36 per cent of the French population. They can be considered as covering French rural areas with its network of small towns.

There have been attempts to assess the extent of urban and rural England on the basis of the influence of large urban areas, using the social and economic characteristics of areas rather than commuting patterns. The ONS Area Classifications 1991 (Bailey et al. 2000) used a range of indicators to identify the characteristics of different administrative areas and the similarity between areas. The resulting classification allows areas to be described in relation to how 'urban' they are. Some local authority districts in this approach are thus described as 'rural areas' whilst 'inner London' is at the other end of the rural-urban continuum. Local authority districts are quite large in spatial extent and thus it is obviously possible for some small towns (measured on a land use and population basis) to be set within this broader rural context. Another Countryside Agency definitional approach, used in some analyses of rural England has also recognised differences *within* rural areas, classifying local authority areas (districts) into urban, accessible rural and remote rural areas.

In England, the basic building block for identifying towns or urban areas in the census has not been very different in concept from the French approach but rather than using the lowest level of the administrative hierarchy to define the boundaries of towns, settlement boundaries are based on the extent of urban land uses. Settlements with a minimum population size of 1,000 people are counted as urban areas for census purposes. By this definition the rest of the land is 'rural' and composed mainly of open land and 'countryside'.

The government's Rural White Paper (November 2000) emphasised the importance of 'market towns' and growing concern about their future. These market towns were defined by the Countryside Agency as towns in rural England 'usually with a population from 2,000 to 20,000'. Subsequent work analysing market town characteristics and performance has used the range of 2,000–30,000 population. This work has also attempted to assess the degree to which towns within this size range act as 'service hubs' with 'a proper complement of services'. This included the following:

- a bank or building society or solicitor;
- more than 10 retail outlets;
- an above average number of shops (2.4 per 1,000 residents);
- a doctor's surgery;
- a small or large supermarket.

Subsequently there has been a review of urban and rural area definitions (Countryside Agency 2004a). This rejected the utility of social and economic criteria claiming that these no longer distinguished urban from rural areas, and proposed the adoption of the land use definition of 'urban areas' discussed above. However, any places which had a population of less than 10,000 population in 2001 were to be counted as rural settlements. These therefore include urbanised areas on the old definition with populations between 10,000 and about 1,500. But it also includes small villages, hamlets and isolated dwellings not distinguished in previous definitions. These settlements are officially divided into three types: 'town and fringe'; 'village' and 'dispersed' based on their 'density profile' (dwellings per hectare). Small rural towns in England are now those with less than 10,000 population but with a distinctive density profile. The new definition also distinguishes between the context within which rural settlements are located based on the surrounding population density. Two levels are distinguished: 'sparse' and 'less sparse'. Sparsely settled areas are remote from the large urban centres and to some degree overlap with the types of areas identified by the 1991 ONS classification of local authorities areas as 'remoter rural areas'.

The consequence is that there is remarkably little consistency between the two countries in approaches to the definition of a small town or to rural areas. The insignificance of agriculture as a source of employment nationally, the growing links between larger urban settlements and the areas of open countryside and smaller settlements between them means that, in England unlike in France, the project of distinguishing areas by the degree of urban influence (as measured by their social and economic characteristics) has officially been abandoned, though not without criticism (see, for example, Green 2004).

The performance of small towns in national perspective

Analyses by INSEE suggest that small towns as a group (i.e. those with populations between 5,000 and 20,000) maintained their position in terms of population growth in the 1990s. But this analysis is based on a sample which changes with demographic trends and includes all small towns. In France there is, in fact, considerable diversity in the situation of small towns, particularly growing differences between two groups of towns: first, small towns within the catchment area (villes périurbaines) of one of the 354 large urban employment centres and those on the coast; and, second, small towns within rural areas remote from the large urban employment centres. The first group have experienced a notable and rapid growth since 1970. The results of the partial census in 2005 in France published in January 2006 has shown that the periurban growth has remained very strong being the area which experienced the fastest growth in the early 2000s. Half of the French population lives in towns of less than 10,000 inhabitants and the growth rate of these towns has doubled (0.5 per cent per annum 1990–9 compared with 0.9 per cent 1999–2005). Small town growth has been accelerating within 25 km of large urban centres. A second group have shown some weakening in growth rates from about 1980 onwards. Some stability has been regained in the 1990s with some towns showing renewed dynamism. Many, however, are in decline. This is true particularly of very isolated small towns in rural areas or those with a former industrial specialism (Fournier 2005). This mixed picture of small town growth is confirmed by Laborie (2004) who using the same sample of 533 small towns since 1968 has noted that 250 (47 per cent) have lost population and are still experiencing difficulty.

The performance of small towns in England in recent years has not been researched in a systematic way. Problems arise largely because of the changing definitions over time. However, Brown *et al.* (2005) have tried to assess the performance of all 369 small towns (2,000–30,000 population in the settlement) within the more rural districts of England and Wales based on the ONS classification discussed above. This research could not obtain population data for the whole sample but obtained data on change in the number of dwellings in the towns over the 1990s. This showed that these small towns as a group were growing faster than the England and Wales average. This does not automatically translate into population growth in these towns since this will also be affected by trends in the number of persons per dwelling (which may well be falling in these areas). In terms of housing growth, the small towns that were showing the weakest performance were those located in coastal areas (an interesting contrast with the French situation), those which were in former mining areas and those which had relatively large social housing stock.

Small towns in rural areas as a policy issue

How significant politically at the national level has the role and performance of small towns in rural areas been? In France, the question of the future of small towns in rural areas has been the object of research by DATAR from the 1960s and a number of researchers have addressed the issue (for example, Kayser 1979; Laborie 1979). Public policy has also been committed to this issue. In 1975, DATAR launched its small towns policy (Politique des Petites Villes) complementing policies already developed for regional metropolises (Métropoles d'Équilibre) in 1963 and medium-sized towns (Villes Moyennes) from 1973 to 1979. They aimed to maintain and support the development and social and economic vitality of these towns and their surrounding rural catchment areas. The measures taken were concerned with supporting the industrial and agricultural sectors. Nearly 300 agreements were concluded between the State, regional bodies and local authorities under this policy.

The recent burst of national level interest in the role and performance of small towns in England dates from 2000 and the Rural White Paper (DETR 2000), *Our Countryside: The Future. A Fair Deal for Rural England.* When described as 'market towns', a label which conjures up a rural and agricultural heritage, they were seen as playing a significant service role for a surrounding rural hinterland and a significant role in rural regeneration policy. Before that date, small towns away from the big cities were in the 1950s seen as possible partners of large urban local authorities under the Expanded Towns Act. This Act, complementary to the new towns policy, aimed to help with the planned decentralisation of population from large cities to smaller towns in order to improve living conditions in the big cities. But in general terms, the goal of urban containment has meant that policy has aimed to constrain growth and development outside major urban areas. Small towns have in general been seen to need protection from urban growth pressures, and only limited expansion has been encouraged. This growth has been focused on certain selected small towns or smaller settlements (key or selected settlements) with a view to supporting the viability of local public and private services. It is important to note that the Rural Strategy of 2004 has failed to mention market towns. With institutional reorganisation, responsibility has been left to Regional Development Agencies (RDAs).

Problems for small towns in rural areas

Despite historical and cultural differences, there are some common themes in official discourses about small towns in rural areas in England and France: employment and prosperity, transport issues in rural areas and service provision. There are also some acknowledged differences between types of rural area reflecting the accessibility of small towns in rural areas to larger urban centres.

In France, whilst some recent policy developments (la Loi Relative à la Solidarité et au Renouvellement Urbains (SRU), for example) might be seen to threaten continued periurban growth, current population trends mean that a major concern for many small towns in accessible rural areas and on the coast is that they remain attractive as places to live. Since employment has remained much more centralised than population within aires urbaines, these small towns have a role as dormitory towns for the large urban areas. They need to offer a good quality environment in which to live, and service provision is an important aspect of this deaal. Population growth might contribute to the maintenance of local services but a study of small towns in Loire-Atlantique by Fournier (2005) has shown that this is not always the case with a decline in cultural facilities in towns in the hinterland of Nantes. Transport issues are of growing importance given the mobility of the population and growing dependence on the car.

In remote rural areas the question of the attractiveness of the town as a place to live has become the central development issue. Small towns furthest from large urban centres, for example in Limousin, have had the greatest difficulty in keeping their population as illustrated by recent studies by Fournier (2005). In this process, the continued provision of services is seen to be essential from the point of view of local decision-makers. Many small towns are engaged in a struggle to keep open hospitals which were established in the 1950s but which are now under threat of closure. There are also experiments with the development of 'Maisons de services publics' (Chambly dans l'Oise) (APVF 2005).

Another asset for a small town is its built environment/heritage. Laborie (2004) has shown that towns which were the least industrialised in the postwar period have succeeded in the growing 'residential economy' of recent years. Many of these are in the South West of France. By contrast the industrialised towns have been less attractive as places to live and have found it difficult to adapt to changed circumstances, the towns in Limousin once again being a good illustration of these trends (Fournier 2005).

It is difficult to separate out the problems in rural areas more generally from the problems specific to small towns in rural areas in England. And there are some important regional dimensions to the perceived nature of the problems. In the Rural White Paper (DETR 2000) there is a concern for the serious economic difficulties faced in some rural areas (the 'predominantly rural' areas) with a loss of young people, high unemployment and low wages and low investment. In these areas small towns too are likely to be sharing these problems. In the more remote rural areas Brown *et al.* (2005) show that in general, manufacturing employment has been growing though there is a great variation from town to town in this performance and there is no consistent link between economic specialisation and employment growth. Elsewhere in more accessible rural areas there is greater prosperity with high growth rates, increasing employment and business activity in which small towns are likely to share. There is general evidence that rural areas tend to have lower unemployment rates than larger urban areas and that they have higher economic activity rates. There are differences within rural areas, with the 'accessible' rural areas showing the highest rates of economic activity. Economic activity rates in recent years have been rising in rural areas whilst they have been declining in urban areas (Countryside Agency 2004b) The fastest growth has been in the 'remote rural areas'.

Unemployment rates in markets towns follow a north west–south east pattern with the lowest rates of unemployment in accessible rural areas around London and particularly to the south and east of London, reflecting local labour market conditions in different regions of England (Countryside Agency 2004b). Within labour markets in more remote rural areas, unemployment rates tend to be higher in small towns than in the areas surrounding them. This reflects housing market processes by which the poorest members of the rural community are channelled into housing in small towns. High and more persistent unemployment is found in the largest towns in employment terms within a labour market (within the 2,000–30,000 range) associated with high levels of social housing in these towns (Brown *et al.* 2005). Employment growth has not been favouring the main employment centres in rural areas. It has been fastest in the smallest towns within labour markets, and even faster in rural hinterlands of these small towns.

Another more general concern for small towns in rural areas (including the more prosperous areas) is the threat to their service role as services (both public and private) shift to the larger towns because of economies of scale; as large supermarkets on the edge of towns destroy the viability and vitality of the town centre and its shops; and as internet-based services undermine further traditional activities such as banking, estate agencies and travel agencies. The knock-on effect of these changes will be felt in the appearance of the town, loss of jobs and economic vitality, and lower quality of life for people in the town and surrounding area (Simms *et al.* 2003).

A strong contrast with the situation in France is a general preoccupation in rural areas with the problem of housing affordability, as planning controls have limited new housing development whilst there is a strong desire for rural living amongst the urban population. At the same time there is seen to be shortage of social housing in rural areas, despite efforts to allow land normally protected from development to be 'released' for 'affordable housing' (often, though not restricted to, social housing) development. There is clear evidence that small towns have been the focus of housing growth, out-performing villages in their hinterlands, a pattern consistent with the long term aim of policy in rural areas to channel new housing to small towns rather than the open countryside (Brown *et al.* 2005). But many communities in small towns are keen to protect their town from further housing development and are strong supporters of planning control.

Small towns and changing rural governance

Britain and France have radically different administrative traditions and structures. The rural commune is a key part of the national identity (Bodiguel *et al.* 1990). The political issues involved in the restructuring of rural governance are likely therefore to be radically different.

How has the State initiated these new institutional forms?

Consistent with the expectations of the new rural governance, the central State in France and the UK has not imposed organisational solutions on the local level but has encouraged self-organisation from the bottom up. In 2000, 'a new commitment to market towns' was announced in the Rural White Paper. (This of course applied to England, not the UK as a whole.) The broad strategy for the Market Town Initiative (MTI) was set out in the White Paper. Market towns were invited to participate in the initiative under regional regeneration programmes. The White Paper set out guidance on the number of towns to be involved, the sorts of measures to be taken, and the criteria by which towns would be selected for inclusion in the programme. It also committed some additional funding for market town regeneration in the programmes of the Regional Development Agencies (RDAs) and the Countryside Agency. These bodies, together with a voluntary body – Action for Market Towns – worked in partnership to articulate the policy in more detail and acted in an 'enabling role' for initiatives at the market town level. The emphasis was in developing a local partnership, bringing together a number of agencies and the local population in and around the small towns to diagnose the nature of the problems in the town (to carry out a 'health check') and to develop an action plan to solve those problems. Funding would then be sought from a variety of bodies to implement the action plan.

In France there have been a number of incentives to the creation of new institutional forms from the 'bottom up', in a way that was not typical of the traditional French approach to these matters (Marconis 2005). The 'quiet revolution' produced by the Loi Chevènement in France has encouraged the formation of Établissements Publics de Coopération Intercommunale (EPCI) which has addressed the fragmentation of French local government (described in Chapter 5) and encouraged the adoption of common local taxation policies. Small towns are thus incorporated into a number of different inter-communal organisations. They can be part of the 14 Communauté Urbaines (more than 500,000 in population), the 162 Communautés d'Agglomération (less than 500,000 in population) or the 2,343 Communautés de Communes (less than 50,000 in population).

Another impetus to the creation of new organisations at the local level has been the creation of *pays* under the Loi d'Orientation pour l'Aménagement et le Développement Durable du Territoire (LOADDT) 1995 and 1999. These are intended to bring together local politicians, local service organisations of the central State, and leaders of business and voluntary organisations in a Conseil de développement to develop strategy for their area (Charte de développement in a 'pays'). Where the proposals are consistent with regional and departmental priorities, a contract can be signed with the State for a seven-year period in order to finance the planned developments (drawing on funds from the State, the region, the department or Europe). This is a unique feature of the French system.

Further encouragement for inter-communal cooperation for small-town development has appeared in the guise of a call by DATAR in 2005 (to be repeated in 2006) for proposals to support the process of territorial development around small and medium-sized towns, focusing on their role as centres for employment, services and local facilities.

The development of the new institutional arrangements in England and France have been influenced by policy discourses about the nature of rural areas and their economies and by how space is imagined. There are clearly somewhat different 'spatial imaginaries' for rural space. As already remarked, the French official statistical division of the French territory recognises that a significant proportion of France is remote from major urban areas and is mainly rural. With a very substantial proportion of its national territory covered by this rural designation, French proposals emphasise the importance of small and medium-sized towns as motors or drivers of the rural economy, and the necessity of linking urban and rural areas in strategic planning. Within small towns accessible to the larger urban areas in France, the Loi

SRU influenced by environmental considerations is obviously attempting to restrain further periurban development and refocus development in urban areas, as discussed in Chapter 2.

Sustainable development, as originally interpreted in England, highlighted the essential aim of protecting rural areas from large scale physical development by concentrating most new development, particularly housing, on 'brownfield land' within existing large urban areas. The English approach reveals an ambivalence about the nature of rural areas and their economies. On the one hand, some urban–rural differences have been acknowledged. The 2000 White Paper (DETR 2000) recognised that the poorest counties were those which were 'rural' and suggested that there are links between small town prosperity and the prosperity of the rural region around it, hence small town regeneration is also part of rural regeneration more broadly. On the other hand, the latest Rural White Paper 2004 (DEFRA 2004) and work around the new rural definition (Countryside Agency 2004b), suggest that there is no systematic distinction between the economies of rural and urban England. This strand of thinking means that urban-based concepts of competitiveness and, more importantly, of regeneration can be appropriately imported into rural areas. In this respect, the Market Towns Initiative can be seen to share a number of features with urban regeneration policy as it has evolved in England under the Labour government: it is focused on small areas; it is about inter-agency and partnership working which is intended to encourage integrated policies; it has a strong emphasis on community involvement; community 'ownership' of problems; and it has tried to mobilise local leadership in resolving these problems. Officials working within the initiative explicitly drew parallels with the urban-based Neighbourhood Renewal Programme.

The rescaling of governance

The direction of rescaling and its relationship to the existing levels of governance varies between the countries, reflecting in part the existing local government structure in the two countries and the perceived strengths and weaknesses of these arrangements in debates about new institutional arrangements.

In England, responsibilities for small towns and the rural economy moved both up and down from the spatial level of districts and counties. In England it moved to regional scale and became a regional level responsibility with RDAs (introduced in 1999 to promote regional economic development) taking over responsibility for these issues. The move to the 'market town' level saw new initiatives at a scale below that of local authority districts nearer to the level of the town or parish council. This was prompted by a desire to engage with local communities, in a move that was in many ways similar to more urban-based regeneration policies.

In France, the shift has been to define new levels of operation and responsibility at a scale above the level of commune but below that of département and région. The logic here is also to do with the selection of more appropriate areas for the delivery of public services as well as lobbying or strategic planning. The mutual development of small towns and their hinterlands is the focus of strategies for the remote rural areas. Two hundred and fifty-one 'pays' were recognised at the end of 2004, with 90 more planned. Sixty per cent of 'pays' have a small town of between 5,000 and 20,000 as the main centre; a further 20 per cent have a smaller settlement (bourg) as the main centre.

The setting of boundaries

In France, communes have been encouraged to look for new partnerships at a range of spatial scales (State, region, European Union) but mainly with neighbouring communes and here the setting of boundaries has been a very significant issue. Recent legislation requires local actors to consider the geographic realities of the area in which they are located identified through the work of INSEE. A new planning tool – the SCOT (Schéma de Cohérence Territorial) – requires a consideration of 'aires urbaines', and in rural areas the organisation of space around rural employment centres or around towns at the centre of service catchment areas. The Loi SRU and the Loi Urbanisme et Habitat are also explicit that places with strong geographic, cultural, economic or social ties at the scale of the local service catchment area or the labour market, should organise themselves in 'pays'. But there is a great deal of variety. The medium-sized town of Saumur illustrates the divergence between these concepts and the importance of local political considerations to boundary setting (Fournier 2005). The Communauté d'Agglomération (Saumur Loire Développement) has 32 communes, wider than the 'aire urbaine' which according to INSEE consists of only 22 communes, whilst the local labour market according to INSEE covers a total of 103 communes. Meanwhile the SCOT and the 'pays' around Saumur cover different sets of communes again.

In England, the MTI left the definition of boundaries to the market town as one to be decided by local actors in the partnership. The idea behind the policy encapsulated in the name is that the town acts as a central place (following Chintaller) which serves people not only in the town but also in the surrounding countryside. A number of towns had existing partnerships before they became part of the MTI and in these cases the boundaries reflected those of the pre-existing partnership. Many towns focused on the existing local government boundaries using those of the town council to demarcate the town and often those of contiguous parishes to identify the outer limits of the partnership boundary. But many partnerships have reported problems in engaging the hinterland in the process, recognising that despite the supposed service role of market towns in the more accessible and higher density rural areas of England, many parishes have links with a number of towns (Entec 2004) and many towns do not have a significant service role.

The geometry of power and its construction: who are the key actors?

In the introduction we raised the question of whether the new institutional forms through which policy for small towns in rural areas is formulated and implemented represented significant differences in the 'geometry of power' between England and France. In France, whilst the new rural spaces of 'agglomérations' and 'pays' are intended to bring together local politicians, local service organisations of the central State, and leaders of business and voluntary organisations in a 'Conseil de Développement' to develop strategy for their area, and whilst the strategy has to be developed in association with the local population, this process is a consultative one and it is clear that the key actors in the new structures are local public bodies and local mayors. The Président de la Communauté de Communes, for example, within the 'pays' plays a crucial role in setting the agenda for local development. At the same time the recent process of decentralisation has transferred responsibilities for some important local policy issues to départements and régions, but few to communes, particularly those in rural areas.

In England, rural development partnerships of the 1990s have in general been criticised for being dominated by local government. The impetus behind the MTI was to give an important leadership role to the local community. But the dominance of the local authorities in MTI has remained a feature. It seems clear that local government representatives (both officers and councillors) – at parish/town council, district and county level – represent a significant proportion of the membership of MTI partnerships. County councils are less often represented in partnerships. The public sector more generally represents around two-thirds of seats. Community and voluntary representation is about one-quarter of members. There is therefore less private sector representation (Entec 2004).

Where there is a dominant group in the partnership it tends to be the district council, which is not surprising given that they provide most of the funding for regeneration projects, are an important regulatory body for planning and have considerable experience in regeneration.

Conclusions

Policy for small towns in rural areas is an interesting prism through which to study national differences in attitudes to, and concepts of, the 'rural' as well as changing governance in rural areas. The socio-political process of creating new institutional forms has been simultaneously a process involving the social construction of the geographic scale at which governance is to operate. Edwards *et al.* (2001) claim that whatever the rhetoric, partnerships have tended to shift the locus of operation between *existing* scales of government. By contrast in France the rescaling of governance has seen a clear attempt to create a *new* scale of operation for both strategic planning and also for implementation (existing competences/powers can be transferred from commune level to the intercommunal level). Of course there have been various attempts to encourage intercommunal working in the past. What is new is the pace with which these new arrangements in rural areas have been adopted. In January 2005, 2,343 'Communautés de Communes' were recorded bringing together 29,172 communes. In England, the impact of the MTI has been to shift the locus of action to the lowest tier of local government – the town or parish council which covers the market town – and to the regional level with responsibilities being given to Regional Development Agencies for rural development.

In relation to the debate about the changing geometries of power in rural areas, our interpretation of trends in both England and France suggests that whilst, at first sight, the new institutional forms appear very different in terms of the actors involved, they are very similar in their operation. Local authorities have remained the dominant actors within these new organisations.

References

APVF (2005) *L'Adaptation des services publics territoriaux aux changements: qualité de service, évaluation des politiques publiques, enjeux de la proximité.* Paris: Association des Petites Villes de la France.

Bailey, S., Charlton, J., Dollamore, G. and Fitzpatrick, J. (1999) 'Families, groups and clusters of local and health authorities of Great Britain: revised for authorities in 1999', *Population Trends*, 99: 37–52.

Bodiguel, M. (1986) *Le Rural en Question*, Paris: L'Harmattan.

Brown, C., Farthing, S., Nadin, V. and Smith, I. (2005) *Dynamic Smaller Towns: Identification of Critical Success Factors*, Cardiff: Welsh Assembly Government.

Buller, H. and Lowe, P. (1990) 'Historical and cultural contexts', in P. Lowe and M. Bodiguel (eds) *Rural Studies in Britain and France*, London: Bellhaven Press.

Countryside Agency (2004a) *The New Definition of Urban and Rural Areas of England and Wales*, Research Notes CRN 86, Cheltenham: Countryside Agency.

Countryside Agency (2004b) *The State of the Countryside* (June), Cheltenham: Countryside Agency.

Department for Environment, Food and Rural Affairs (DEFRA) (2004) *Rural Strategy*, London: Department for Environment, Food and Rural Affairs.

Department of the Environment, Transport and the Regions (DETR) (2000) *Our Countryside: The Future. A Fair Deal for Rural England.* Department of the Environment, Transport and the Regions CM 4909, Norwich: HMSO.

Edwards, B., Goodwin, M., Pemberton, S. and Woods, M. (2001) 'Partnerships, power and scale in rural governance', *Environment and Planning C: Government and Policy*, 19: 289–310.

ENTEC (2004) *Assessment of the Market Towns Initiative: A Summary*, Cheltenham: Countryside Agency, Market Towns Team.

Fournier, M. (2005) *Les Petites Villes de l'Espace Atlantique Français*, Tours: École Polytechnique de l'Université de Tours.

Green, R. (2005) 'Redefining rurality', *Town & Country Planning*, June: 202–5.

INSEE/INRA (1998) *Les Campagnes et leurs Villes*, Paris: Collection Portrait Social, Contours et Caractères INSEE/INRA.

Kayser, B. (1979) *Petites Villes et Pays dans l'Aménagement Rural*, Paris: Association des ruralistes français/CNRS.

Laborie, J.-P. (1997) *Les petites villes*, Paris: Editions du CNRS.

Laborie, J.-P. (2004) 'Les petites villes face à la métropolisation: la perte d'une spécificité'. Associations des Directeurs de Bibliothèques Départementales de Pret. Available http://www.adbdp.asso.fr/association/je2004/laborie.htm.

Little, J. (2001) 'New rural governance?', *Progress in Human Geography*, 25(1): 97–102.

Lowe, P. and Buller, H. (1990) 'Rural development in post war Britain and France', in P. Lowe and M. Bodiguel (eds) *Rural Studies in Britain and France*, London: Bellhaven Press.

MacLeod, G. and Goodwin, M. (1999) 'Reconstructing an urban and regional political economy: on the state, politics and explanation', *Political Geography*, 18: 697–730.

Marconis, R. (2005) 'Les aires régionales et les pays: France', in F. Bost, L. Carroué, C. Girault, J.-L. Racine, J. Radvanyi, T. Sanjuan and O. Sanmartin (eds) *Images Économiques du Monde 2006*, Paris: Armand Colin.

Simms, A., Oram, J., Macgillivray, A. and Drury, J. (2003) *Ghost Town Britain*, London: New Economics Foundation.

Chapter 9

The evolution of urban policy

Gay Fraser and Florence Lerique

Introduction

Two important considerations, constitutional and historic, underlie urban policy in both the UK and France. First, each of the four constituent parts of the UK, England, Scotland, Wales and Northern Ireland, has policy responsibility in this area and while there are similarities in approach there are differences in development and application. France, however, is a unitary state covered by a single policy approach. This chapter focuses primarily on comparing England and France but includes brief references to policy elsewhere in the UK. Second, the national approach to urban policy in each country has evolved in relation to shifting social and economic conditions over the last few decades and consequently comparisons are made from a historical perspective. The funding context for the regeneration aspects of urban policy is broadly covered in Chapters 10 and 11.

There is no simple definition of a distinctive urban policy. While national mainstream policies have affected people living in urban areas, historically in the UK what is known as urban policy is rooted in the targeting of resources on area regeneration initiatives. These have been largely, though by no means exclusively, in parts of the inner city experiencing the most concentrated areas of social deprivation, including unemployment, crime, drug abuse, poor housing and environment, poor health, social disruption and a high proportion of ethnic minorities. Only relatively recently has urban policy, in practice, expanded into a more strategic approach embracing the range of issues facing towns and cities as a whole. In France urban policy started in a similar way and is predominantly directed at deprived areas which are, through geographical circumstance, mainly in peripheral social housing estates. The background socio-economic trends are outlined in Chapter 2.

Origins of urban policy

In the postwar years, the UK government established a land-use planning system to steer development together with economic initiatives, housing renewal programmes and a New Towns programme which led to loss of skilled population and industry from the core areas of major cities. These areas became more socially deprived, with increasing overseas immigration, racial tensions and riots in London. Mindful of the lessons of civil unrest in the USA the then Labour government responded with basically social and community-based legislation between 1966 and 1969. This provided the foundation for the Educational Priority Areas (EPAs) programme to assist integration of immigrants and the Urban Aid programme, which became the Urban Programme (UP), involving Home Office grants to Local Authorities (LAs) in various large towns and cities for mainly social projects, later broadened to include voluntary organisations and infrastructure. The Community Development Projects of 1970 undertook action research with residents to tackle their problems in selected areas, but these became increasingly radicalised and were closed by 1976.

The structural nature of inner city problems and the need to provide economic opportunities were highlighted by three Inner Area Studies, in Liverpool, Birmingham and Lambeth, commissioned by the next Conservative government and reporting between 1972 and 1976. But it was a Labour government, returned to power in 1974, that used these studies as the basis for the first White Paper concerning urban policy in 1977. More emphasis was given to the impact of economic decline and LAs were encouraged to stimulate industrial investment though policies also aimed to alleviate social problems, improve the physical fabric and bring about a population and employment balance between inner cities and the rest of the city region. The White Paper introduced a more focused approach to urban regeneration, with targeting of expenditure on specific areas of need through local programmes. It recognised the need for partnership between central and local government and for main policies and programmes to take into account the inner areas. The UP was transferred to the Department of the Environment. The subsequent Inner Urban Areas Act 1978 implemented a tiered system of resource allocations, through Partnerships, Programme Authorities and Other Designated Districts and enabled LAs to designate Industrial Improvement Areas.

France had also concentrated in the postwar years on land management to accommodate urban growth and economic development, in response to a period of planned industrialisation. The Zone à Urbaniser en Priorité (ZUP) was the major tool used for the construction of massive housing schemes, the Grands Ensembles. This was followed in 1964 by Métropoles d'Équilibres, to spread development to major urban centres outside Paris, and a New Towns programme. While by this time concerns in the UK were already directed at areas of severe deprivation, France was still in the process of dealing with rapid urbanisation. It was not, therefore, until some 10 years later that a similar pattern of ethnic change, social problems and disturbances led to the first measures in urban policy. The Habitat et Vie Sociale programme, introduced in 1977, applied to 50 zones in certain districts or social housing estates, especially the Grands Ensembles. Using mostly Caisse des Dépôts funding, it aimed to coordinate improvements in housing, management of local services, construction of public facilities and support for families, though in practice tended to deal mainly with the first.

So by 1980 the idea of directing a range of actions to defined urban areas experiencing deprivation was established in both countries. While there was growing recognition of social and economic needs, the response was primarily in terms of physical development and improvements, especially in France. Around this time the political pendulum swung to a Conservative government in the UK in 1979 and a Socialist one in France in 1981, which led to more divergent ways of tackling the issues.

Development of urban area regeneration

Although continuing to operate within the preceding policy framework, the Conservative government in the UK signalled two new directions which had a marked effect on urban policy. The private sector was encouraged to take the lead in regeneration and the physical reclamation and re-use of derelict land was seen as the key to economic investment. The Local Government, Planning and Land Act 1980 introduced Urban Development Corporations (UDCs), short-life public bodies aimed at securing regeneration of derelict areas and bringing in as much private sector investment as possible. It also allowed for the designation of Enterprise Zones (EZs), giving financial and planning incentives to businesses over a fixed period. The UDCs provided the main thrust of urban regeneration policy during the 1980s, taking over various LA powers. Funding regimes for inner city authorities were also altered by central government, leading to ideological disagreements with, and marginalisation of, local government.

Serious rioting in several major cities in 1981 led to an increase in the UP and moves to increase private sector involvement, through investment as well as bringing in more entrepreneurs. The Financial Institutions Group was set up to advise on possible initiatives, as a result of which 'Urban Development Grant' was introduced, a public subsidy to counter constraints to private sector investment in the inner city by bridging the gap between costs of development and its resultant value. It was later combined with Urban Regeneration Grant, which was applied to larger scale projects and paid directly by the Department of the Environment, to form City Grant in 1988.

Many other initiatives were introduced, generally all backing up this policy approach. For instance, four National Garden Festivals were set up between 1984 and 1992, to rapidly reclaim large derelict sites, attract tourists and subsequent inward investment. Estate Action begun in 1985 was a way of allocating resources on a competitive basis to run-down council estates, to tackle social, economic and physical problems and improve local housing management. The Church of England added its voice to concern about inner city problems with a report by the Archbishop of Canterbury's Commission on Urban Priority Areas in the same year, putting pressure on the government to take further action. In the later 1980s this was mainly concerned with attempts to provide better coordination of policy, including City Action Teams of various government departments to coordinate public and private sector initiatives under programmes dealing with job creation, local training and enterprise development and Task Forces of central and local government and the private sector to focus government help in specific areas and foster a local approach to programme management. These were transferred from the Department of Employment to the Department of Trade and Industry in 1988 and then to the Department of the Environment in 1992. In 1988 the government relaunched its urban regeneration policies as part of the Action For Cities Initiative, with a unit temporarily in the Cabinet Office to coordinate government departments involved in regeneration activities and present urban policy more clearly. Some level of commitment across government was achieved but reduction in the direct involvement of local government continued through the introduction of initiatives such as Housing Action Trusts, to take over from LAs and improve public housing stock, and Compacts, a partnership between local employers, schools and Training and Enterprise Councils, to improve skills.

France followed a different path during this period. After riots in Les Minguettes in Lyon, the Socialist government rapidly expanded policies in favour of run-down urban areas. Foreign examples were studied and the English EPAs of the late 1960s formed a model over twelve years later for Zones d'Éducation Prioritaire, to reduce educational inequality. The Habitat et Vie Sociale programme was relaunched from 1982 as Développement Social des Quartiers, expanding from 22 pilots to 148 areas by 1988 and encompassing renovation of social housing stock, public spaces, and social and cultural activities. Progressively, urban regeneration sought to become more integrated, covering a range of local authority functions such as housing, public service provision, accessibility and participation of local inhabitants. Three thematic commissions were also set up, the Schwartz, Bonnemaison and Doubedout, reporting respectively on youth employment, training and skills, juvenile crime and safety, and community co-operation in social development of urban districts. Practical actions included youth employment information and guidance centres, communal councils for preventing youth crime, and action funds for social affairs and the voluntary sector, while the 1982 Banlieue 89 programme aimed to physically renovate many of the run-down Grands Ensembles.

A significant further development, after the return of another Socialist government in 1988, was the setting up of new permanent agencies to manage urban policy. The burden of developing policy and its implementation fell mainly on the Délégation Interministérielle à la Ville (DIV), which was responsible to the Prime Minister and set up to cut across existing government departments, similar to DATAR. As a first measure to combat social exclusion, the Contrat de Ville was formally launched in 1988, a co-operative arrangement linking various public funds for projects and programmes for a specified period within a particular geographic area. It was concerned with improving the quality of service delivery, consideration of all sections of the population as well as co-operation between adjoining authorities. The formation in 1991 of a special ministry, the Ministère de la Ville with a designated minister, which subsumed DIV, sought to strengthen these arrangements. As with the initial efforts in 1982/3 these innovations followed a further series of riots in disadvantaged suburban housing estates in Lyon. This cycle of intervention concluded with measures to combat the effects of local administration upon housing programmes. The many small communes making up the suburbs of French cities led to politically motivated avoidance of the need to construct more and better social housing in these areas, especially the more affluent. A new act, the Loi d'Orientation pour la Ville 1991, therefore, abolished the ZUP development zone process in favour of an improved Zone d'Aménagement Concerté (ZAC) process under which mixed uses could be constructed. It also introduced the Dotation de Solidarité a subsidy to the most disadvantaged communes to co-operate in building social housing over a wider area. Youth activity projects were started through the Opérations Été-jeunes to provide leisure opportunities and keep younger members of society off the streets.

During this decade, coordination of initiatives was seen by government as an increasing problem, though each country sought a different solution. In England the measures to bring together the various interests evolved and further rationalisation of policy initiatives took place within existing structures. France undertook more major reforms to government machinery which, at that time, seemed to give this policy area a greater recognition and higher profile than that experienced in the UK. Physical regeneration and development continued to be important in both the UK and France but whereas private sector enterprise and economic aspects spearheaded the urban policy approach in the former, the emphasis in the latter was on social measures. Paradoxically, the limitations of pursuing each of these to the relative exclusion of the other aspects became increasingly apparent.

Consolidation of the area approach

Indeed, there had been growing recognition in the UK that area regeneration needed to embrace a much wider range of issues than just the physical and local players were alarmed about the proliferation of initiatives and the lack of adequate policy coordination. Commitment to a comprehensive/holistic approach to regeneration increased during the 1990s, accompanied by a heightened emphasis on competitive allocation of resources through the launch of City Challenge, superseding the UP, in 1991. Schemes now had to show an innovative approach to solving a wider range of problems in targeted deprived areas based on 57 Urban Priority Areas, as well as attracting private capital. Key features included partnerships between local authorities and other players, annual bidding rounds, time limits on schemes and a concentration on delivery. The initiative pulled together funds from existing regeneration and housing programmes under the Department of the Environment (Parkinson and Le Galès 1994).

The 1992 election in the UK again returned a Conservative government which took forward a package of associated measures. In the same year representatives of the five largest faith communities were assembled in a forum, the Inner Cities Religious Council, to work with government particularly on regeneration, neighbourhood renewal and social inclusion. New integrated regional offices of central government were established in 1994, the Government Offices for the Regions, replacing the City Action Teams. The competitive basis for regeneration was extended further with the introduction of the Single Regeneration Budget Challenge Fund (SRB) which brought together a number of programmes from several government departments aimed at simplifying and streamlining regeneration resources. Priorities were set locally and outputs to measure performance were put in place. Participation of the local community, as well as the private and voluntary sectors, became a major aspect of the local regeneration partnerships which formulated bids. This process contrasted with the negotiated approach taken by all relevant public bodies under the French Contrat de Ville. Physical renewal was still considered important in tackling dereliction and a regeneration agency, English Partnerships, was formed in 1993 to promote economic and environmental regeneration through reclamation and development of vacant, derelict and underused or contaminated land and buildings. It took over responsibilities from the UDCs which were wound up during the 1990s as areas were redeveloped, amidst criticism that social aspects had been ignored.

Interestingly, at this time, a first attempt was made to give urban policy a broader dimension through City Pride. Selected local authorities with other key players were invited to put together a vision for the future of their city and the action necessary to achieve it. No extra funds were involved but it kick-started a process of discussions, through three pilots in London, Birmingham and Manchester, aiming at more strategic frameworks for urban policy and the relationships involved in pursuing them.

The SRB bidding rounds were developed and refined during the 1990s resulting in generally better quality proposals. Although detailed operational aspects were widely criticised, there was a general consensus that a holistic policy approach was necessary to deal with the multi-faceted problems of the areas concerned. However, integration of mainstream programmes, an aim since the 1977 White Paper, remained elusive. In the UK, as in France, area regeneration was carried out alongside European programmes such as URBAN, as the European Commission became increasingly interested in urban aspects of Structural Funds policy, and a range of environment initiatives.

During the earlier years of urban policy through to devolution (Chapter 4), the swings in approach to area regeneration in England were broadly mirrored in the other parts of the UK. However, in Scotland in particular, the relatively smaller population, smaller number of deprived areas and smaller size of government department made greater policy integration and innovation possible (McCarthy 1999).

The measures put in place in the period 1988/91 in France were administered by DIV, the main tool being 'Insertion', namely economic skills development programme which focused on language training and work skills to counter exclusion in the job market but paid less attention to wider educational issues, wider economic development, consultation or local participation. Other ministries, and especially DATAR which saw employment and economic development as its responsibility, resented DIV's remit and it gradually lost influence. Le Galès and Mawson (1994) concluded paradoxically that when the 'Délégation' became yet another ministry, it became like all the other ministries dependent on ministerial interest and co-operation from other departments. Thus 'urban policy became isolated within the bureaucracy' and became marginalised. Although a separate minister with responsibility for urban affairs was retained, DIV became part of the longer established Ministère d'Emploi et de la Solidarité in 1993.

The Grands Projets Urbains (GPU), large-scale regeneration projects initially proposed by the Comité Interministériel des Villes (CIV) and begun in 1994 became the responsibility of the transport department. Continuing disaffection in the deprived areas led to special areas for economic development under the 1995 Loi d'Orientation pour l'Aménagement et le Développement du Territoire (LOADT). Reinforced the following year by the Pacte de la Relance de la Ville, areas suffering from 30 per cent unemployment and concentrations of long-term, young and female unemployed were targeted. Various zones were defined in these areas, including Zones Urbaines Sensibles (ZUS) to tackle social issues, Zones de Redynamisation Urbain (ZRU) to encourage small industries and commerce together with mixed uses in the Grands Ensembles and Zones Franches Urbaines (ZFU) on the lines of the English EZs (Chaline 1998). In effect these measures represented a shift back to economic development and revitalisation.

But the direction of urban policy was influenced further by a major report in 1998 by J.P. Sueur, which analysed the 20 years of tackling the problems of deprived areas and found that, despite government policy to combat social exclusion, conditions had significantly worsened, sometimes aided by the Zones concept which often stigmatised the inhabitants of specific areas and stultified economic growth. He proposed a more locally based agenda with greater community involvement leading to the 1999 Loi Chevènement, which rationalised the concept of 'Intercommunality' and encouraged Communes to group together to tackle local problems, including the devolved responsibility for social housing (Chapter 4). A major measure, the Plan Local de l'Habitat (PLH), directed such groups to look at housing problems on a wider scale. However, as observed in the Lille area (Booth and Green 1999), there was a marked reluctance to take such action for political reasons, reinforcing the need for government to give greater powers to social housing agencies through the 2000 Loi relative à la Solidarité et au Renouvellement Urbains (SRU).

The 1990s thus saw a steady consolidation of a holistic approach to urban area regeneration with local community participation in England while in France the emphasis in the earlier part of this period was on economic measures, which partly reflected what had taken place during the 1980s in England. This later changed to attempts to reintroduce a social agenda with a more comprehensive approach and greater community involvement. In England area regeneration resources were gradually concentrated within the Department of the Environment, while the new national structures put in place in France to deal with urban policy became relatively weaker. Tackling particular urban problem areas remained the priority in both countries. Some initial steps were also taken by the British government to think about the wider policy framework for particular cities, though in France strong civic leadership in some cities, such as Lille and Lyon, had initiated a process of metropolitan enhancement through large-scale schemes (Chapter 5).

Recent policy directions

At the same time as the French Government was rethinking the social and economic balance in regenerating deprived urban areas, the new UK Labour government of 1997 came in with a political will to look at fresh ideas and take positive action. Evaluations of area regeneration programmes during the 1990s showed that there were many successful aspects of community-led and bottom-up initiatives which had come to form a central plank of government policy. But weaknesses persisted, including the continued relative decline of deprived areas, the compartmentalism of local and central government departments, and the lack of cohesion between mainstream and specific regeneration programmes. Following a review of all government spending, a rash of policy initiatives was unleashed over the next two years, some concerning area regeneration directly and others having an impact on urban areas.

This review brought about the New Deal for Regeneration, with two main strands. The SRB was revamped and became part of the resources managed by the Regional Development Agencies (RDAs), set up in 1999

(2000 in London) to prepare regional economic strategies and taking over the responsibilities of English Partnerships. The New Deal for Communities, continuing the comprehensive approach based on local partnership, sought to achieve maximum impact by focusing resources on small deprived areas of 1–4,000 households. With a return to a social agenda, the Prime Minister set up the Social Exclusion Unit in 1997 with a remit to help improve and coordinate government action to reduce social exclusion by producing 'joined-up solutions to joined-up problems'. A national strategy 'A New Commitment to Neighbourhood Renewal' 2001 proposed a 10-year programme to improve the worst areas and tackle the barriers to work and enterprise.

Many other related activities were put in place, for instance the Environment Task Force for young unemployed to deliver projects with sustainable environmental benefits. Other initiatives contributed to the debate on community-based regeneration such as credit unions and local exchange and trading schemes. The various government departments promoted their own policy ideas, including specific area based initiatives such as Health Action Zones, Employment Zones, Education Action Zones, and a new structure, an Urban Regeneration Company, was established so that LAs could sign up local and regional stakeholders to fund a company with a remit to prepare a vision and deliver a masterplan for regenerating a problem area.

However, wider issues were also coming to the fore, especially the need to accommodate household growth combined with pressures to encroach on the countryside and the economic decline of many cities and towns. Work started on modernising the planning system to promote more sustainable patterns of development, on guidance to integrate planning and transport to reduce the need for car travel, and on a review of compulsory purchase of land and compensation. A range of activities on urban greening was initiated and planning policy on informal recreation space developed. The concept of Urban Villages, incorporating mixed and sustainable development in relatively compact village form, was part of the response to the need for homes coupled with the need to regenerate many run-down areas in towns and cities.

Against this background and increasing concern that yet a further spate of initiatives was perpetuating a fragmented approach, the government decided to produce a White Paper on urban policy. This was given impetus by the work of the Urban Task Force (UTF), chaired by Lord Rogers and set up by the Department of the Environment, Transport and the Regions (DETR) in 1998. The UTF's mission was to identify the causes of urban decline in England and recommend practical solutions to bring back people into cities, towns and urban neighbourhoods, to establish a new vision for urban regeneration based on design excellence, social well-being and environmental responsibility, and to improve the quality of both towns and countryside while providing for significant household growth over some twenty years. Its report set out a detailed agenda for securing an urban renaissance which LAs were seen as best placed to lead in partnership with their communities.

As preparatory work for the White Paper the department also commissioned other studies. The 'State of English Cities' report reviewed the economic role and performance of cities, socio-economic patterns and governance arrangements for local regeneration, while 'Living in Urban England: Attitudes and Aspirations' brought together evidence from surveys in the late 1990s about residents' views on the areas in which they lived. Political interest was shown through the work of the Environment, Transport and Regional Affairs Select Committee of the House of Commons which reported in July 2000. The government decided that the White Paper would, in effect, form the response to the committee's recommendations as well as the strategic response to the UTF Report.

Publication of the English Urban White Paper 'Our Towns and Cities: The Future' (UWP) in November 2000 marked a step change in thinking on urban policy. Although many of the ideas had been raised at various times since the White Paper over 20 years earlier, this was the first concerted attempt to look not just at area regeneration but at the range of issues facing towns and cities and to pull together policies and programmes from right across government. The UWP provided a strategic framework for delivering an urban renaissance, putting forward a long-term vision of towns, cities and suburbs offering a high quality of life and opportunity for everyone, with attractive and well kept towns and cities; use of brownfield land and sustainable forms of development; good design and planning; creation and sharing of prosperity through measures to stimulate innovation and enterprise and equip people with necessary skills; good quality services across education, health, housing, crime prevention, culture/leisure/sport; approaches to bring disadvantaged areas up to levels enjoyed elsewhere; and a variety of fiscal measures at national and local levels.

Another key aspect of the UWP was the emphasis on policy delivery and arrangements for ensuring follow up. It stressed the critical role of local government in working with the community, service providers, business and others in Local Strategic Partnerships to develop a vision for their area in a Community Strategy. A Community Empowerment Fund was introduced to develop community networks and give a voice to communities in the 88 most deprived areas in the country. The WP also put in place new central structures to take the White Paper forward, including a Cabinet Committee which agreed a remit to coordinate action across government departments and between urban and rural policies, a Sounding Board with members drawn from a wide spectrum to advise the minister responsible, and an urban group formed from a partnership of government department and LA representatives. The Office of the Deputy Prime Minister (ODPM), formerly DETR, published an Implementation Plan to track progress on all main initiatives in the UWP along with information on mainstream programmes having some relevance to urban policy.

Part of the Government's commitment to making towns and cities better places commenced through the Working with Towns and Cities Initiative under which 24 towns and cities were selected to work with the government to examine their visions, priorities, means of delivery and measures for assessing progress and provide feedback on government policies and initiatives. An action research programme was developed with consultants to consider progress in changing various aspects of urban living. The final report, published at the same time as the Urban Summit October 2002 found that 'progress is often patchy, and is not necessarily engaging or benefiting all parts of the community'. The summit highlighted a range of urban issues and policy achievements and also set the scene for further changes in emphasis in urban policy. While the broad framework set out in the UWP continued to be implemented, including tackling deprived areas through the work of both the Neighbourhood Renewal Unit and the Social Exclusion Unit, which became part of ODPM in 2002, the themes of developing sustainable communities and economic competitiveness were gaining political attention.

In order to meet the government's objective of raising the quality of life in England's urban and rural communities, a £38 billion Sustainable Communities Plan up to 2005/6 formed part of the 'Sustainable Communities: Building for the Future' report of 2003. The aim was to support the principles of sustainable development by balancing and integrating social, economic and environmental components of the community for existing and future needs. The funding package essentially related to physical aspects of regeneration and development within ODPM's responsibilities but sought to integrate at the outset facilities and services within the remit of other government departments.

During this time, parallel work was being pursued in Scotland with a major review of Scotland's cities followed by the Scottish Executive's overall policy framework Building Better Cities 2003 and the Cities Growth Fund, to help each city to deliver its vision.

The other main policy thrust for towns and cities in England stemmed from concern about regional competitiveness and the gap in growth between regions as well as the performance of cities in their own right. Delivering economic prosperity was also an important element underlying the Sustainable Communities Plan. The ODPM's role covered the coordination of key stakeholders at national, regional and local levels to build closer linkages between urban policy and the work of the RDAs on economic performance. The Core Cities, the eight major regional cities in England, were pivotal to this. A Joint Working Group of various government departments, the RDAs and local government was set up by ODPM early 2002 to make recommendations for policy changes and practical actions, to enable these cities to fulfil their potential as drivers of the urban renaissance and of economic competitiveness in their regions. An initial set of 10 key 'success' factors for city competitiveness was considered at the Core Cities Summit June 2003. Subsequently, ODPM commissioned two independent studies to inform the debate, 'Competitive European Cities: Where do the Core Cities Stand?' 2004, which compared various characteristics of urban competitiveness between a range of successful cities in continental Europe and the Core Cities and 'Our Cities are Back' 2004, which contained the results of work undertaken since 2002 to identify the economic role major regional cities must play in a modern knowledge-based economy and to set out a comprehensive action plan. The first of these was extended by similar research for the Scottish Executive. As part of the English agenda, three northern RDAs looked at ways to reduce the gap between northern and southern economies, preparing the 'Northern Way Growth Strategy' 2004 which emphasised urban-regional as well as inter-regional links and provided a spur to similar work in other regions.

Development of these particular strands of urban policy was bound up with moves to speed up and streamline the planning system through the Planning and Compulsory Purchase Act 2004. Under this, proposals contained in documents forming the new statutory planning framework needed to contribute to the achievement of sustainable development while provisions for the preparation of Regional Spatial Strategies complemented the work underway on the regional economic context for cities. Various issues were brought together at the Sustainable Communities Summit January 2005, which followed up the earlier Urban Summit. Its main aim was to share expertise and experience with key people delivering the Sustainable Communities Plan and related reports, 'Homes for All' and 'People, Places and Prosperity', were published around this summit. Debate waged across a wide range of issues, not just the physical, and progress on the Northern Way Growth Strategy and on the forthcoming State of the Cities report was considered.

Regeneration of deprived areas continued to form an important aspect of urban policy in Scotland as well as in England, the most recent approach, outlined in a Regeneration Policy Statement within the Scottish cities policy framework, concentrating on tightly targeted action in such areas. Under a flagship Welsh Assembly programme, Communities First, social inclusion in poorer urban and other areas provided the focus for urban policy since devolution. However, the collapse of the power sharing assembly in Northern Ireland hindered progress in the development of urban policy.

French urban policy had undergone three cycles of legislative and governmental action followed by a lack of delivery of tangible socially acceptable results and by 2003 it had, in practice, returned to a more traditional and small-scale physical and economic focus, with little social dimension. Further legislation that year, the Loi sur la Rénovation Urbaine, strengthened this more physical approach by providing for the renovation of older housing properties. As a result urban policy in France was refocused in a rather different way from that in the UK. Action was mainly at neighbourhood level with urban renovation agreements between the Agence Nationale de Rénovation Urbaine, communes and local social housing agencies. Urban policy objectives essentially remained concerned with variety in housing, the right to decent housing and more generally the challenge of social segregation.

However, initial steps were taken to bring wider economic concerns to bear, owing to increasing governmental concern about the state of the French economy. The launch of the European Commission's Urban Audit in 2002, following a pilot study, showed that French cities were performing more sluggishly than those in other EU member states. A further strengthening of the economic strand to all policies was translated into the urban sphere through a new competitive programme for all the major French cities launched by DATAR in 2004, when they were invited to submit schemes for the enhancement of their European economic and cultural profile. Fifteen city regions were selected for further government assistance to help implement these proposals. A major recipient, the Lille Métropole, proposed a three-pronged programme encompassing new marketing initiatives, the promotion of the area's important science, medical and IT industries and the strengthening of the integration of the Métropole. There has been no real perceived need to address some underlying social tensions here or elsewhere (Agence Lille 2005).

In December 2005, France was once more engulfed in riots in the same deprived areas which had erupted in previous years; many observers put the blame on the government's retreat from the social objectives of the measures put in place in 1996–2000 and the return to the more traditional mix of economic incentives and physical regeneration. The response to these recent eruptions has again been familiar. An Act of March 2006 proposed discontinuation of the Contrat de Ville and replacement by a Contrat de Cohésion Sociale and a public Agence Nationale de Cohesion Sociale et pour l'Égalité des Chances, responsible for equal opportunities in employment and housing and for social cohesion.

Up to the last few years there were similarities, though on different time scales, between English and French approaches to urban policy but some differences in emphasis have become apparent. There has been a period of intense activity in this policy area in England, also in Scotland, resulting in new directions in tackling the problems facing towns and cities. The drive has been on pulling together all key strands of policy affecting urban areas, of which social exclusion in deprived areas is a key aspect among others, within the context of sustainable communities and underpinned by a push to improve the economic performance of cities and their related regions. Deprived areas have continued to be the focus for urban policy in France, with a strong physical housing element, though with a renewed emphasis on social cohesion. Separately there have been embryonic measures to increase the economic competitiveness of some city regions.

Evaluating urban policy

While it has always been common practice to evaluate independently individual government policies and programmes in the UK, including a long tradition of evaluating area regeneration programmes, the government recognised the need for a better understanding of urban trends and conditions and the need for a comprehensive picture of the impact of policy in delivering an urban renaissance. The State of the Cities report was an UWP commitment, reflecting UN recommendations in the 'State of the World's Cities', similar reports in the USA and work by the European Commission on the urban audit. The ODPM commissioned work on a database of town and city indicators to provide the basis for analysis and act as a baseline for the future, using Urban Area definitions by the Office of National Statistics, and in 2004 commissioned a consortium of research organisations to prepare the 'State of the Cities' report, to provide a comprehensive audit of urban conditions in England and to review policy performance in urban areas.

Pending this report, several related progress reports were produced including a 'Tale of Eight Cities' which showed a revitalisation of leading cities outside London, and some preliminary findings on the State of the Cities work. The UTF also decided to carry out further work to check progress on its original recommendations six years earlier, as it was concerned that, despite considerable progress, some key recommendations had still not been met and some new issues needed to be addressed.

The 'State of the English Cities' report 2006 provided an analysis of the condition of the cities, how they could improve and some detailed ideas for change. It looked at demographics, social cohesion, economic competitiveness and performance, liveability concerned with the public realm and the built environment, governance and public attitudes in English cities and the impact of policy. It concluded that progress had been made in recent years and cities were now better placed to meet the opportunities and challenges still evident. However, the economic recovery in some cities needed to be extended and sustained and cities still faced challenges of social exclusion and inequality, which economic growth would not necessarily solve. The main messages were similar to those debated at the time of the UWP.

Evaluation of policy in deprived urban areas in France has been pursued mainly through DIV and a National Observatory concerned with ZUS set up by statute in August 2003, providing annual reports on the objectives of urban policy and the procedures put in place. The observatory's 2004 report considered the gaps in social and economic conditions between these areas and their wider context, pointing out the main trends since the 1980s, particularly in terms of population and housing. Its report the following year presented data on the basis of monitoring indicators defined in 2003 and added to them, giving a more detailed and systematic account. It projected the trends using the most recent reliable data on the actual state of the ZUS. Generally this report was sceptical about the effectiveness of urban policy, noting a growth in the number of unskilled people in the ZUS between 1990 and 1999. In effect, these people remained concentrated in these areas, while often at the same time the more upwardly mobile left.

Other institutions also assessed urban policy, including the Court of Accounts which produced a critical report in 2002 concluding that urban policy was marked by imprecise objectives and strategy and lacked transparency, despite some interesting innovations. Some suggestions regarding rationalisation and evaluation of certain aspects were taken on board. In 2005, Senator P. André, member of the Senate Commission des Affaires Économiques, reported on the Contrat de Ville, pointing to the complexity and lack of transparency in a process concerning 2,200 communes and 247 contracts between 2000 and 2006.

Both countries have been concerned to monitor and evaluate urban policy, whether individual policy approaches, on an area basis or city-wide. In many ways the general conclusions have been, to date, the same, that progress has been made in certain aspects of policy but that many issues remain to be tackled.

Conclusions

Over the last 40 years many similar urban policy ideas have developed in both countries, though at different stages and with varying approaches to operational aspects. Within deprived urban areas the balance between social, economic and physical actions has varied not only in response to the need to try new approaches but also, critically, in response to the political complexion of the government at any given time. With right-wing parties broadly favouring private sector and economic measures and left-wing parties favouring measures for social cohesion, the result has been alternating sets of policies between the two countries. By the mid-1990s both the UK and France were committed to a holistic approach implemented through local partnerships, in which the private sector was more effectively involved in the UK as France placed greater reliance on State actors. Since 1997 in the UK social inclusion has formed a key aspect of policy in deprived neighbourhoods, with new proposals in France to refocus on this issue.

This has been accompanied in the UK by what is, in effect, a comprehensive approach to the wide spectrum of problems facing towns and cities, not solely deprived areas. Positive steps are being taken to improve the quality of life in cities and to improve their economic performance, in order to underpin both the mainstream policies affecting urban areas and specific actions in deprived areas. Work is also now in progress in France to make its major cities more economically competitive.

While urban policy has been handled in a different institutional framework in each country with, for instance, some undoubted advantages in having a range of urban-policy-related responsibilities including planning, regeneration, housing, neighbourhood renewal, social exclusion, regional development and local government in one department, the ODPM in England, this has probably been less important than the political leadership. Urban policy has generally been driven forward, in the UK and in France, when the Prime Minister or Deputy Prime Minister has taken an interest or a particularly influential minister has had the political will to forge the necessary coordination of policies, programmes and resources across government departments. The extent to which this is being fully achieved is still uncertain.

The bulk of urban policy evaluation work in both countries has been on actions in deprived urban areas. What is plain is that the problems in these areas – which essentially kicked off urban policy – remain an issue in the UK as well as France. It is early days to assess the overall impact of more recent policies on cities, as in the 'State of the English Cities' report, given the complex and dynamic nature of towns and cities, their relationship to national and global economies and the long-term scale for policy effects to be felt. But again, clearly, more needs to be done. Urban policy has had a historic tendency in the UK and France to be based on a political reaction to specific events, such as civil disturbances or economic decline, but both countries require a consistent and long-term commitment to the ongoing challenge of urban change.

References

Agence de Développement et d'Urbanisme de Lille Métropole (2005) 'Déclaration d'Intention de l'Aire Métropolitaine de Lille', Lille Métropole.

Archbishop of Canterbury's Commission for Urban Priority Areas (1985) 'Faith in the City', London: Archbishop of Canterbury's Commission for Urban Priority Areas.

Booth, P. and Green, H. (1999) 'The Programme local de l'habitat: preparing a housing strategy for Lille', *European Planning Studies*, 7(3): 283–94.

Chaline, C. (1998) *Les Politiques de la Ville*, Paris: Presses Universitaires de France.

Commission Bonnemaison (1982) *Face à la Délinquence*, Paris: Documentation Française.

Commission Doubedout (1983) *Ensemble Refaire la Ville*, Paris: Documentation Française.

Commission Schwartz (1981) *L'Insertion Professionelle et Sociale des Jeunes*, Paris: Documentation Française.

Department for Communities and Local Government: www.communities.gov.uk.

Department of the Environment (DoE) (1977a) *Policy for the Inner Cities*, CMND6845, London: HMSO.

Department of the Environment (DoE) (1977b) *Change or Decay: Final reports on Inner Area Studies: Birmingham, Lambeth and Liverpool*, London: HMSO.

Department of the Environment, Transport and the Regions (DETR) (2000a) *Our Towns and Cities: the Future. Delivering an Urban Renaissance*, White Paper CM 4911, London: HMSO.

Department of the Environment, Transport and the Regions (DETR) (2000a) *Living in Urban England: Attitudes and Aspirations*, London: HMSO.

Environment, Transport and Regional Affairs Select Committee (2000) Report and Proceedings on the Proposed Urban White Paper', House of Commons, 185–I.

European Commission (2000) *Urban Audit*, Brussels: DG Regio.

Hutchins, M. and Parkinson, M. (2005) *Competitive Scottish Cities? Placing Scotland's Cities in a European Context, Edinburgh:* Scottish Executive.

Le Galès, P. and Mawson, J. (1994) *Management Innovations in Urban Policy: Lessons from France*, London: Local Government Management Board.

McCarthy, J. (1999) 'Urban regeneration in Scotland: an agenda for the Scottish Parliament', *Regional Studies*, 33(6): 559–66.

Northern Ireland Office: Information on Northern Irish developments can be obtained on www.nio.gov.uk.

Office of the Deputy Prime Minister (ODPM) (2003) *Sustainable Communities: Building for the Future*, London: ODPM.

Office of the Deputy Prime Minister (ODPM) (2004a) *Moving Forward: Northern Way*, London: ODPM.

Office of the Deputy Prime Minister (ODPM) (2004b) *'Making it Happen': A Tale of Eight Cities*, London: ODPM.

Office of the Deputy Prime Minister (ODPM) (2005a) *State of the Cities: A Progress Report to the Delivering Sustainable Communities Summit*, London: ODPM.

Office of the Deputy Prime Minister (ODPM) (2005b) *Sustainable Communities: Homes for All*, London: ODPM.

Office of the Deputy Prime Minister (ODPM) (2005c) *Sustainable Communities: People, Places and Prosperity*, London: ODPM.

Office of National Statistics (2004) *Urban Area Definitions*, London: ODPM.

Parkinson, M. and Le Galès, P. (1994) *Policies for Cities in Britain and France: A Comparative Assessment*, London: Franco-British Council.

Parkinson, M., Hutchins, M., Simmie, J.M., Clark, G. and Verdonk, H. (2004) *Competitive European Cities: Where do the Core Cities Stand?*, London: ODPM.

Parkinson, M., Champion, T., Dorling, D., Parks, A., Simmie, J. and Turok, I. (2005) *State of the English Cities*, London: ODPM.

Robson, B., Parkinson, M., Boddy, M. and Maclennan, D. (2000) *The State of the English Cities*, London: DETR.

Scottish Executive (2002) *Review of Scotland's Cities*, (2003) *Building Better Cities, Cities Growth Fund*, (2006) *Regeneration Policy Statement*, and other relevant documents are available on www.scotland.gov.uk/Topics/Government/Cities.

Social Exclusion Unit (2001) *A New Commitment to Neighbourhood Renewal* National Strategy Action Plan, London: HMSO.

Sueuer, J.P. (1998) *Demain la Ville*, Paris: Documentation Française.

UN-Habitat and Earthscan (2004) *The State of the World's Cities*, New York: United Nations.

Urban Task Force (1999) *Towards an Urban Renaissance*, Lord Rogers of Riverside, London: Spon.

Urban Task Force (2005) *The Urban Renaissance Six Years on*, Lord Rogers of Riverside, London: Urban Task Force.

URBED (2000) *Towns and Cities: Partners in Urban Renaissance*, London: URBED.

Welsh Assembly Government: www.wales.gov.uk.

Wong, C., Jeffery, P., Green, A., Owen, D., Coombes, M. and Raybould, S. (2004) *Town and City Indicators Database*, Final Report, Universities of Liverpool, Warwick and Newcastle-upon-Tyne.

Working Group on Cities, Regions and Competitiveness (2003) *Progress Report: Core Cities Summit*, London: ODPM.

Working Group on Cities, Regions and Competitiveness (2004) *Third Report: Our Cities are Back*, London: ODPM.

Chapter 10

The financing of development

Charles Fraser in collaboration with
Pascal Hoffmann

Introduction

An apparent difference between the French and British systems of everything
from planning control to the completion of regional strategies or regeneration
projects is the fact that in France the final stage of financing the construction
of the project is as much a part of the process as the preparation of the
documents and the acquisition of approvals and consents, whereas in the
UK the last stages are often left to the happenstance of the attractiveness
of any proposal to the private investment market. It could be argued that
in France, planning and regeneration strategies are complete when the last
brick has been laid and that in Britain they are complete when the documents
of guidance have been completed for the private property investment sector
to consider.

This has several implications. First, ensuring that investment can be relied
upon, as part of the long-term strategy for any project of public or private
development is implicit to any French planning strategy. In few cases, in
the normal planning process or development funding process is such a
link commonplace in the UK: the New Towns and Urban Development
Corporations (UDCs), etc., may have this but they are by their nature
exceptional and outside the normal planning system.

Second, there is the implication that in France there must be some form
of public influence or control over the flow of funds into urban regeneration
projects and strategic public investments if this security is to be maintained.
Such security is erratic in the UK, for example, even housing associations
and companies, etc., have to rely on very erratic flows of funding, despite
the existence of investment strategy documents, now the Social Housing
Grant Programme.

As other chapters in this volume will demonstrate, much of this long-
term view of investment in and the management of the territory of France
is enshrined in the processes of Aménagement du Territoire and the series
of national Contrats de Plan which run from the national to the local level;
but equally important is the fact that financial investment planning is part

of this process. The question is not merely how, but also why is it that the subjugation of the private property development industry to a public strategy appears to yield such satisfactory results in all parts of the country.

In the UK, investment in the territory of the kingdom has been, apart from basic public works, a matter for the investment market, which has the liberty to disinvest in areas where no profit can be made and transfer investment to those regions and cities where a return can be guaranteed. Public funding is there to serve the interests of private capital to whom land development is just another investment opportunity. In the UK planners struggle in many places to attract development and crave some stable long-term process for planning the secure future of a town or region.

In attempting to discover why these differences occur it is clear that we are comparing two very different processes of investment control based on two very different conceptions of how the public good/l'intérêt public is best served. This hints at the fact that governments behave differently towards the private investment market, presenting different options to the investors of capital, large or small, and acting during the process of this investment to channel funds to different outlets.

In attempting to compare these two systems there are two basic starting points. One can begin by examining the origin of the financial flows, who invests, for what purpose are they allowed to invest and how are their choices guided. Alternatively one can look at the outcomes and compare the funding patterns in comparable major regeneration projects or other similar strategic land investments.

Finally, there is evidence which shall be examined to demonstrate that neither system is static and that in the UK, for example, each of the four territorial authorities have become aware of the fact that the emergence of strategic national urban and rural strategies demand that better long-term planning of financial investments is a critical part of them. Conversely, in France there are pressures to end the traditional national insulation of their investment processes from the emerging global investment mechanisms if economic stagnation is to be avoided and a more open economy created. Where these trends are leading is the key to whether the UK and French systems are converging or remaining totally different in objective, structure and social utility.

To begin at the end

Normally, describing the structures of a process might precede the description of specific case studies; however, in this case it may be salutary to begin with a comparison of the funding of two major flagship projects which are similar in their end product and objectives, and two small-scale urban regeneration projects, all in the planning strategy of their parent cities but which have been financed and brought into being by entirely different processes and actors.

In 1998 a football match between Brazil, the World Cup holders, and Scotland inaugurated the new Stade de France; in 2006 it was intended that the new Wembley Stadium would host the FA Cup Final and be the inaugurating match at this spectacular sporting venue. Both stadia are more than just pitches but multi-functional centres for sport at the centre of major regeneration schemes for their part of their host city, Paris and London respectively. In the case of London the new Wembley is part of the strategy for the development of the facilities for the Olympic Games in 2012 and provides a more modern home for English football. In the case of the Stade de France the stadium area was the first part of a major regeneration process for the Plaine de St-Denis which stretches from the stadium to the Boulevard Périphérique. The differences however go much deeper than this.

In the case of Wembley the owners are Wembley National Stadium Ltd (WNSL), a conglomerate of interests led by the English Football Association, but essentially a private company; the constructors are Multiplex, an Australian company which specialises in stadia and sports facility construction; the main sources of funding are private and largely German.

Indeed the funding of the project has a long and chequered history and at certain points it seemed that the project would fail to be financed since the British government would not involve itself in a rescue exercise. Football, the main motor of the project, was perceived as a part of the entertainment industry, a privately owned and operated sector. In the end the funding was, to be precise, scraped together from a variety of sources just in time to render the project (apparently) viable.

The saviour of the project was the West Deutsche Landesbank (paradoxically a German State Bank), which contributed £433m in loans to the project. The next major contributors were the English Football Association at £148m and Sport England with £120m. The government's direct contribution from the Department of Culture Media and Sport was a mere £20m, less than the contribution of £21m from the new London Development Agency, the financing section of the London Assembly and Mayor's office. The remaining £15m of the £757m total will come from sponsorship and sales. The local authority, the London Borough of Brent will contribute small sums to assist with access and service provision (Carter 2002).

Unlike the Stade de France which is integrated with the surrounding developments of the Plaine St-Denis, the 55ha site adjacent to Wembley Stadium is in the process of redevelopment for complementary uses by a totally separate company Quintain. Thus Wembley, serving only one part of the United Kingdom, was constructed by Australians and significantly lies in the investment portfolio of a German State Bank. While it may be politically useful to point out that the 'taxpayer' contributed less than 20 per cent of the cost of construction it is equally true that the public 'stake' in the project is nil since it is owned by a private company to whom all profits will flow. The project is currently running behind schedule and over budget.

The construction of the Stade de France has, however, a very different history. There was a need in Paris to replace the ageing Parc des Princes, especially as France wished to host the 1998 World Cup. The choice for the French State was either to wait for a private entrepreneur to rebuild the Parc des Princes or build another new stadium, or to take the initiative itself in planning and overseeing the construction of a new national stadium to ensure the success of the World Cup bid. In fact there never really was any doubt, and it is obvious that the area, the Plaine St-Denis, had been earmarked by government and regional authorities for some time as a potential site for some major national project. Thus in 1991 the government set up a 'mission' to work out the programme for the construction of the stadium, organise and judge a competition for its design and set the construction process in motion. The task was made easier by the fact that the site had belonged to a former public utility operator, Gaz de France, and was therefore available for redevelopment. The overseers of this stage were the state banking organisation, the Caisse des Dépôts et Consignations (CDC), who funded this stage to the tune of 14m French Francs (2.1m euros). From then, after the choice of the winning design, a private/public partnership was set up to deliver the project. A public agency was set up to manage the delivery and a private consortium was given a concession to construct, finance and manage the stadium for a period of 30 years from 1995 to 2025. The consortium established in 1994 as a private company (Société Anonyme), comprised three separate agencies with different skills. They were Bouyges, the giant French construction company, GTM Entreprise (Groupe Lyonnais des Eaux), and SGE, Groupe Générale des Eaux, the latter two partners being the funders and managers of the project. The stadium cost between 300 and 400m euros, a fraction of the Wembley total. Significantly, it was built and opened on time!

However, the State has provided 600m euros/£400m for the entire regeneration project, one half to the stadium and the rest to the planning of the surrounding area and to a range of transport upgrades, metro, RER and autoroute, to make the venue viable. The planning of the main building is therefore only a part of the regeneration of the entire Plaine St-Denis area. The 'concession' formula is very similar to that used to construct toll autoroutes where public agencies assist private constructors to build and run motorways.

At the other end of the scale it is equally instructive to compare two small housing renewal projects identified in the Interreg IIc project, *Living in Towns* (Fraser *et al.* 2001). The first is the St Peter's Street area of Maidstone, Kent. It was previously a gas works and nearby industrial area which had become derelict around the mid-1990s. The borough council and the county council identified it as a possible housing redevelopment site with some commercial use. However, apart from intimating this, no other steps were taken to initiate the redevelopment of the area and private investors were awaited. None came until 2004 and the area is now part redeveloped for housing and a retail park. The redevelopment does not link to the rest of the town in any cohesive way. It is a tale which could be repeated in almost every British town.

By contrast in the small French town of Armentières, the closure of factories left several waste sites. However, in all cases the town council in coordination with the Metropolitan Planning agency for Lille and national government agencies have declared certain areas such as Le Bizet as Zones d'Aménagement Concerté (ZACs), and initiated measures thereby to ensure the redevelopment of the site for housing. In analysing this development the study team noted that it appeared axiomatic that such development opportunities would be developed in conformity with local planning initiatives and that funding from the CDC would be available as a matter of course.

From this brief glance at some cases of development in both countries the following can be discerned:

- That there are a wide range of sources of implementation funding in the two countries.
- That in France there is a greater willingness to use 'public' funds to ensure that this final stage is achieved and not to let land lie unused until some commercial operator decides to develop it.
- That there is greater willingness in France for the government to control and utilise funding directed towards project implementation.
- That in France the plan dictates what will be developed and therefore the final stage of the development process is always plan led. In Britain the plan is shaped much more by the needs for investment by the private development industry.

The chapter will in turn proceed to examine, first what funds are available for development, across the range from private commercial to totally public; second what types of public funds are available in each country and how each government controls or directs the investment of these, either in themselves or in conjunction with private investors. Finally, the extent to which there is a funding plan to parallel the physical development plan will be explored.

Sources of finance

We are thus considering projects in a paradigm wider than that of private/ public partnerships (PPPs), in that the process of construction especially of public works and of publicly sponsored projects now encompasses a range of combinations of private and public interests, mainly capital and land but also including various services and supporting actors.

Thus the *Flow of Funds* in each country into major projects or long-term planning strategies varies considerably. The concept of the management of the financial system as being akin to a plumbing system is derived from a 1970s work by Mason (1976), which approached the subject by analysing the transfer of funds, capital, etc. between institutions as if it were a liquid flow of funds. No similar analysis has been discovered in France and the only comparable effort charts intra-public sector flows in the housing market, (Domo Quintet 1988). A more recent attempt to categorise the various ways in which different forms of funding are utilised occurs in Couch *et al.* (2003) where the analysis of funding contributors to inner area residential markets revealed an emphasis to public or commercial funding in British cities, and to State agencies, but not governmental tax-derived sources, in France and Germany.

This approach is used to construct a range of funding sources set out below.

Private commercial 'risk' capital

British readers will be aware of the dominant role played in property development by major financial institutions and the way in which they use property as an investment target for funds often raised across the globe. They are also liable to the vagaries of markets and the risks of speculation beyond market realities. The tale of the Canary Wharf development in London's Docklands and the excellent chronicle of the 'boom and bust' of the 1980s in *Bricks and Mortals* where Ross Goobey (1992) describes the pitfalls of this mega-investment industry. It is a cultural aspect of British planning that a comprehension of the motives and strategies of this industry is essential if a planning authority wishes to see investment in their area and to have whatever plans have been devised for an area implemented. Often the strategy for a site or even a sizeable area of a town is dictated by the attitude of the property development industry to it. At one extreme it can by mere force of investment value alter the approved strategy for an area, as at Bluewater Shopping Centre in Kent; at the other it can, by disinvesting or by refusing to invest in an area, lead to prolonged dereliction which the public sector is powerless to rectify, as in the St Peter's Street example, or more currently in countless towns and cities across the North of England where the regional economy yields no prospect of profit. The reasons for this are inextricably linked to the internal economics of such companies and their place as 'profit deliverers' in often larger and more complex corporate structures, e.g. Bovis Homes group which appears to be a housebuilding company, but is in fact a subsidiary of a subsidiary of the international conglomerate, Lonhro. The mechanics of their operations are a study in themselves. In the investment structure of the United Kingdom they dominate investment in retail, commercial office, industrial, leisure, and even residential, both private and social, property. In the UK, perhaps by default but most certainly due to the long period of market-dominated economics, the choice has been made to go along with this investment sector but to try to use it to deliver social goods such as housing, schools and hospitals as a by-product. This is particularly true of the current government who look to private funding institutions to realise new property developments and to assist the economy to prosper in those regions which are perceived to be growth regions.

Their place in the spectrum of investment institutions in France is, however, more problematic. International conglomerate development companies are a virtually absent species and the 'private sector' by definition is restricted to national banks and local companies, chambers of commerce, etc. In the Stade de France case the 'private investors' such as Compagnie Générale des Eaux were once public companies and retain something of the concept of 'l'intérêt public' in their operations. What is unique about the French banking system is the existence of two distinct sectors. The first is the purely commercial, represented by banks such as Crédit Lyonnais, Banque Nationale de Paris, etc. The second is the mutual sector which has three major groups, Crédit Agricole, the Banque Populaire network, and the Caisse des Dépôts et Consignations and its itinerant savings banks, the Caisse d'Épargne and the Crédit Foncier.

Whilst the former sector plays a major part in financing development it is virtually impossible for commercial companies to dictate the plan for an area mainly because they cannot override the many safeguards built into the French planning process.

Private finance initiative (PFI)

The Private Finance Initiative (PFI), a funding mechanism which brings private financing into the construction and management of such basic public services as hospitals and schools, was originally introduced in the early 1980s in the UK ostensibly to lift the burden of providing public services from the public purse and to extend the potential investment range for private capital. By 1992 there was still no great incentive for private interests to lend money to the public sector which still had end control of the investment. Thus the market was made more attractive to the private sector. First, the need to demonstrate that a project, a school or hospital, could be built better by the private sector than by the public, was discontinued and the private sector was free to take the initiative and submit schemes for the construction or reconstruction of public sector facilities which they were free to design, build and operate. At the same time it was considered that in so doing the private sector was also assuming certain areas of risk which had been absorbed by the public purse beforehand.

Needless to say the PFI initiative has not been without its critics in the UK on many different grounds (Elliot 2005). The general criticism being that short-term private gain is not a proper rationale to guide the planning of the construction of the country's social infrastructure.

Contrary to expectation the concept of PFI is not unknown in France where the State is increasingly looking to private finance to fill the funding gap where public finances are unable to meet a need. The Stade de France example is very close to a British PFI model although the land was in public ownership. However, a recent venture to construct and manage a new hospital in Caen in Normandy is almost totally private in structure and follows precisely the model set out in the most recent British PFI guidelines.

Private/public partnerships

In the United Kingdom PPPs are usually the result of collaboration between public authorities or utilities which have land which is surplus to requirement, and often derelict or polluted, but no financial resources to develop it, and private financiers, banks, insurance companies, property development companies, etc. which have capital to invest in property ventures. The two together may form a partnership to realise a development project which otherwise would not happen. In France such co-operation is in its infancy and the Stade de France is a major venture into such co-operation. Normally 'partnerships' in France are between various levels of government and the truly private sector is seldom involved beyond local chambers of commerce or local companies. The financing of major regeneration efforts usually depends on the Caisse des Dépôts being the prime source of the fundamental initiating finance, such as in the case of Euralille (Baert and Fraser 2003).

The economics and structures of such ventures are dealt with in depth in the following chapter and the differences between the two countries in how they manage such co-operation illustrated. For the purposes of this chapter the salient differences seem to be, first, that in France the public authorities are more proactive in the early parts of the process, site assembly, site preparation, etc. to facilitate the development than their UK counterparts. Second, the scope of private capital available in the UK is much greater and more international than in France, since property development and investment is a much more highly developed industry than in France. The reasons for this are alluded to in Chapter 3, and are rooted in the differing social nature of property rights.

Mutual funding

In the case studies examined above a major player in the French financing process was the Caisse des Dépôts et Consignations which with its associated Caisse d'Épargne network is one of the three mutual banking organisations mentioned previously and for which there is no equivalent in the United Kingdom.

The Caisse is a financial funding agency managed by a board of directors appointed by the State through the National Assembly and therefore free from direct control by the government. This in itself is a difficult concept for British readers since in the UK the State, the government and the monarchy are constitutionally the same, whereas in France the President's office, the State Assembly and the elected government of the day are separate branches of the country's administration. Its role is essentially to provide a means for citizens to invest *their* savings to undertake works necessary for *their* State. Thus its prime source of funds is from the Livret A savings accounts of the network of High Street savings banks, the Caisse d'Épargnes, the former mortgage bank the Crédit Foncier de France (CFF) and other public investments such as notaire investment funds. It also manages the investment portfolios of public sector pension funds, as well as having its own historic funds built up over its almost 200-year history. What is more remarkable is that it was founded in 1816 to ensure that in future the savings of ordinary citizens were protected from the excesses of governments which over the preceding century had used them and every other financial source for military expansion. It is thus not a modern financial mechanism developed in response to the need for managing the economy in the post-war era but a mutual institution founded in the interests of citizens in the early years of the French Republic (Dusart 1980).

The funds derived from these sources, accumulated and invested over nearly two centuries, are essentially targeted to specific types of investment now related to urban regeneration and social housing. In 2004 the annual budget of the CDC totalled 242,000m euros of which nearly 100m were derived from the savings system such as Livret A. This money is targeted at the social housing sector (HLMs) (85m euros in 2003–4) and urban regeneration generally.

By contrast in the UK, this intermediate area of funding, neither private commercial nor government programme funding, is weakly developed. The British equivalent of the Caisse d'Épargne in a social sense are the building societies but those that remain in the true building society sector. Now only some 60 societies are restricted in their investment target to the mortgage market. In the 1970s there were over 2,000 such societies but the changes to the Building Societies Acts in the 1980s encouraged the larger ones to become mainstream banks, e.g. Abbey National, and the smaller ones to amalgamate to remain financially viable in the face of a more aggressive national and international mortgage market.

At the same time the only bank which could be considered local and which catered for small local borrowers and investors, the Trustee Savings Bank, was controversially taken over by Lloyds and incorporated into the mainstream banking world. Thus in Britain the process to date has been to exterminate the local savings bank industry and channel such savings into the corporate international investment industry.

What takes its place in terms of funding by the public which is neither derived from the commercial sector nor direct government funding is a plethora of mini funds which add up to very small sources of funding usually very local in their control and investment target, e.g. credit unions, lottery funds, venture capital, development trusts and a range of local initiatives to attract liquid funds.

Public investment

Deriving their funding from taxation and investments in government schemes, both national governments have the budgets of their main departments as a basic source of funding for infrastructure, regeneration, etc. Health, education, transport and social services are the big consumers of these funds but significantly in both countries housing has a peripheral place. In France, as has been shown, social housing finance is derived from CDC investment and in Britain only annual funding from the Housing Corporation is now available from public funds for social housing programmes. Housing agencies, no longer dominated by local authorities, must scour the markets and the banking sector for the bulk of their funding.

However, having noted that there is a parallel system of funding by the governments of both countries to these mainstream sectors, what differentiates the two is the way in which governments coordinate and plan the investment of that finance both between sectors and over time.

In France such intervention is pervasive and historically long established so that a series of financial plans set out over time the extent and the amount which will be invested by the State and other public agencies. This process has become formalised in the process known as the Contrat de Plan between the State and the regions. It was inaugurated as part of the process of regionalisation by the Mitterand government in 1982, but was in fact really an updating for new administrative circumstances of a very old tradition of State budgeting for the delivery of the infrastructure and social facilities which were perceived to be needed in the interests of the French State at any given time and were implemented through the parallel process of Aménagement du Territoire.

The Contrat is a programme for a specific period, e.g. 1994–8, determining the strategic choices and the mean-term objectives for economic, social and cultural needs of the nation and 'coordinating the investments of the national and the local, regional/local authorities to attain these objectives' (Pontier 1998). In 1998 the regular four-year cycle was changed to 2000–6 to fit in with the changes to the cycle of European ERDF funding and the management was delegated to a state commissioner instead of a government minister. Despite these managerial changes the process remains the same and the emphasis under Pontier's observations is intended to highlight the fact that the plan is not considered complete until the objectives are delivered and that thereby the plan has an attached budget to ensure this. Equally important is the fact that the Contrat is agreed between equal partners at five levels: central government, regional government, departmental level, commune level and with inter-communal agencies.

The budget for the 2000–6 period is a total of 17m euros from central government and a matching sum from the regional and local levels, approximately 35m euros in total. However there are a series of additional special budgets usually administered at the regional level which boost this total, e.g. FRAM, funds for the acquisition of museums, etc. (DIACT). While the plan is advisory and flexible and can be amended to meet changing needs, it does provide clear guidance to the agencies engaged in plan delivery of where priorities for physical development and capital investment lie.

To date there has been no parallel of the Contrat de Plan in the UK. The only incidence of such national planning linking economic development loosely to physical development was in the days of the Wilson government 1966–70 with the production of the National Plan. This was the brainchild of George Brown who headed the newly created Department of Economic Affairs which was charged with the overseeing of long-term economic policy including spatial policy and was from the beginning set in conflict with the Treasury which had a tradition of short-term 'tweaking' of the economy. Short-term economic turbulence soon ended this venture (Ward 1994). Since then the most common budgeting device in the UK has been the Annual Spending Round, when competing government department claims are discussed and budgeted for. A major difference to the Contrat de Plan is that this mechanism is for central government departments only, since other levels of government have no independent constitutionally guaranteed existence. Local spending in large part is at the mercy of central government programmes.

However, the Treasury recently has not only tried to set the economy and its financial policy on a long-term basis with a three-year horizon to the Annual Spending Round; it has also set the parameters for all areas of national policy, including spatial policy, within this. Thus the development of more long-term spending targetted funding mechanisms is emerging as a possibility in the British budgeting process. This trend has been encouraged by the report, *Towards an Urban Renaissance* (Urban Task Force 1999), which makes a clear recommendation to 'Introduce a new financial instrument for attracting institutional investment into the private rented market'.

Similarly the more recent Urban Policy White Paper, *Our Towns and Cities: The Future* (DETR 2000) in recommendations 99 and 100 calls for the establishment of funding mechanisms, such as a funding bank, to invest both private and public funds in a strategic planned way over time at regional level.

The relationship of financial planning to physical planning

There has been some progress towards these goals in that there has been a coalescing both of organisations and budgets to a contemporary situation where the key agencies are now the regional development agencies, of which there are nine in England, which now coordinate the activities of the remodelled English partnerships, local strategic partnerships and urban regeneration companies. At the same time the main budget for regeneration, the Single Regeneration Challenge Fund and other ODPM budgets, has been combined with budgets from the Department of Trade and Industry (DTI) and the Department of Rural Affairs (DEFRA) to form the new 'single budget'. In 2005 the total budget for the nine regions was £1.2bn (€1.8bn).

This budget will be in turn linked in to the regional strategic plans which are now being prepared under the new Planning and Compensation Act 2004. The Act does not, however, have any provision for a financial appendix to the planning process in its provisions. Therefore the 'single budget' can be seen as no more than a tentative step towards a form of Contrat de Plan, but it is a step towards linking the physical plan and a financial plan.

In France, as has been demonstrated, there has always been a link between the two and until the recent legislative changes the national planning process of Aménagement du Territoire was inextricably linked with the Contrat de Plan process, working from national through regional to local planning strategies such the Zones d'Aménagement Concerté (ZACs), and other area specific strategies. This has continued in the new structure of SCOT and PLU plans.

The Contrats de Villes and more recent Contrats d'Agglomérations are, however, not part of the Contrat de Plan structure and have been a secondary budgeting system between the central government and city/metropolitan governments, and may be abolished due to criticism.

The only situation in the UK where budgets were linked to a physical strategy was the Housing Strategy and Investment Programmes, which were introduced in 1977. However these were soon shortened to Housing Investment Programmes controlled by the Housing Corporation and the strategy links to the physical environment dropped. However, these budgets, now operating as the four-year rolling Social Housing Grant programme are only a small part of the financial provision for housing as providers seek finance from the many private sector agencies, banks, etc. and some with a tradition of housing finance, namely Abbey, setting up their own homes agency. However whether this link will be maintained as these ex-building societies become part of global investment companies remains to be seen.

In parallel with the 2004 Act for England and Wales there have been similar policy reviews for Scotland and Northern Ireland. In Scotland the comprehensive 'Review of Scotland's Cities' (Scottish Executive

2003) examines the entire range of urban problems and makes wide recommendations and led to the creation of the Cities Growth Fund, and the recent report on regeneration which includes a full investment statement (Scottish Executive 2006). In Northern Ireland and Wales although policy documents have been produced recently they do not address funding processes. However there is a sense that these 'territorial' governments are closer to integrating their financial and physical planning processes than the ODPM and the Regional Development Agencies in England.

Conclusions: problems and prospects

The purpose of this chapter has been to explore the nature of the links between the planning and regeneration processes of the two countries and the financing mechanisms which facilitate the translation of their proposals into actual developments, without becoming lost in a comparative study of public finance systems.

At the fundamental level there is a basic difference between the two countries. In the UK, all of it, since devolution has not changed this, there is no implication in a planning or regeneration strategy document that the public authorities have a duty or even an expectation that they will initiate the realisation of their proposals. They may, and the recent Scottish Executive report on regeneration has taken steps to do this (Scottish Executive 2006), but in general they leave this stage to the development agencies of the private market. Therefore axiomatically they leave the process of seeking finance to these agencies. Even ostensibly 'public' agencies such as English Partnerships or housing associations can depend on very little direct 'public' funding and will also have to seek funding from commercial financial sources.

In France there is an implied link between plans of all types, from the basic POS/SCOT system to major regeneration initiatives such as the 'grands projets', and the funding agencies, especially the Caisse des Dépôts, which will be programmed through national strategies, such as the Contrat de Plan or more specific strategies such as the Contrat d'Agglomération, to finance the initiation of development and see it through to its realisation.

This highlights the differences in both the structure of 'public' funding and the nature of the commercial property investment 'industry'. In the UK property and land development is a major adjunct of the financial investment industry. Commercial investors may be local, national or international; they may be banks, pension funds or speculators. They invest where a profit acceptable within the business plan of the company can be had. Where the profit margins are not acceptable they will not invest and this can apply to places which are in economic decline or to sectors such as social housing where margins are tight. The public strategist, central or local, is engaged in a battle to encourage commercial interests to invest in these spatially and sectorally marginal areas. PFI is just such a mechanism. In France, by contrast, land and property have been traditionally less of an investment 'good', and the commercial property investment industry is much less developed. Where 'private' capital is invested it comes from local and national banks or chambers of commerce, rather than from specific property investment companies. Development is evaluated within the paradigm of its place in the land development strategy for the nation, a region or even a commune, not whether it yields a commercial gain to a company and shareholders based in some remote corner of the globe. Thus the case studies of Wembley and the Stade de France reflect this mind set. Wembley is a private commercial venture with 'public' interest; the Stade de France is an integral part of the national plan for the State. The St Peter's Street development in Maidstone was left for years until the economics of investment in it changed in favour of commercial profit margins; the derelict industrial sites of Armentières were immediately built into a regeneration strategy to provide housing, etc. needed by the town and the metropolitan area.

The converse is not reflected in what can be termed strictly 'public' finance in both countries. Here State finances are remarkably similar. Both countries derive such funds from taxation, public investment in government savings, etc. although the management of these does differ. In France the tradition of long-term investment in public goods and infrastructure predates the current form of the Contrat de Plan going back to the strategic investment plans of the postwar era. In Britain the recent move to a three year spending round and the creation of the 'single budget' even if it coordinates the spending of only three government departments marks a move to a more 'continental' money management system. Such funding may pay for basic infrastructure, although in both cases the emergence of PFI style programmes to attract private, commercial capital to invest in this shows the pressure that public purses are under to meet the growing demand for such social capital.

In the case of Britain, this is where it ends. If the private sector does not care to invest and the public sector cannot afford to, the process comes to a halt. In France the existence of a healthy mutual savings and banking sector directed in its investment strategy to the realisation of public strategies in the interests of its citizen investors, rural in the case of Crédit Agricole, urban in the case of the Caisse des Dépôts, means that the planning system in the broadest sense has that vital financial tool to initiate and realise development projects at almost every scale, from a local social housing scheme to a major metropolitan statement such as Euralille. The funding for these agencies comes from citizen investments; it is *their* money invested in the public works in *their* Republic. This sector has virtually disappeared in the United Kingdom. A few building societies are all that remain.

However, the dynamics of change in the financial world mean that these models of funding flows, simplified for the needs of comparison, are subject to certain pressures. In France they are threatening, in the UK encouraging. As evidenced by the creation of a PFI hospital in Caen, French public spending is under pressure. This led to a serious possibility that the funds of the mutual sector would be pressed into more direct service for the government. However, a combination of several factors, the constitutional position of the agencies, their central place in the investment culture of the citizen and their value as guarantors of mainstream public spending agencies has lifted the pressure. What is more threatening is the fact that even the mutual agencies must yield a return to their investors which competes with alternative investments. Slowly but inexorably the annual investment in this mutual sector is declining as alternatives are 'marketed'. This pressure on the sector has been demonstrated recently with the inception of merger talks between the Caisse d'Épargne group and the Société Générale, another large mutual bank. The Caisse des Dépôts has naturally attempted to stop this move but it does indicate a need for rationalisation in the sector (Tran 2006). The opening of the French market in an uncontrolled way, as with the 'big bang' in the London financial markets, would surely have grave consequences for them. The speed at which this is allowed to occur is now a central political argument in France; the final arbiter may be the European Union.

In Britain through the 1980s the country was swept into the globalised capital market economy and is if anything now 'rowing back' from its effects. More strategic financial planning to parallel physical and social planning is now part of government thinking; the Treasury is the controller of strategic investment in all sectors. However, it has looked only at the capital markets as an ally in the delivery of its strategies. Only recently has the possibility of incorporating other funding sources been given any thought. The third sector in the UK is, however, fragmented and limited in resources and much as one would encourage credit unions, lottery funds, etc. to be invested in communal ventures, there is no cohesive strategy for their management as an investment arm. The concept of local personal savings being invested in local communal developments is curiously peripheral; in France it is *central* to their delivery.

Thus the French system presents a challenge to the UK to rethink the link, not only between the strategies of planning and the financial structures to deliver them, but also between the citizen and the development of his or her own locality; to the French the British example provides some lessons on how to, and how not to, engage with the international corporate financial system.

As hinted, the final arbiter of where the lines will be drawn may be the European Union. At present the French government is under attack for its attempt to shelter some 11/12 economic sectors from the effects of international competition (Tran 2006). The European Union is unlikely to support this policy and will press for France to open up its financial sector in the interests of the citizen and the investor. However, given the obvious benefits that the French mutual investment sector has conferred on the physical development process in France, why is there no balancing

European concern to encourage the 'social' banking sector as part of the so-called 'social model' for Europe's future? This could save the British citizen from an unbalanced pattern of property investment which 'globalisation' has ushered in.

References

Baert, T. and Fraser, C. (2003) 'Lille: from textile giant to tertiary turbine', in C. Couch, C. Fraser and S. Percy (eds) *Urban Regeneration in Europe*, Oxford: Blackwell Publishing, Chapter 6.

Caisse des Dépôts et Consignations (2005) *Rapport Annuel 2004* and *Fonds d'Épargne: Présentation des Comptes 2004*, Paris: Caisse des Dépôts et Consignations.

Carter, P. (2002) *The English National Stadium Review: Final Report*, London: The Stationery Office.

Couch, C., Fraser, C. and Percy, S. (2003) *Urban Regeneration in Europe*, Oxford: Blackwell Publishing.

DETR (Department of the Environment, Transport and the Regions) (2000) *'Our Towns and Cities: The Future': Delivering an Urban Renaissance*, London: DETR.

Domo Quintet (1988) *Les HLM: Approches Sociales, Économiques et Juridiques*, Paris: Adels.

Dusart, G. (1980) *La Caisse des Dépôts et Consignations*, Notes et Études Documentaires, Paris: La Documentation française.

Elliot, L. (2005) 'Public building and private finance? That's a formula for tomorrow's slums', *Guardian*, 29 August.

Fraser, C., Le Ny, L. and Redding, B. (2001) 'Living in Towns', Interreg IIc Project', London South Bank University.

HM Treasury (1995) *Private Opportunity, Public Benefit*, London: The Private Finance Panel.

Mason, G. (1976) *The Flow of Funds in Britain*, London: Paul Elek.

Pontier, J.-M. (1998) *Les Contrats de Plan entre L'État et les Régions*, Paris: Presses Universitaires de France, Que sais-je? 3281.

Ross Goobey, A. (1992) *Bricks and Mortals: The Story of the 1980s Property Boom – and Slump – and Those Who Made It*, London: Century Business.

Scottish Executive (2002) *Review of Scotland's Cities*, (2003) *Cities Growth Fund*, (2006) *People and Places Regeneration Policy Statement*, and other relevant documents available on www.scotland.gov.uk/Topics/Government/Cities.

Tran, P. (2006) 'French mutuals in merger talks', *The Business*, 19–20 March.

Ward, S. (1994) *Planning and Urban Change*, London: Paul Chapman Publishing

Chapter 11

Public-private partnership in urban regeneration

Hichem Trache, Howard Green and Florence Menez

Introduction

Partnership, whether it be between the public and private sector, the public and public sector, or other combinations, is the buzz word in many aspects of contemporary society. The partnership approach is seen as the most effective way of working in a wide range of settings as it has at its heart the notion of shared responsibility, accountability and in a practical sense, shared know-how in the implementation of strategies and projects. This chapter examines the concept of partnership particularly in urban regeneration in the UK and France and seeks to demonstrate how two countries, each with their own legal, administrative and cultural traditions are developing the partnership approach and how the different backgrounds are leading to particular approaches.

It is arguable that the overall approach to partnership emanates from these differences – the French adopting partnership as a development principle whilst in the UK it is seen more as a tool of development. What emerges is a picture in which PPP is used loosely in a wide range of situations and with models which move from straightforward privatisation of service to genuine joint venturing. It is this latter model which we argue is the emerging form of PPP in the two countries.

The chapter begins with an overview of the growing importance of partnership in the two countries before unpicking some of the definitional problems in the use of the terminology. It then examines the expectations we have for partnership before assessing some of the key issues which are emerging. The chapter concludes with the observation that this bilateral comparison highlights the tensions in developing a common understanding of partnership and the dangers in attempting to develop a single, tightly delineated framework for the development of partnership across Europe.

What are we regenerating: defining the problem

France, since the end of the 1970s, has witnessed fundamental changes in its economic structures with the collapse of some of the industrial sectors and the rise in importance of services. An inevitable consequence of these changes has been industrial dereliction often within the urban core. Many of these sites are of strategic and emotional significance and as such pose a major policy challenge. At the same time decentralisation has transferred responsibility for dealing with such development challenges to the local authorities without at the same time transferring the funds to accomplish the task. Local authorities are therefore faced with a double challenge: to engage in urban regeneration but at the same time without putting significant new demands on the local tax base. So with industry wanting to develop new uses for its land and local authorities anxious to modernise and adopt their urban structures, the PPP offers an attractive solution for collaboration in urban change. This approach has been increasingly observed and discussed in the literature since the early 1990s (Gaudin 1999; Jacquier 1993).

Change in UK towns and cities began earlier. In 1977 the White Paper 'Policy for the Inner Cities' (DOE 1977) set out what had emerged as the conventional wisdom on the nature of the urban problem in the UK. Economic decline, associated with industrial restructuring, has led to physical destruction and decay with the inevitable growth in social disadvantage and poverty (see, for example, Atkinson and Moon 1994; Hambleton and Thomas 1995; Imrie and Thomas 1993; Booth *et al.* 2003). Unlike in France the role of local government has fluctuated widely. In the late 1970s it was seen as a key player in partnership with central government. During the 1980s there was a move away from the idea that central government should provide all of the resources necessary to support policy intervention. This period was marked by the emergence of new institutions such as the Urban Development Corporations (UDCs). In the mid-1990s City Challenge and the Single Regeneration Budget brought the local authority back into the regeneration game. At the same time selected decentralisation of service provision and transfer of funding from public to private organisations provided an environment in which business increasingly engaged in public policy (Cochrane 1993; Hill 2000).

The situation in France is rather different. PPP is emerging when the 'État providence' is under challenge. There is scarcity of public funding and the neo-liberalism of the UK is taking on greater significance. At a time when the legitimacy of the politician is being questioned and the business ethic is bringing new commercialism into strategic thinking in the public sector, PPP is gaining ground. PPP is helping to redefine the role, purpose and approach of the public sector.

In both countries, we might therefore suggest that the drivers towards a PPP approach have certain common characteristics:

- an emerging urban problem – although with different timetables and causes;
- a change in the role of the local authority with consequent effects including local capacity, expertise and funding limitations;
- the political necessity to act.

All this is happening in two countries with very different socio-cultural contexts: one with an underlying culture of doing, which is taking on and adopting a neo-liberal approach and the other with a predominantly conservative approach which resists change and reform.

Definitions of regeneration and partnership

What do we mean by urban regeneration? Earlier we identified briefly the nature of the urban problem – we therefore argue that regeneration is the programme of action to ameliorate problems and indeed to transform towns and cities into places in which all citizens can participate in urban activities – work, leisure and the associated democratic activities.

Critically, urban regeneration moves beyond the aims, aspirations and achievements of urban renewal, which is seen by Couch as 'a process of essentially physical change' (Couch 1992: 2), urban development (or redevelopment) with its general mission and less well-defined purpose, and urban revitalisation which, whilst suggesting the need for action, falls short in prescribing a precise method of approach.

Eurocities concluded that,

> Urban regeneration is the sustainable development of cities, i.e. a new holistic and integrated approach to urban problems, which is holistic in approach, targeted at economic and cultural (re)development, social cohesion and physical rehabilitation of cities.
>
> (Eurocities 1996: 5)

Whilst to Roberts it is a

> Comprehensive and integrated vision and action which leads to the resolution of urban problems and seeks to bring about lasting improvements in the economic, physical, social and environmental condition of an area that has been subject to change.
>
> (Roberts 2000: 17)

Most definitions articulate the importance of a holistic approach to urban regeneration which combines both physical and non-physical activities. Most emphasise the notion of sustainability and the coordination of public and private policy activities consistent with with the principles of sustainable development. The key then is the notion of a holistic approach to change. Our examination of the role of PPP will retain this as an underlying element.

The importance of the private sector

Finally, it is important to recognise differences in the importance and structure of the private sector in the UK and France. In the early parts of the twentieth century, other than a number of municipal services, the majority of activity and production in the UK was undertaken by the private sector. By the 1960s, the major nationalisation programmes had brought sectors of strategic importance into public ownership such as coal, steel and the railways. The private sector did though remain significant. During the 1980s and early 1990s the Thatcher government returned most if not all publicly owned companies to partial or full private ownership. Thus the private sector is of fundamental importance to the delivery of goods and services.

It is not our place to comment here on the impact of the transfer of ownership. However, the importance of the private sector with its legal responsibility to shareholders dictates that in many areas of urban development, it is virtually impossible to act without the sector's involvement.

In France, private developers or 'promoteurs privés' are often classified as the 'the private sector' in the regeneration literature, yet when investigated in further detail they are more accurately land-use change intermediaries. The private sector in reality is far broader than that and consists of structures of strategic importance engaging in the delivery of goods and services for the general public. We can include companies such as Vivendi and Suez-Lyonnaise-Dalkia and Elyo respectively in this context. Notwithstanding this definition, the role of the private sector in France was historically associated with industrial production such as the textiles whilst the State assumed the delivery of public services and amenities as part of its role as 'garant de l'intérêt général'. It is nonetheless worthwhile emphasising that the dominance of the public sector over the private sector in France is a key characteristic of the French system and worth considering within such a comparative context.

Partnership in France

In France, PPP refers vaguely at both project and service level to an approach in which the public and private sectors work together adding value to a public sector alone approach (Marcou 2002; Gaudin 2004). PPP is primarily perceived as a tool enabling the financing of public buildings and it is within this perspective that the concept originated in the 1980s. The aim was to find new means of financing public buildings given the economic crisis experienced by France at that time (Prud'homme and Terny 1986; Martinand 1993; Chatelus and Perrot 2000). This concept was short-lived and it soon became apparent that PPP could be more than a financing tool to become a 'principe d'action' (a new departure) underpinning public intervention. Such directional change was motivated by a lack of confidence in the role of the local authority, and in the public sector more generally, and its efficiency in delivering regeneration projects. This led in some instances to the involvement of the private sector, with its experience, efficiency and ability to manage the development process.

The most common form of PPP in France is a public-public partnership which is a contractual agreement between central government and local authorities to develop and implement urban policy objectives (Loi relative aux libertés et responsabilités locales 2004). This was the cornerstone of public action after decentralisation subsequently extended to the contrat de plan État-Région which is currently the main contractual procedure in urban policy delivery.

In France the PPP takes the form more of an operating principle rather than a toolbox in the regeneration process. It may take one of several forms – all forms of contract (concession, convention, délégation) including the highly formalised structure of the SEM (Société d'Économie Mixte). The precision which characterises the French approach is essentially about creating rules for the management of public capital projects (Albouy 1991; Lafay and Lecaillon 1992; Caillosse et al. 1997).

The SEM can be seen as a tool enabling redevelopment and regeneration or an actor or institution delivering regeneration. Initially introduced in 1926 with the overall aim to develop or improve the quality of public services, the main thrust of the SEM was largely driven by the lack of private sector involvement in the provision of public amenities. The SEM reduced the financial risks to the local authorities. From 1955 onwards, the SEM shifted its activities towards urban renewal and transport, both urban and motorways. In the 1980s, and following decentralisation, the creation of the SEM was primarily under the control of the State. The pool of funding resulting from such partnership mechanisms comes from largely public monies whilst the share of private monies is relatively minor. This means the public sector bears most of the financial risk, somewhat at odds with the notion of partnership and shared risk. The property market crisis of the 1990s led to a series of speculative and high-risk investment ventures by SEMs, usually undertaken by private sector investors. Bearing the financial risk meant that local authorities faced severe financial difficulties which subsequently led to the questioning of the Zone d'Aménagement Concerté procedure and the SEMs.

SEMs have been criticised for their lack of transparency, corruption and poor management, yet praised for their proactive and long term investment initiatives especially in some deprived areas (Diagonal 1998). Notwithstanding these criticisms, the SEM, essentially a hybrid system, continues to operate because it permits responsive behaviour and long-term investment which the local authority, because of its political and administrative structures, is unable to do (Cossalter 2003). The Law of 12 January 2002 attempts to bring more transparency to the contracting and tendering process. It envisages the separation of roles between those elected members who are on the board of the SEM from those who have responsibility for the tendering process and the allocation of public services. However, complete clarity on the essential question of the separation of roles, a key issue at the heart of the SEM, remains largely unresolved. How can a local authority finance a private company, but with public funds, hoping to have a return on its investments – a laudable and legitimate objective – and not at the same time benefit other companies? So all the ambiguities of the SEM are still with us. It is hard to be both judge and jury.

Partnership in the UK

It became evident in the 1980s that single-sector and single-agency approaches to urban development had fundamental limitations in trying to tackle the multi-layered and complex nature of urban problems. 'Gone are the quick fix schemes of the early 1980s. in the place of opportunism and an obsession with getting things done, there is a model of integrated development based on a comprehensive, multi-agency approach' (Roberts 1997: 4). It became evident that public agencies needed substantial private capital and expertise to deal with the problems that cities faced, hence the need for a public-private approach to urban regeneration.

The notion of PPP is similarly broad in its application in the UK and includes formal structures such as Private Finance Initiative (PFI) discussed below and less formal partnerships built less formally around memoranda of understanding or agreement. The concept of partnership has evolved over many years and whilst it is perhaps recognised most easily in the formalised Private Finance Initiative, the approach has a much longer history often underpinned in the late 1980s and early 1990s by a vision jointly held by both public and private sectors that there is substantial benefit to both to cooperate. The concept of public sector funding levering in private sector investment and the notion of partnership between different agencies and organisations became the cornerstone of urban policy through to the mid-1990s. We can recognise three distinct strands to this evolution.

In the early days of partnership, many of the projects in the City Challenge initiative were jointly developed and funded by public and private sectors alike. Similarly, many of the projects in the Urban Task Force initiatives in the early 1990s were joint ventures, in the loosest sense of the word between the public and private sector. Many of the initiatives associated with these activities were quite small scale and involved small environmental improvement, training programmes and workspace developments.

A further strand in the developing relationship between the public and private sector was the emerging approach to town centre management now a common feature of the management of our town and city centres given the increased competition between UK cities. In the various models adopted in town centre management, the importance of the private sector working in partnership with the local authority and other public bodies is evident. Interestingly in early examples the local authority took the initial lead and the private sector was difficult to attract. Stubbs *et al.* (2002), for example, note that many were content to free-ride on local authority initiatives (Medway *et al.* 1999, 2000). More recently the private sector has played a more dominant role as in the case in Edinburgh (Anon. 1999). Smith (1998) notes the growing importance of property owners and retailers with companies such as Boots, Land Securities and NatWest Bank playing important roles. All are realising that such investments are beneficial to both the public and private sectors. As early as 1996, Hirst noted that survey evidence suggested that 71 per cent of stores in town centre management schemes had experienced higher takings. The successful development of organisations such as Business in the Community (BITC) with a membership of over 700 major UK employers is a further example of the developing role of the private sector in all aspects of urban regeneration and change.

Finally, we should also recognise the relationship between the public and private sector in the development process itself, particularly in the application of so-called Section 106 agreements. Planning gain agreements are another means for engaging the private sector in, for instance, public realm improvements as financial compensation for permissible development rights on specific sites. This relationship is however contractual yet negotiated between the public and private parties.

Involvement of the private sector in urban issues has then been evolving over many years and can be recognised in several areas of activity. This evolution does perhaps emphasise that for many private sector organisations there is an interest beyond that of simple profit in the motivation to engage in partnership and that the overall motivations for entering partnerships go much further than simply those of getting the job done. Corporate and financial institutions have a long-term investment strategy that exceeds by far those of property developers and such a strategic investment perspective leads to partnership agreements that can potentially fit within the wider regeneration framework in terms of urban, economic and social objectives. Some of those issues will be discussed in the subsequent sections of this chapter.

The UK has latterly, some might argue belatedly, focused on developing tools for partnership, when compared with the long history of the SEM in France. The PFI, possibly the most well-known form of PPP, refers to a strictly defined legal contract for involving private companies in the provision of public services, particularly public buildings.

The PFI was introduced by the Conservative government in 1992 and then radically amended to give more scope to, and attract, investors; it was subsequently inherited by the Labour government when they took office. According to the Nation Health Service (NHS) plan, more than 100 new hospitals will be provided using the PFI by 2010. Perhaps the largest PFI is the new University College Hospital in London. In 2001/2 the PFI accounted for 9 per cent of public investment.

Under a PFI scheme, a capital project such as a school, hospital or housing estate is designed, built, financed and managed by a private sector consortium, under a contract that typically lasts for 30 years. The private consortium will be paid regularly from public money depending on its performance throughout that period. If the consortium misses performance targets, it will be paid less.

The attraction of PFI for the government is that it avoids making expensive one-off capital payments to build large-scale projects and hence it does not show up as increased public borrowing. Risk is also transferred to the private sector. Critics claim that as with any form of hire purchase, buying over a long period of time is more expensive than buying up-front with cash. Governments can borrow cash at a cheaper rate than the private sector. Growing concern has recently been expressed amongst experts about the cost of PFI. It will take at least a further 20 years, when the first PFI contracts have been completed, before the real cost of PFI can be judged.

Whilst the PFI is the principal formal structure, a plethora of specific individually defined structures have come into place to frame the agreed partnerships. These will usually take the form of a joint venture in which each of the potential several partners agrees to deliver an element of the project. The precise nature of the contract will be specific to individual projects and may be as simple as a memorandum of understanding to a formally constituted joint venture involving the establishment of a new company.

In 1999/2000 and following recommendations in the Urban Task Force Report, the government established three pilot Urban Regeneration Companies (URCs) in Liverpool, East Manchester and Sheffield. The Urban White Paper (2000) proposed a programme of about 12 more Urban Regeneration Companies over the following two to three years – bringing the total to 16. The purpose of URCs was to 'work with a range of private and public sector partners, including the Local Strategic Partnerships, to redevelop and bring investment back to the worst areas in our cities and towns'. URCs have been promoted by the government and established by local partners, in order to achieve a focused, integrated regeneration strategy for key towns and cities. They coordinate investment plans from both the public and the private sectors and attract new investment through the purposeful and imaginative promotion and regeneration of their areas. Their role consists primarily in producing a powerful and coherent single vision for the future of an area and then coordinating its implementation in a way that, previously, could not be achieved through individual ad hoc decisions.

Importantly the URCs are separate private legal entities. URCs are experts in their local areas and the local authority, local employers, amenity groups and community representatives play an important part, with the regional context represented by the Regional Development Agencies (RDAs) and the national dimension by English Partnerships. Their operation is not isolated from wider regional and local contexts.

Developing a typology

The characteristics discussed above have been formalised into a loose typology of partnership, the synergy model, the budget enlargement model and the transformational model (Mackintosh 1992). Each of these is outlined below.

A synergy model

In the synergy model of partnerships, by combining their knowledge, resources, approaches and operational culture, partners (or partner organisations) will be able to achieve more together than they would by working on their own. It is based on the principle that the whole is greater than the sum of the parts.

A budget enlargement model

As argued earlier in this chapter, access to wider and additional funding opportunities could be one of the objectives of a partnership model. Within the budget enlargement model of partnerships, partners working together will gain access to a pool of funds that neither could access on their own.

A transformational model

The third model of partnerships, the transformational model, suggests that there are benefits to be gained by exposing the different partners to the working methods of the other partners. Arguably, the process will stimulate innovation as part of an ongoing process of development and change. Partners will be able to learn from each other and synchronise their working culture with that of the other partners involved in a PPP. The issue of trust emerges as a key issue within these models. In France it seems that trusting the private sector in terms of their motivation and profit-making while entering into a PPP remains a key barrier to PPP.

At present we are unable to demonstrate the importance of each of these models to the two countries. We would simply want to suggest that as partnership working develops in both countries it is this transformational approach which should drive change.

What can partnership deliver?

Changing working practices

There has been a consistent argument in this chapter that the traditional culture of doing identifies government and the public sector in general as the one responsible for the creation of public value. With the increased pressure on local government to deliver 'best-value', the latter had to be creative to deliver its policy objectives. It meant that the traditional public administration (TPA) which entailed a Weberian organisation of civil servants administering and managing public policy objectives had their limitations given the complexity of the urban, social economic and environmental problems that urban regeneration deals with. Such a challenge of the TPA structure meant that new forms of governance – New Public Management (NPM) – were much needed to deal with such complexities. Jurgen (2005) argues that the key challenge is to bring new methods and cultures of doing from the business community into government sectors, stressing that delivering best value can be done through the involvement of private companies, the partnership approach leading to what Jurgen refers to as Public Value Management.

An alternative approach to delivery

As we have noted partnerships are involved at various levels and in many sectors, so, simplistically, we can suggest that they are capable of delivery. But closer scrutiny suggests that their influence can be more fundamental to thinking about provision more generally.

Partnerships have the potential to ensure that the weaknesses of previous approaches to urban regeneration are overcome by concentrating on those elements which have a maximum impact upon urban problems. Partnerships can bring together social, economic and physical activities within the same strategy. This has the potential to bring a new dynamism to old problems as they are not dealt with in isolation but within a coherent urban regeneration strategy.

While the assumption that the public sector is responsible for the delivery of basic services remains deeply entrenched in many countries (such as France and Germany), the methods by which these services are created, procured and delivered are changing. This reflects a greater need and desire for the public sector to work and harness the benefits of the private sector.

Partnership arrangements could be strategic or localised given the nature of activities involved. At a strategic level, Strategic Service-delivery Partnerships (SSPs) have been perceived by many local authorities, particularly the larger ones as essential tools for service delivery. Those SSPs constitute substantial contracts involving a PPP, whereby the public sector gains investment and significant risk transfer. Such partnership agreements are long term, and for some, such long-term commitment to a single partner for the delivery of essential services is seen as high risk. Offsetting the risks against the long-term benefits is for many a difficult act to balance.

At a local level, LSPs have been seen by central government as a key driver for change in the deliver of regeneration both physical and non-physical at the neighbourhood level. LSPs are a single body that brings together at local level the different elements of the public sector as well as private, voluntary and community sectors in order that different initiatives and services support rather than contradict each other.

Additional funding

Funding benefits come in a variety of ways from simple leverage, base funding and funding enhancement. Accessing a wider pool of funding is of particular relevance especially that partners entering into a partnership have access to funds that neither of them has access on their own. This is of critical importance when tackling large-scale and complex urban problems.

Expertise and know-how

In many cases partnership is able to make significant contributions through the expertise of the individuals and teams involved. For many local authorities, development professions are now frequently absent particularly in the context of large physical projects. Specific skills and enterprise are equally important where partner companies and organisations have specialised skills which are less likely to be found in the average local authority.

Organisational simplicity

PPPs offer the opportunity to overcome the weaknesses of local individual partners through joint action. Frequently the private partners are able to bring essential project management and organisational simplicity to projects which the administrative complexities of the public sector are unable to match.

Community involvement and partnerships working are key factors in the success of many regeneration schemes. Community organisations are flexible, close to informal networks and support long-term interests of the community. Their knowledge of local issues, problems and opportunities is a valuable asset despite their limited financial resources.

Governments, local and national, have key roles to play in encouraging cooperation, initiating and supporting local initiatives and decision-making. Bureaucracy and duplication could be an issue. In the UK the notion of one-stop shop is currently being promoted by central government so streamlining provision of advice, support and contact to the private sector.

Organisational learning

A major impact of the partnership approach has been in the field of what we might refer to as organisational learning. In both countries both the public and private sector have in the past approached development from different perspectives with different approaches to achieve those objectives. For the public sector, this reflects their need to complete activity within prevailing statutes and derived responsibilities. For the private sector, an obligation to shareholders is an overarching responsibility. As a consequence, cultural and operational approaches are different. Historically this has often led to tensions and disagreements. Increasingly partnership is leading to change. This may be simply in terms of 'there are better ways of doing this' in a technical sense. Or perhaps more importantly it is changing the way each partner views the position and approach of the other.

This learning has to be two-way. Smith (1998) notes that the strengths of the public sector are often forgotten in the heady search for private involvement. He voices concern that the public input can often be discarded as the public involvement in the partnership declines. He asks, 'wouldn't it be better to have companies transfer their experience and resources into local government in such a way that it meant local authority workforces did not have to transfer themselves out?' (Smith 1998: 30). Perhaps part of this learning will emphasise the notion of public enterprise rather than privatisation.

In what sectors do we find partnerships playing an important role?

Beyond the physical regeneration activities, PPPs can help deliver in activities such as education, enterprise, crime, employment and waste. As we have noted above, public-private partnerships have characterised activity in both countries for many years – and indeed in the specific structures such as the SEM, partnership has been a characteristic of a many sectors and particularly in major infrastructural and development projects. For example, the development and maintenance of the motorway system in France is undertaken within the SEM structure, where since 1985 the State is the major shareholder, except in the case of Cofiroute, the funding comes from State grants and toll revenue.

More recently in France other sectors have been involved in partnership development, in many cases moving away from the SEM structure towards private provision with service level agreements. It is often however difficult to distinguish between what is essentially privatisation or straightforward contracting and partnership. For example, in urban heating programmes, 95 per cent of the production and distribution is undertaken by private companies through a service agreement (délégation de service); 75 per cent of public transport outside Paris is delivered by private companies. Neither of these would we suggest are partnerships. In the development of cable networks, 99 per cent of the infrastructure and subsequent maintenance is undertaken by the private sector which invoices either the local authority or the user for the cost of provision and service.

Following some of the recent improprieties of the private providers such as Veolia Environment, Vivendi and Lyonnaise des Eaux, local authorities have been drawing back from this approach.

Looking at the sectors in which both countries have involved the private sector, we are immediately struck by a similarity between countries. This is perhaps not surprising as they represent the major areas of public service and infrastructure in which transfer to partnership approaches are likely. There is also a similarity in the nature of the partnerships involved. In both countries, many of the cases represent the delivery of a service – whether it be the collection of rubbish or the provision of public transport. In all

Table 11.1 UK PPPs by sector

Health	11%
Transport	6%
Defence	4%
Water and waste water	6%
Accommodation: police	4%
Accommodation: education	21%
Accommodation: health	17%
Accommodation: other	11%
IT: education	1%
IT: health	3%
IT: other	12%
Prisons	4%
Total	100%

Source: Sectors of PPP activity, *Infrastructure Journal*, August 2002.

cases, as we will note below, this is often more akin to the quasi or total privatisation of a service rather than the joint delivery of the service.

Who takes the lead?

Concessions or delegation of activities to the private sector are widely recognised forms of contractual agreements. In France, large water companies such as Vivendi (formerly Compagnie Générale des Eaux) and Lyonnaise des Eaux-Dumezn Bougues have developed a close working relationship with local authorities. Investment activity in the sector is recent yet it has grown steadily since decentralisation and as a result of portfolio diversification from those private corporate institutions (Campagnac 1992). Private developers were assuming the majority of the financial risk. More recently new enterprising companies have become heavily involved in the development process, specialising in the delivery of a specific service or a certain type of development. Altaréa Gerec is an example of this, investing in the retail sector. It could be argued that with the increasing number of players in the property development sector, new models of 'doing' will be developed in France.

In France, public-private partnerships is a much criticised approach as it is characterised by lengthy negotiations between both parties seeking a consensus. In some instances, local authorities have a rather weak position within the framework of action compared with the private sector actors, notwithstanding their statutory powers to deliver planning permissions and develop local plans. Similarly, contractual agreements seem to be the norm rather than a partnership framework for action (Marcou et al. 1997; Gaudin 1999). Such contractual agreements are also used as key negotiating tool by the local authority. This is the case in the Carré de Soie project in Vaulx en Velin where the local authority entered into a contractual agreement with Altaréa Gerec on the basis of a flexible schedule of development and accommodation. It was nonetheless necessary for the local authority to agree on some key developmental issues so that the deal and the developer could be secured. Land ownership had a direct impact on the way deals were brokered in this case as the private sector, not the local authority, owned the land.

Dynamics: how are things changing?

Partnership and its significance to the regeneration process is constantly evolving and we have already seen in the French example how attitudes and approaches to the SEM and private subcontracting are changing.

It appears that there is a movement away from public intervention *per se*, albeit very cautious, towards one in which funding streams are emerging which are both public and privately resourced. In this sense, partnership development reinforces rather than minimising or removing the importance of the public sector. Several evaluations of urban development projects have argued for a better management of public expenditure, not a reduction, and the development of a clear strategy for regeneration on the part of the local authority. In essence the implementation of partnership approaches imposes a constant challenge to the local authority in matters of strategy and clarity of funding.

A quick review of current projects highlights the emergence of new approaches and structures embedded in both the public and private sectors. The development of 'SEM locales' (Euralille in Lille, Cité Internationale and Confluent in Lyon) or specific structures, an approach developed by the Communauté Urbaine de Lyon, has allowed the uncoupling and division of financial, human and technical resources of the local authority. In addition, in recent years there has been a change from a climate perhaps of mistrust between the various groups towards one in which trust and understanding have been progressively built up. However, these developments should not be overstated as the cultural and philosophical underpinnings of French republicanism remain significant. It is worth noting that from the point of view of city planners, the dearth of studies on the workings and impacts particularly of the SEM is worrying. Such studies would help local authorities develop more effectively new tools for partnership and understand better the management and project management techniques which are essential for successful public-private partnership.

The current changes in the UK scene are primarily related to the notion of incremental partnering within a PPP. At odds with the notion of 'big bang' partnerships with the private sector, the current partnership strategy is based primarily on the notion of local authorities adopting a low-risk stage-by-stage approach, allowing confidence in the partnership to be built up before moving into the next level. Maybe this is what is needed for the French context – to build trust and a good working relationship. This also has attractions to both the private and public sectors as they can evaluate how things are evolving through time. In addition this means the need for flexibility in agreements and fine tuning as work progresses. Whilst this is feasible in the UK it is less easy to see how the French will respond, given that their system is predicated on codes and legal structures and the practice of PPP is dominated by the public sector.

Incremental partnering involves working with a strategic partner or partners, initially without a long-term commitment to a partnership covering a range of core activities.

In the UK, the changes are directly linked to the methodology of doing PPP rather than the principle. This is primarily a fine-tuning exercise given the long experience that local authorities and private sector as well as community and voluntary groups have developed over the years. The substantial changes are also linked to the deliverables. Are PPPs delivering on the ground, given all the debates regarding their timely relevance and importance in urban regeneration?

Looking to the future, both countries are recognising the need to resolve some of the constraints imposed by the rigours of Brussels such as processes of procurement and the limitations imposed by state aid rules. From the very divergent contexts, these may be matters which bring a greater degree of commonality to the respective approaches to PPP.

Conclusion

Throughout the chapter we have noted a simple confusion in the use of language and meaning of public-private partnership. In both countries there is a tendency to confuse the three areas of interest:

1   the development of services or infrastructure provision in which the public and private sectors are straightforward shareholders;
2   the clear-cut privatisation of services in which the private sector agrees to deliver to the public sector under given conditions in terms of price, period and quality;
3   the joint provision of infrastructure or service involving some form of joint venture agreement.

It is this latter form of involvement which is of particular interest as it adds something new to the approach to development. Whether it is an approach which can be accommodated in the institutional and administrative structures of the two countries to a similar degree is perhaps open to discussion. In this sense there is much thar we can learn from the way in which partnership working is developing in both countries. It is clear that the evolution of partnership, whilst driven by similar imperatives, is shaped by the political and administrative environments in which they exist. Our observations on the differences between Britain and France suggest that the development of a common framework more widely across Europe is an unrealisable goal.

References

Albouy, C. (1991) *Sociétés d'Économie Mixte Locales*, Collection pratiques de l'Immobilier, Paris: Éditions Masson.

Anon. (1999) 'Joint firm to manage city centre', *Planning*, Issue 1,305, 12 February: 4.

Ascher, F. (1994) 'Le partenariat public-privé dans le (re)développement. Le cas de la France', in W. Hainz (ed.) *Partenariats Publics-Privés dans l'Aménagement Urbain*, Paris: Éditions l'Harmattan, pp. 197–248.

Ascher, F. (2001) *Les Nouveaux Principes de l'Urbanisme: La Fin des Villes n'est pas à l'Ordre du Jour*, Paris: Éditions de l'Aube.

Bezançon, X. (2004) *2000 Ans d'Histoire du Partenariat Public-Privé: Pour la Réalisation des Équipements et Services Collectifs*, Paris: Presses de l'École Nationale des Ponts et Chaussées.

Booth, P. (2004) *Le Partenariat Public Privé en Grande-Bretagne, in Partenariat Public-Privé et Collectivités Territoriales*, Paris: La Documentation française, pp. 109–32.

Booth, P., Green, H. and Trache, H. (2003) 'British urban policy since 1997: change and continuity', *Hommes et Terres du Nord*, 2002–2003, pp. 116–24.

Cabinet Office (2001) A *New Commitment to Neighbourhood Renewal: National Strategy Action Plan*, London: HMSO.

Caillosse, J., Le Galès, P. and Loncle-Moriceau, P. (1997) 'Les sociétés d'économie mixte locales: outils de quelle action publique?', in F. Godard (ed.) *Le Gouvernement des Villes: Territoire et Pouvoir*, Paris: Éditions Descartes et Cie, pp. 23–96.

Campagnac, E. (ed.) (1992) *Les Grands Groupes de la Construction: de Nouveaux Acteurs Urbains*, collection Villes et Entreprises, Paris: Éditions l'Harmattan.

Chatelus, P. and Perrot, J.Y. (2000) *Financement des Infrastructures et des Services Collectifs: Le Recours au Partenariat Public-Priivé, les Enseignements des Expériences Françaises dans le Monde*, Paris: Presses de l'École Nationale des Ponts et Chaussées.

Choay, F. (1985) 'Production de la ville, esthétique urbaine et architecture', in G. Duby (ed.) *Histoire de la France Urbaine: La Ville Aujourd'hui*, Vol. 5, Paris: Éditions du Seuil.

Cochrane, A. (1993) *Whatever Happened to Local Government?*, Milton Keynes: Open University Press.

Cossalter, P. (2003) 'Sociétés d'économie mixte locales: les SEML dans le collimateur du droit européen', *Le Moniteur*, 2 May: 62–3.

Couch, C. (1990) *Urban Renewal Theory and Practice*, London: Macmillan.

Couch, C., Fraser, C. and Percy, S. (2003) *Urban Regeneration in Europe*, Oxford: Blackwell.

Decoutère, S., Mettan, N. and Ruegg, J. (1994) *Le Partenariat Public-Privé: Un Atout pour l'Aménagement du Territoire et la Protection de l'Environnement?* Lausanne: Presses Polytechniques et Universitaires Romandes.

Department of the Environment (DOE) (1977) *Policy for the Inner Cities*, Cmnd 6845, London: HMSO.

Department of the Environment, Transport and Regions (DETR) (2001) *Local Strategic Partnerships: Government Guidance*, London: The Stationery Office.

Diagonal (1998) 'Dossier SEM sur la sellette', No. 133, September–October: 300.

Gaudin, J.P. (1999) *Gouverner par Contrat*, Paris: Presses de Sciences Po.

Gaudin, J.P. (2004) *L'Action Publique: Sociologie et Politique*, collection Amphi, Paris: Presses de Sciences Po and Éditions Dalloz.

Hambleton, R. and Thomas, H. (1995) *Urban Policy Evaluation: Challenge and Change*, London: Paul Chapman.

Hill, D.M. (2000) *Urban Policy and Politics in Britain*, London: Macmillan.

Hirst, C. (1996) 'Town centre management boosts takings', *Planning Week*, 4(17): 4.

Imrie, R. and Thomas, H. (1993) *British Urban Policy and the Urban Development Corporations*, London: Paul Chapman.

Jacquier, C. (1993) *Voyage dans dix Quartiers Européens en Crise*, Paris: L'Harmattan.

Janvier, Y. (1996) 'Nouveaux enjeux de société', in J. Landrieu and C. Martinand (eds) *L'aménagement en Questions*, Paris: Éditions de l'ADEF.

Jurgen van der Heijden (2005) 'Towards an understanding of public-private dialogue', unpublished working paper, University of Amsterdam.

Lafay, J.D. and Lecaillon, J. (1992) *L'économie Mixte*, Collection Que Sais-je?, Paris: Presses Universitaires de France.

Landrieu, J. and Martinand, C. (eds) (1996) *L'aménagement en Questions*, Paris: Éditions de l'ADEF, Paris.

Le Galès, P. (1995) 'Du gouvernement des villes à la gouvernance urbaine', *Revue Française de Sciences Politiques*, 45 (February): 57–95.

Lorrain, D. (1992) 'Le modèle ensemblier en France (la production urbaine après la décentralisation)', in E. Campagnac (ed.) *Les Grands Groupes de la Construction: de Nouveaux Acteurs Urbains*, collection Villes et Entreprises, Paris: Éditions l'Harmattan, pp. 71–82.

Lorrain, D. (1993) 'Après la décentralisation: l'action publique flexible', *Sociologie du Travail*, 36 (March): 285–307.

Mackintosh, M. (1992) 'Partnerships: issues of policy and negotiation', *Local Economy*, 3(7): 210–24.

Marcou, G. (2002) 'Le partenariat public-privé: retrait ou renouveau de l'intervention publique?', in *Partenariat public-privé et collectivités territoriales*, Paris: Éditions La Documentation française, pp. 13–50.

Marcou, G., Rangeon, F. and Thiebault, J.L. (1997) *La Coopération Contractuelle et le Gouvernement des Villes*, Collection logiques juridiques, Paris: Éditions l'Harmattan.

Martinand, C. (1993) *L'Expérience Française du Financement Privé des Équipements Publics*, Paris: DAEI, Éditions Economica.

Medway, D., Warnaby, G., Bennison, D. and Alexander, A. (1999) 'Retailers' financial support for town centre management', *International Journal of Retail and Distribution Management*, 27(6): 246–55.

Medway, D., Warnaby, G., Bennison, D. and Alexander, A. (2000) 'Reasons for retailers' involvement in town centre management', *International Journal of Retail and Distribution Management*, 28(8): 368–78.

Novarina, G. (ed.) (2003) *Plan et Projet: l'Urbanisme en France et en Italie*, Collection villes, Paris: Éditions Anthropos.

Office of the Deputy Prime Minister (2003) *Cities, Regions and Competitiveness*, Core Cities Report, London: HMSO.

Prud'homme, R. and Terny, G. (1986) *Le Financement des Équipements Publics de Demain*, Paris: Éditions Economica.

Roberts, P. (1997) 'Sustainable development strategies for regional development in Europe: an ecological modernisation approach', *Regional Contact*, XI: 92–104.

Roberts, P. (2000) 'The evolution, definition and purpose of urban regeneration', in *Urban regeneration: A Handbook*, London: Sage Publications.

Smith, R. (1998) 'Improving the company you keep', *Municipal Journal*, 3 July: 30–1.

Smith, S. (1998) 'Time to take town centre management seriously', *Chartered Surveyor Monthly*, 7 (9): 34–5.

Chapter 12

Public transport in cities and regions

Facing an uncertain future?

*Reg Harman, Alain l'Hostis
and Philippe Ménerault*

Introduction

This chapter addresses transport policies in the two countries. Transport
is a crucial factor in spatial planning. At its simplest, the quality and speed
of transport affects the area within which people can live their lives and
obtain goods and services. In turn the shape and scale of settlements has a
significant impact on the forms of transport that are used. In consequence
changes in transport have paralleled changes in settlement structure, both
being driven by improved technology and growth in the economy.

The twentieth century has seen massive growth in mobility levels, with
complex travel patterns reflecting dispersed development. This has led to
congestion, delay, pollution, traffic accidents, economic inefficiency and
social inequity. Public transport services, which can play a crucial role
in solving these problems, are becoming ever more difficult to sustain
on a purely commercial basis. So transport policies in both countries are
changing, with the stated aims of supporting the demand for wider access
while constraining the use of motor vehicles. But in practice they have so far
had little impact on the demand for ever greater mobility.

This chapter outlines the main aspects of British and French transport
policies, especially for urban and regional public transport, against this
background. The first section reviews the development of major transport
policy instruments in recent years. The following sections consider some
specific aspects, including the roles of regional agencies and local authorities,
the links between transport and spatial development, and the administration
of public transport. Each section contains a brief review of the British and
French approaches and some comparative remarks. A concluding section
draws out some key points of similarity and difference.

Stubbs, B., Warnby, G. and Medway, D. (2002) 'Marketing at the public/private sector interface; town centre management schemes in the south of England', *Cities*, 19(5): 317–26.

Trache, H. and Green, H. (2001) *The Involvement of Private Sector Investors in Urban Regeneration Projects: The Case of Birmingham, Brussels, Lille Métropole, Roubaix, Manchester, Rotterdam and Valenciennes*, Paris: Caisse des Dépôts et Consignations.

Urban Task Force (1999) *Towards and Urban Renaissance: Final Report*, London: E&FN Spon.

Werner, H. (ed.) (1994) *Partenariats Publics-Privés dans l'Aménagement Urbain*, Paris: Éditions l'Harmattan.

The development of transport policy in recent years

British policy has evolved primarily in line with the main themes of the two White Papers discussed below. These in principle apply to all parts of the United Kingdom; in practice there are some real differences. Northern Ireland has a distinct policy regime, largely reflecting serious social unrest experienced over recent decades: most transport is centrally managed by the province's administration. Within Great Britain, following an Act of 2001, Scotland has its own Parliament, with significant powers, and Wales has a separate Assembly, with more limited powers. Both are now developing policies for the administration and development of transport which differ from those in England. The majority of Great Britain's population lives in England, and in practice most of this review applies primarily to transport policy in England. London also has very different powers.

In France the key document which defines transport policy is the Loi d'Orientation des Transports Interieurs (LOTI), of 31 December 1982. This act was initially motivated by the need to revise the statutory position of the SNCF but became a document of general application. Its aim as such was to set out a comprehensive legal framework for the organisation of transport, covering all modes and all spatial levels, for both freight and passengers. Drawn up under a left-wing government by a communist minister, LOTI comprises a flexible framework which rests on establishing public regulation within a market economy. This principle is formalised in the combination of ideas of 'right to transport for everyone', 'public service', and 'freedom of choice for the user'. The act envisaged a sharing of roles, between central government and the local authorities on one hand and the public authorities and the operators on the other. Furthermore, Paris, like London, forms a special case in view of its national significance.

British transport policy has changed substantially over the last decade. The Conservative government in power during the 1980s and 1990s pursued two simple policy strands. It transferred the ownership and management of most public transport into private hands, through the Transport Act 1985 (buses) and the Railways Act 1993 (railways). It envisaged road movement as the keystone of transport policy, and so in 1989 published a strategy document called 'Roads to Prosperity', setting out a significant programme for expanding the trunk road network. This brought a substantial reaction from environmental groups and the wider public too, and the government slowly changed its approach to recognise that its policy of 'predict and provide' would not solve problems of access and congestion. The economic downturn of the early 1990s reduced public funds available for road building anyway.

The Labour administration elected in 1997 carried out a widespread consultation on transport and in 1998 published a White Paper 'A New

Deal for Transport: Better for Everyone'. This identified the positive benefits of increasing transport but also saw the negative impact, in terms of poor quality of life for many. It set out as key objectives:

- An integrated transport policy is essential, in which transport supports spatial planning aimed at improving sustainable travel, environmental improvement, and education, health and employment policies.
- Public transport should play a greater role in travel and should be improved to attract people out of their cars.
- Good transport planning should happen mostly at local level, providing much better walking, cycling and bus services.
- Improvements to the environment should not mean forcing people out of their cars.
- More sustainable modes for freight movement should be encouraged.

The White Paper was linked to a number of supporting policy documents – the 'daughter documents' – which set out policy intentions for railways, buses, road pricing, and also guidance on the links between spatial planning and transport.

To implement these policies, the government adopted new powers, through the Transport Act 2000. The main changes established in this included:

- reorganisation of administration of the national railway system, notably through creation of the Strategic Rail Authority to develop and implement a strategy and manage the franchising of passenger services;
- creation of new powers, processes and duties for local transport authorities to prepare and implement a Local Transport Plan (LTP), covering local highways and bus services, financed largely by government grants;
- creation of powers and processes for bringing in road pricing and workplace charging schemes.

In 2000 the government also published a plan for investment and action, 'Transport 2010 – The 10 Year Plan', which defined the intended funding for transport over the decade, both capital and revenue. It aimed to encourage capital expenditure by private interests, through public-private partnerships. Its aims were to achieve the White Paper objectives through reducing congestion, encouraging higher use of public transport, supporting economic growth and improving the environment. This formed the economic justification for increased spending on transport, as the government was committed to tight fiscal management.

The new policies and action plans received widespread support. However, there remained some concern about whether the policies could be achieved, while some motoring and business interests considered that the policies would constrain the freedom to travel, and could lead to poorer economic performance. These negative aspects were widely reported in the media. Negative views eventually gained dominance after two key events. One was a campaign against fuel price rises in autumn 2001, when some groups of independent road freight drivers blockaded oil depots; this led government to abandon its petrol tax 'escalator'. Then government declared bankrupt the private owner of the national rail infrastructure (Railtrack PLC) and established a 'stakeholder company' (Network Rail) to run it, following a period of rapid increase in railway maintenance costs and growing public concern over four crashes in the London area (even though the total number of casualties was relatively small).

Other indicators also suggested that the new policies were not working: bus service passenger levels and operations continued to decline outside London; the condition of roads remained poor and that of footways declined. Implementation of local authority LTP projects was generally held back by government controls, so that congestion continued to increase while local transport and environmental conditions generally got worse. In response, the government issued two more White Papers in 2004, one proposing a review of railway administration, the other setting out policies for the other areas of transport. The second document – 'The Future of Transport', subtitled 'A network for 2030' – stressed the increased public funding which government was awarding to the transport sector, and set out a series of new initiatives for various parts of the transport sector, aimed at taking forward the principles of 'Transport 2010'. Many commentators saw this as moving transport policy away from environmental and social goals and back towards more road building.

In contrast to Great Britain, French transport policy has not seen any real change since the publication of LOTI. While its application has run into several difficulties, subsequent legal documents have sought to remove blockages rather than restructure it. Two points should be stressed: the difficulty of an intermodal approach; and the problem of interaction between transport systems and decentralisation.

On one hand the multimodal and intermodal approach of LOTI has in practice seen little development. Thus the first national strategic plans, proposed by LOTI, for infrastructure were single mode: they covered respectively inland waterways (1985), motorways (1990) and high speed rail links (1991). It was not until 1999 that the Loi d'Orientation pour l'Aménagement et le Développement Durable du Territoire (LOADDT) replaced the sectoral strategies for transport, implemented through the Loi Pasqua of 1995, by two multimodal strategies for coordinated services, one for passenger transport and the other for freight. However, despite the concern expressed for altering the balance of modes in favour of public transport, especially rail, there remains a wide gap between intentions and implementation. Planning for transport networks and establishing complete travel systems, key factors in such a policy, remain limited, while the road network continues to grow, notably through more bypasses round conurbations.

On the other hand it is important to note the problems resulting from the telescoping of two separate policy strands: the transport sector and the process of decentralisation. From 1982 the organisation of administrative areas was defined as having three tiers, one above the other (the region elevated to be a public authority, the department, and the municipality), linked to the principle that no authority has control over any other. In this framework LOTI allocates to each area level the power of Autorité Organisatrice (AO) for the defined system of public transport. The growth of mobility and the expansion of functions over wider areas meant that the institutional areas became more and more inappropriate. Coordinating transport networks has become more difficult because of the multiplicity of responsible authorities: the French system always tries to maintain the balance between seeking to establish comprehensive networks and strictly maintaining the autonomy of local authorities.

Regional agencies and local authorities

As discussed elsewhere, England's structure of local administration includes non-elected regional bodies and elected local authorities. The regional assemblies, made up of members from local authorities with some representatives of business and community interests, draw up a regional planning strategy, and this must incorporate a regional transport strategy (RTS). The transport policies in the RTS should support the spatial and land-use objectives; they also act as the guiding framework for LTPs in the region. The action and investment programmes of the regional development agencies (RDAs), which represent mainly the businesses in each region, support mostly development and regeneration projects, but may also cover some transport projects as well.

Greater London has a unique structure, reflecting its size and its central role as a national capital and international finance centre. The Greater London Authority (GLA), led by the (elected) Mayor, is responsible for strategic planning (led by the London Development Agency, LDA) and for most aspects of transport (led by Transport for London, TfL). But this level of control is to some extent limited. Development of the London Underground system is defined through a long term public-private partnership (PPP) contract agreed between the government and private consortia before the Underground was handed over to TfL. TfL has no direct responsibility for the national railway network around London (though this is being sought). TfL does have full control over highways, and over bus services, which are run by private companies under short-term franchises for groups of routes. Policies and programmes are set out in the London Transport Strategy, formulated under the leadership of the Mayor.

In England the structure and powers of local authorities outside London vary widely, following significant reorganisation by successive governments over the last two decades. The major conurbations (metropolitan counties) have no county council. Instead the metropolitan district councils, which are elected authorities, cooperate through joint arrangements over strategic planning for their area, while passenger transport functions are overseen by a passenger transport authority (PTA) representing all of them. The PTA's policies are developed and managed by a passenger transport executive (PTE): a body of permanent staff headed by a small group of directors. A joint team from the PTE and the metropolitan districts manages local transport planning matters, including the LTP.

Outside the major conurbations, English local authority areas may have two levels of elected councils or just one. In two-tier authorities the county council is responsible for strategic planning and for transport (together with other functions such as education and social welfare services) and a number of district councils are responsible for local development planning (and some other functions). In single-tier areas a unitary authority has both strategic and local planning and transport responsibilities (and other functions).

The main transport tool for local transport authorities is the LTP, established by the Transport Act 2000. This sets out a five-year programme for all local transport services and facilities, including highways and public transport. The first LTP was prepared and submitted in 2000, to cover the period 2000/1–2005/6. The second LTP has been prepared during 2005, to run for the period 2006/7–2010/11. The LTP is intended to describe the authority's transport policies and programmes for the five-year period, show how these address the government's key transport themes, and set out Key Performance Indicators (KPI) for monitoring progress. It should reflect the regional transport policies set out in the RTS. Implementation of the programmes and projects depends on funding approved annually by government. This is based on an Annual Progress Report (APR) which each local transport authority prepares each year, summarising its activities and updating funding needs. It also reflects the rating awarded by government officials, following procedures set out in government guidance documents, which change from year to year. As a result, spending is strictly controlled, and local transport authorities have little freedom to coordinate or to negotiate.

Apart from London, local transport authorities have little control over public transport. They are required to draw up a bus strategy but they can only fund services to run where commercial operators do not provide them, organise joint tickets in certain circumstances and publish area timetables. They have no real control over rail services, which are planned and administered centrally. They can fund new local infrastructure, such as improvements to bus stations and railway stations, and provide road priorities for bus operation, but the funds they have for these are generally very limited.

In Wales and Scotland all local authorities are unitary. In Scotland statutory Regional Transport Partnerships, bringing together the local authorities in each region, now coordinate planning and investment for transport, under the overall authority of the national Transport Executive. (The Glasgow area's unique PTE has been absorbed by the relevant partnership.) These regional groups are now coordinated by a national Transport Executive established by the Scottish Parliament to develop and manage all transport across Scotland.

In France the institutional structure and its evolution are, for the most part, very different from those of the United Kingdom:

- The influence of elected representatives from the different levels of public authorities is dominant.
- The role of central government is declining more and more in terms of funding and of transfer of responsibilities.
- Business interests are not represented in the decision-making bodies in the fields of transport and of planning.
- The municipality, as the basic tier, remains the key level in local policies.

However, the strengthening of intermediate levels for planning and operations within the framework of districts and regions forms an element of convergence between the two countries.

In France the municipalities in urban areas, on their own or in groups, can establish a Périmètre des Transports Urbains (PTU) for public transport; the PTU forms the geographical framework for the AO. Within the PTU the AO allocates to a single operator the management of an urban transport network comprising one or more modes of public transport (bus, tramway, metro, etc.). Outside the Île-de-France, these authorities, unlike those in England, have at their disposal sufficient financial resources of their own: these include local taxes (31 per cent), income from users (20 per cent) and above all the revenue from a specific tax on the salaries of businesses situated within the PTU, the Versement-Transport (VT), 46 per cent. The modest budget share which central government allocated to urban public transport authorities (3 per cent in 2002) was cut out from 2004. The VT encouraged municipalities to group together in order to have powers over urban public transport, because this tax system could only be set up for levels of population within the PTU above a certain threshold. In addition to the widening of areas, the VT also led to the assembly of groups of municipalities into Syndicats Intercommunaux à Vocation Unique (SIVU), formal associations whose sole responsibility is for public transport. This has contributed to public transport being cut off in its own field of responsibility, supported by funding which separates it from other functions, such as spatial planning.

The reform brought about by the 1999 act on the strengthening and simplification of cooperation between municipalities (the Loi Chevènement) has addressed this gap. It basically establishes a form of local authority association with wide powers, including urban public transport and area planning, obligatory in urban areas. While Communautés Urbaines (CU) existed before this act, they were few in number; in contrast the newly created structure of Communautés d'Agglomérations (CA) has been taken up enthusiastically. Financial incentives from central government have contributed strongly to this development. But grouping together various powers in one joint body does not necessarily lead to the integration of sectoral policies, even if it can make it easier. In fact many urban transport authorities do not have their own developed expertise. They can only carry out the legal supervision of the contract with the operator of the system and rely on the latter for defining the transport services to be provided.

Outside the PTUs the départements are, within their own area, responsible for interurban passenger transport. The powers of the Conseil Général, the elected assembly of the départements, cover scheduled coach services, on-demand services and school transport; the latter forms the principal public transport activity at this level. In practice coordination between urban and interurban transport is often poor, and the imbalance between the resources of the two types of authority does not help to integrate them. In addition, the départements have a major role in the management of the road network, and this continues to grow, with transfer of 18,000 kilometres of national roads from 2006.

The regions, which became public authorities through the Decentralisation Act (1982), constitute the third level for organisation of local transport. They are responsible for regional rail transport. The annual budget allocated to public transport by the regions forms their second highest item of spending. The transfer of railway services from central government to the regions has increased the disparity of service provision between the regions and has also led to the running down of inter-regional services not on the network of 'trains à grande vitesse' (TGV). Under LOTI it is possible to set up formal agreements establishing the relationship between the responsible regional authorities and one operator: SNCF. However, in a system where central government continues to subsidise rail significantly, the cash flow appropriate to organisation on a regional basis was set up only in 2002, following a period of experiment carried out in seven regions. Implementing this regionalisation raises several difficulties, including: the scale of investment needed; congestion and allocation of train paths, which raises the issue of infrastructure charges; the dependence of the regions on the national system of passenger fares; the need to establish expertise at regional level. Furthermore the Loi relative à la Solidarité et au Renouvellement

Urbains (SRU) of 2000 proposed policies favouring the creation of Syndicats Mixtes bringing together different levels of responsible authorities (urban, departmental, regional). In this framework, the regions could play better the role of coordinating the actions of different public authorities. However, although this has been discussed, no applications have so far taken place.

Within the overall national picture the Île-de-France forms a separate case in terms of both local authority structure and of transport organisation. Under a regime which differs from LOTI, central government controlled the authority responsible for urban and regional transport until 2005. The departments were represented on it but it was not until SRU that the region gained a seat on the Syndicat des Transports d'Île-de-France (STIF), which remained under the direction of central government. The latest situation is that the Act on 'Local Responsibilities' of 2004 has proposed withdrawal of central government and transfer of the responsibilities for transport to the region. However, the process of bringing the Île-de-France in line with this standard approach is proving difficult. The current difficulties essentially reflect the debate on maintaining central government's financial contribution after its withdrawal from the decision-making bodies.

Transport and spatial development

The British 1998 White Paper envisaged close links between transport policy and land-use development. Effective spatial planning would encourage the right choices of travel, leading to more sustainable transport. To achieve these objectives, clear links were established through mechanisms at both regional and local level, and were set out in various guidance documents on planning strategy (PPGs and PPSs).

Following radical changes to the UK planning system (discussed elsewhere), links between the new local Development Framework (LDF) and the LTP are set out in the Government's Planning Policy Statement 12 (PPS12). This states that

> The integration of transport and spatial planning is central to the development and delivery of effective local development frameworks. Local transport policies need to reflect and support the aims of the core strategy development plan document. Land use planning, in turn, needs to take account of the existing transport network and plans for its development. To deliver integration, local development documents outside London should be consistent with the local transport planning policies of the local transport authority for their area. The local transport plan sets out the local authority's transport policies and detailed investment priorities over a five year period.

It adds that

> Consistency between local development documents and local transport
> planning policy (as set out in the local transport plan or equivalent)
> is particularly crucial in shire counties where the district authority
> prepares local development documents and the county is responsible
> for transport planning.

However, the formal mechanisms for ensuring that such integration
actually happens are in practice very limited. In two-tier areas especially,
the county council retains its transport powers but no longer has its former
powers to prepare the planning strategy; all spatial planning powers are in the
hands of district councils. Furthermore, there are also timescale differences.
The LDF sets out policies for a 10-year period, and there are no defined
periods, so that one local authority's LDF may cover a different period
from that of its neighbours. In contrast the LTP is produced for defined five-
year periods. This can make it very difficult to evaluate and fund transport
projects to properly reflect spatial planning policies.

While the concern for better integration of transport and urban planning
is common to the two countries, the overall structure for putting it into
practice follows fundamentally different principles. In England each level
of authority is allocated a single power; in France powers in both fields are
available at both regional and local level.

In this context, recent French legislation has encouraged planning which
links transport and spatial planning on two levels: on the one hand, the
conurbations, with the authorities responsible for urban transport charged with
creating Plans de Déplacements Urbains (PDU) and the municipal associations
responsible for Schémas de Cohérence Territoriales (SCOT); on the other, the
regions, which draw up Schémas Regionaux de Transport (SRT) within the
framework of Schémas Régionaux d'Aménagement du Territoire.

The PDU is an old process, established by LOTI (1982) but changed by
recent acts. Thus in 2000 the SRU Act extended the reform of the PDU
in the context of municipal coordination renewed by the emergence of
Communautés d'Agglomération, and brought together policies on housing,
transport and urban planning in the same document to create conditions for
better coordination. For the current Plans Locaux d'Urbanisme (PLU), the
allocations must be compatible with the PDU, and this can particularly affect
the standards for parking provision. The SRU Act however cannot avoid the
contradictions which reflect the difficult compromise between network and
area. In particular it provides that the joint municipal bodies responsible for
the SCOT can take responsibility for drawing up a PDU. While it is satisfactory
from the viewpoint of geographical coherence, this provision deprives the
organisation responsible for urban transport – defined within the PTU, whose
boundaries are much smaller than those of SCOT – of the principal mechanism
which they have to promote coherence between sectors.

At the regional scale, the linking of transport and spatial planning was, following the first Act of Decentralisation (1982), solely achieved through the Contrats de Plan État-Région (CPER). In these contracts, of five to seven years' length, which set out the agreed choices in terms of facilities, notably transport, central government's decision is dominant. However, the evolution of the planning system has provided the regional tier with new tools for coordinating sectoral processes. Thus the Loi Pasqua introduced Schémas Régionaux d'Aménagement et de Développement du Territoire (SRADT) and the Loi Voynet integrated the Schémas Régionaux de Transport (SRT) into them. Through this strategic step the connections between transport and planning are explicitly defined at regional level. However, the regions do not have available all the levers needed to ensure coordination of spatial policies. On the one hand, the municipalities remain in control of land-use planning and on the other, the requirement for coherence between different levels of authorities is now unbalanced: the SRADT must oversee the coordination of the various SCOTs but the latter do not have to follow regional choices, and links between the PDUs and the SRADT are non-existent.

Public transport provision – railways, buses and trams

Public transport in Great Britain is provided on a basis that is both centrally controlled and yet fragmented. Railways, buses and tramways each have their own regime and set of controlling policies.

The former national railway corporation, British Railways (BR), was totally restructured by the 1993 Railways Act. Despite some major changes (through Acts of 2000 and 2005), the 1993 structure remains largely intact:

* The infrastructure, initially allocated to a new private company, Railtrack PLC, is now managed by a non-profit 'stakeholder company', Network Rail, which is responsible for maintaining the network and producing plans for investment in it.
* Provision of passenger services is through franchises, let for periods of seven to 15 years. Between 2000 and 2005 the Strategic Rail Authority was responsible for letting franchises but it is now the duty of the Department of Transport. The powers formerly held by the PTEs have been withdrawn.
* All rail freight operations are now owned and managed by private companies.
* Regulation of the system, including guidance on the level of funding required for the infrastructure over five-year periods, is the responsibility of the Office for Rail Regulation (formerly the Office of the Rail Regulator).

Under the Transport Act 2000 central government created the Strategic Rail Authority (SRA) to be responsible for strategic planning for the railway network, the franchising of passenger services, and other functions. The Railways Act 2005 disbanded the SRA, its functions being split between the Department of Transport and Network Rail. There is now no statutory requirement for long-term network planning, even though growth in traffic has caused serious problems from lack of track capacity. Network Rail continues to prepare route utilisation strategies for groups of lines, a process started by the SRA: these look to identify the most efficient way to operate the maximum number of trains. There has been little investment in new infrastructure for many years (apart from the Channel Tunnel Link), and significant increases in national rail capacity appear unlikely for the foreseeable future.

Bus services outside London operated until 1986 under a system of route licences, regulated by each region's traffic commissioners. Most bus companies were owned either by a municipal authority or by the state-owned National Bus Company (in England; the Scottish Transport Group in Scotland). The 1985 Transport Act removed this regulation, so that most bus services are now provided on a commercial basis by operators. The municipal and NBC (and STG) companies were sold off as individual small companies. A high proportion of most bus services are now run by subsidiaries of four large private corporations: First Group, National Express, Arriva, Go-Ahead. These groups also operate most passenger rail services under franchise. A few medium-size independent companies and many very small ones also operate bus services. All three large French corporations (described in a later paragraph) are building up operations in Great Britain.

The PTEs and local transport authorities have powers to provide contract services over routes which are not served commercially but these are limited by budget considerations. PTEs and local transport authorities may also publicise services and provide bus priorities on their roads. Many places have seen the establishment of bus Quality Partnerships, whereby the public authority cooperates with one or more bus operators over major improvement to a group of routes: the bus operators put new buses on the route, the local authorities provide local infrastructure (priorities at junctions and lights, bus stops), and both groups cooperate over promoting the services.

These powers were strengthened by clauses in the Transport Act 2000. The Act also established powers for Quality Contracts, under which the public authority becomes responsible for the services and lets contracts to operators to run them; to date these powers have not been used. There remains however a serious barrier to operating bus services in an integrated way. Bus service provision is subject to the regulations of the Competition Acts as applied by the Office for Fair Trading (OFT), and these prevent operators from cooperating in any way which involves 'sharing the market', e.g. through agreements over timetables or common fares systems.

London has seen development of both a light metro (Docklands Light Railway) and a tramway network (Croydon) in the 1990s, and expansion is planned. Outside London only one light metro and one older tramway existed before 1990,[1] but since then four new city tram lines have been opened.[2] In 1998 the government declared a strong interest in seeing more new systems and extensions built; but they insisted that schemes should still be developed by the PPP approach required by the previous administration. Substantial work has taken place since then to develop new systems and extensions to existing ones, but in 2005 the government refused to provide funding for them, because costs had risen well above the budget allocated. The promoters attributed much of the increase to the PPP method of funding, with private companies seeking considerable risk premiums, primarily because they were uncertain about revenue, as unregulated bus operators could compete on any routes.

In the field of public transport provision, the French situation differs from the British as much in its structure as in its evolution. The geographical area remains the basis for organising transport services, whether they are provided by public monopolies or private companies. Furthermore, since the 1980s many local authorities have developed and then implemented guided transport schemes, rail or road.

In France two operators hold a monopoly position on passenger transport: the Société Nationale des Chemins de Fer (SNCF) for national and regional rail links, and the Régie Autonome des Transports Parisiens (RATP) for metro and bus services within Paris. The RATP's area extends into the départements in the inner ring around Paris. Several recent measures have sought to open up these corporations to competitive activity; the extension of RATP's field of interest to provincial and international systems enables it to prepare for the probability of competition in the Île-de-France.

In the provincial cities, the public authorities do not usually operate their own public transport system. They have to deal with a very limited number of transport companies. Three-quarters of the systems are in the hands of one of three groups: Keolis, Connex and Transdev, who carry more than 80 per cent of the trips made in urban public transport. Of these groups, two are predominantly owned by public interests: Keolis, created in 2001, following the purchase of VIA-GTI-Cariane by SNCF, and Transdev, subsidiary of the state-owned financial institution CDC. Only Connex, subsidiary of Veolia-environnement (previously Vivendi-environnement), is fully owned by private funds. Since the middle of the 1980s the strategy of the groups has been marked by four common types of development:

- growth based on the emergence of new transport authorities in small cities;
- growth through concentration by merging large companies and by buying up family-owned companies;

- combining urban and inter-urban transport activities;
- an aggressive international strategy, launched by VIA-GTI in 1989 and followed by Connex in 1996. In contrast, operation of urban transport systems in France by foreign companies remains at present marginal.

In addition to the three groups mentioned, the association AGIR, which represents independent operators, plays an important role (9 per cent of urban systems), essentially in small and medium-size cities.

Different types of contract between the operators and the responsible authorities are possible, depending on the allocation of risk and its form. However, the situation of oligopoly in urban transport which limits the impact of competition means that the public authorities, who often have limited expertise of their own, have to rely on contracts which limit the industrial and commercial risks of the transport companies.

The development of guided transport systems in French cities has seen a striking evolution since the 1980s. Nantes (1985) and Grenoble (1987) started the wave of new tramways, assisted by an industrial policy underpinned by central government. Seven other conurbations followed suit, and from 'standard' the vehicles became 'modular' and 'personalised' in order to meet the conurbations' objectives of a positive image and affirmation of their identity. In addition to its significant impact on the use of urban transport, the tramway formed a tool to revitalise city centres and to create local centres in the suburbs of French conurbations. The new French tramway is thus both a mode of travel and a means of reallocating public urban space. This enthusiasm shows up in the number of schemes: 17 cities currently aim to gain or develop a tramway system, almost half of all identified systems of guided transport on own right of way. In comparison the development of the VAL automated light transport system has been much more limited, and in France has only involved Lille (1983), Toulouse (1993) and Rennes (2002). The range of technological solutions has recently widened to include new intermediate transport systems, both guided and on rubber tyres. They are considered less expensive than the tramway, and their market extends to smaller cities, but also covers major conurbations wishing to complement their heavy transit system (Rouen or Île-de-France). Furthermore, schemes are now coming forward to use the concept of the tram-train to address the problems of outer urban areas. Its implementation will however require the establishment of authorities with specific responsibilities, which will experience problems in finding their place in the current institutional landscape.

Comparison of British and French policies and practices

It is clear from the short reviews of British and French approaches that there are strong differences between the two. Some of these concern matters of detail rather than substance. But some differences are fundamental. The following paragraphs consider those areas where the most significant differences appear to exist.

Perhaps the most crucial is the level at which real influence lies. The form and development of transport affects people and places at local level especially, because most journeys are short distance, carried out as part of people's daily lifestyle. The regional level, in the sense of intermediate level between conurbation and central government, is also important, because regional decisions set the framework for many local ones. Therefore, transport decisions need to be taken primarily at regional and local level. This is the case in France, where intercommunal bodies and regional councils both have substantial responsibilities for transport. The French government's role is mainly limited to providing the broad policy framework, and encouraging and guiding authorities to follow this.

The current trend is for this delegation of responsibilities to continue. By 2002 the regions had taken over full responsibility for administering all regional and local rail passenger services. Strengthening the role of the départements in road transport with the transfer to them, in 2006, of part of the national road network forms another example of this. Government is also withdrawing the substantial funding which it has been granting to conurbation authorities for fixed track urban transit systems. This has led to some authorities becoming doubtful over the effectiveness of developing new public transport; especially as ridership is generally not growing and the systems are facing increased operating losses, which the intercommunal bodies must underpin.

In contrast, the British approach is highlighted by strong central control, with government both setting out policies and keeping a tight control on the programmes and funding of local transport by local authorities. It is in effect micro-management from the centre. The LTP offers in principle the opportunity to establish a strategy for the area's transport. However, its form and contents are closely prescribed by government guidance, and its programmes are approved for funding on a year-on-year basis. This seriously inhibits local transport authorities from acting positively, so they have very little room to achieve real change in their area's transport. This can reduce the morale of both elected members and professional staff and breed cynicism among the public.

The French system has its weaknesses: some of the relationships between municipalities, intercommunal bodies, départements and regions remain unclear; and the links between transport and spatial planning are not fully defined. Because it remains a fundamental principle that no one public authority has control over another, the new planning tools which are aimed at permitting coordination between transport policies and urban development are likely to prove limited in their effectiveness. Thus the coordination of policies is restricted in France by the large number of local authorities which retain their privileges, while in Great Britain the weakness of coordination is due to the centralised control of power and the fragmentation of responsibilities.

This is also reflected in the two countries' widely differing frameworks for public transport administration and investment. Broadly speaking, British public transport is seriously fragmented whereas in France it is strongly integrated. This reflects several factors.

In France most local public transport services are franchised out by the responsible public authority. Some measure of fragmentation exists, because different elements of public transport are the responsibility of different levels: railway passenger services for the regions, inter-urban coach services for the départements and urban transport services for the municipalities. The three levels do not in practice always work together, leading to poor coordination of services; especially a lack of through tickets.

Within each French urban area, however, full responsibility for provision of public transport lies with the conurbation authority, which represents all the municipalities within the conurbation, and sometimes beyond. The whole urban network is let to a concessionaire for a period of years. The network is developed by the conurbation authority, in cooperation with the concessionaire. This approach produces a network that is fully integrated, in terms of operations, tickets, and general promotion. It also enables the public authority to plan system changes and extensions on an integrated basis; and it is able to fund them because it controls much of its funding, especially through the Versement-Transport.

This has led to the construction of 15 new fixed track transit systems of various types, in the last 20 years. However, the new peri-urban areas developing beyond the formerly compact cities are generally not well located for public transport. To address this, plans are now being developed in a few places for tram-train services, applying light rail techniques to under-used local rail lines.

Local railway passenger services in France are now determined by the regions. In principle, this enables them to decide on which services they should develop in relation to their regional spatial strategy and other responsibilities. In practice, the implementation remains limited by the rise of railway transport costs and by the power of SNCF.

In Great Britain public authorities have very limited responsibilities and powers for public transport. Bus services are operated largely on a commercial basis, mostly by the few major public transport companies. Local transport authorities may contract with bus companies to operate services on other routes but this function is limited by legal and budget factors. Coordination of timetables and joint ticketing are prevented by the competition law. In consequence local services are run on a fragmented basis rather than as a cohesive network.

Very few new light rail transit lines have been built outside London; currently six cities have them. Plans for three further systems, together with extensions to the existing ones, have been rejected because their capital costs, under the complex PPP system preferred by government, have risen considerably above original estimates.

Railway service franchises are administered centrally by the Department of Transport, whose main focus is to restrain cost rises, and there has been little real investment for many years. There is no effective link between railways and regional or city planning strategies. Planning strategies such as the Sustainable Communities (major expansion of housing in the regions around London) are not matched by any railway expansion, with even the two cross-London projects (Thameslink 2000 and Crossrail) trapped in uncertain processes.

Public transport in Great Britain is largely controlled by central government and by the transport providers (most of them commercial). Therefore, it is very difficult for local transport authorities to have any meaningful input. Thus public authorities at regional and local level are not in practice able to employ transport as a tool of spatial planning or sustainable development. This is further exaggerated in two-tier areas, where land-use planning is carried out by district councils, who have no real involvement with transport anyway. In contrast, the substantial controls that French conurbations and regions have over their public transport allows them to integrate their planning; especially in the case of new transit systems, which are usually planned to serve the main regeneration and development areas of the city, with the bus network in the area restructured to provide local links, with through travel by integrated ticketing.

In France, in the continued application of LOTI, the tendency is to seek new local contributors to support public transport systems, rather than to leave this primarily to market forces, as is the case in Great Britain.

However, the French system is running up against the problem of scale: the size of responsible urban authorities is too small in relation to the scale of everyday travel and the regional level is too large. In this respect the scale of the British counties where the LTPs are prepared appears more suitable than that of the municipal associations responsible for the PDUs. But this positive factor is rendered ineffective by the loss of the counties' planning powers, which means that they are incapable of ensuring real coordination between planning and transport.

Notes

1 Blackpool Tramway, Tyne and Wear Metro.
2 Birmingham, Manchester, Nottingham, Sheffield.

Chapter 13

So near, yet so far

Michèle Breuillard and Charles Fraser

Comparing challenges and problems

In the Preface to this volume allusions were made to the many examples of contemporary misunderstanding and near conflict between Britain and France; equally it pointed out that in truth the reality contained perhaps more cordial and constructive exchange and co-operation than the media would have us believe. In the field of urban affairs, land management, planning, etc. which is our focus of analysis similar misunderstandings and similar co-operation can equally be found. The Introduction set out the various areas where a dialogue between French and British academics, and some practitioners, is in progress and the challenging questions they have set out to find answers to. The authors of the various chapters have collaborated across the national divide to examine and compare the nature of a problem or issue they face and the response to it. They have set about this by defining the 'problems' and the terminologies used in responding to it in each country and proceeded to examine the respective national policies and programmes in place to deal with them.

How should one proceed in attempting to draw conclusions from their disparate deliberations? Although some common guidelines were set down for each author they were free to approach their subject matter in the way they thought best to draw out differences and illustrate common ground. Thus a historical approach has been taken to show how the field of urban policy has evolved in relation to social, economic and political change. A case study approach has been taken to contrast the methods of tackling metropolitan planning in Manchester and Lyon, a comparison of the legal frameworks to compare land tenure systems, and a comparison of flows and processes to compare development finance mechanisms, etc. Each is appropriate. How can one analyse their efforts and begin to produce meaningful conclusions? First let us examine whether the comparisons were easy and the extent to which some of the stated problems of comparison were encountered and overcome.

The first major barrier to comparison is undoubtedly that of comprehension, not just of a translation of a word or technical term but of the true
meaning in its context of that phrase. The first problem encountered was in
equating the various terms used to describe what we, in general, do. Town
planning is a phrase in the English language which has a connotation far
beyond the planning of towns to encompass the entire land management
intervention, legal and advisory by the public sector in the UK. There is no
equivalent in French, 'urbanisme' being the statutory process of drawing up
and approving legally approved contracts for what will be permitted in a
given area. The wider strategic process ranges from the state-wide exercise of
Aménagement du Territoire, in English management of the national territory
through to local or regional plans, formerly Schéma Directeurs, now the
new SCOT system. Thus a town planner in the UK will have undergone
an approved professional training and work in a range of activities from
local 'development control' to wildlife, economic or housing development
activities often at a regional level. The French equivalent is more likely to
be identified with his or her organisation or public agency engaged in the
delivery of public regulation, policy or project development. In the UK town
planning is defined by its professional context, in France by its administrative
one. However, as far as the activity of planning goes, Booth, Nelson and Paris
point out in Chapter 5 that change may be blurring these differences and the
new planning systems may be more similar than previous ones and therefore
the activity of 'planning' may in a European context be becoming a more
recognisably similar activity in each country although the contexts remain
stubbornly different. Despite the adoption of the term 'spatial planning' to
describe the process in both countries, the activity of 'planning' will remain
bound by the differences in their professional and governmental contexts.
Nothing written so far has clearly articulated any emerging similarity of
terminology which can adequately describe what happens in both cultures.

The difference in the use of words also clouds the examination of the
concept of 'public' and 'private', especially in Chapters 10 and 11 where
financial aspects are discussed. Indeed a major part of the analysis of Trache,
Green and Menez (Chapter 11) is in clarifying definitions. In examining
public-private partnerships, they demonstrate that 'private' agencies are
radically different in both countries and the way that they interact with 'public'
agencies presents a variety of combinations which although superficially
similar are structured to reflect the intrinsic nature of existing administrative
and political systems. The definition of 'private' in particular causes problems.
In the UK context such agencies are large, often multinational, conglomerates
from the property development, banking and insurance investment worlds.
In France they are more often local or national banking agencies from the
mutual banking sector and would not in a British context be considered
strictly 'private'. Conversely, similar forms of partnership or co-operation,
such as those for service delivery, are often labelled in a way to lead to the

belief that they are quite different. One example can be drawn from the health sector. NHS foundation trust status is endowed to publicly owned hospitals while an 'établissement privé conventionné', i.e. a trust hospital, is a French privately-owned hospital, incorporated into the French public health service.

The structure of the two financial systems for funding development activity (described in Chapter 10) equally produces terminological confusions. The Caisse des Dépôts et Consignations is viewed by British observers as a 'public' agency in the sense that it is controlled by the government but in France it is clearly part of the mutual banking sector owned by the 'public' in general through the republican State and kept out of the clutches of the 'government'. Thus even in discussing where finance for development should come from, one is drawn into a discussion of the difference between the State and the government and the fact that in France they are different things while in the UK they are the same, and also of quite different definitions of private and public. Thus the nature of people's perception of how their 'communal' life should be organised differs greatly.

There have been few examples of statistical comparison in the chapters undertaken, although the statistics quoted in Chapter 2 on immigration do require more examination to really compare the extent to which this factor is important in the many facets of urban policy work. However, as the riots of late 2005 in France demonstrated, actually identifying the numbers of a particular ethnic group in an area is extremely difficult as no such statistics are kept. This is not, however, due to bad accounting but due to the fact that in the Republican tradition of the country all races are equal before the law and distinguishing one from the other is considered discriminatory; this merely makes uncovering discrimination more, not less, difficult. Even if British Jacobins do not want to fill in the 'ethnic origin' part of a form, the availability of this information is in fact of great value in identifying the effects and scale of these factors where social problems occur.

Attempts at the comparison of the respective costs of the new Wembley and the Stade de France were equally fraught mainly because the financing of the Stade de France seemed to intermix public and private finances in a way which is unknown in the UK and finding out exactly how much was paid for by the taxpayer, how much by the mutual investor and how much by the market was quite a task. By contrast, the financing of Wembley, even if it is a tragi-comic story, is also a totally transparent one. Thus these two examples indicate that 'statistical' problems are a function of the national administrative culture more than of different accounting processes.

Summary of the chapter conclusions

A primary question in comparing the planning systems of Britain and France is to establish the extent to which they operate in comparable environments in economic and social terms. As Farthing and Carrière (Chapter 2) point out although the two countries have similar-sized populations there are quite significant differences in their geographic sizes and disposition of urban areas which impinge significantly on the nature of their urban problems. Both have large primate cities, London and Paris, but below this level the urban disposition is quite different. In France there is a distinctive layer of major provincial cities, Lyon, Nantes, Toulouse, etc., with perhaps only Lille being at the heart of a larger multi-centred conurbation of industrial origin. In the UK not only are the other centres almost exclusively part of wider conurbations, there is also the complicating factor that at least three of them are major administrative and governmental sub-centres, Edinburgh, Cardiff and Belfast. The difference in the location of these conurbations also means that the problems of decaying industrial cities are disproportionately located in the north and west of the UK whereas again only the Lille conurbation and the northern coalfield area is similar in France. Conversely the areas of growth in the UK are in reality an extension of the greater London conurbation in the south-east of England, while in France although the Greater Paris region, the Île-de-France, is a major growth area, economic and physical growth is more widely spread with strong growth in the south and south-east of the country. This means that the 'regional problem' has a very different flavour in each country.

However, within 'city regions' in both countries the processes of decentralisation and 'periurbanisation', are equally common. This has given both countries policy challenges to confront the need to revitalise city core areas and to curb 'sprawl' into the countryside. In each this process is complicated by the changing social geography of the major urban areas. Thus in Britain, but particularly in England, the emptying city cores have been occupied by immigrant populations moving into older social and private rented housing areas, leading to the coining of the phrase 'inner city' to the problems of racial tension, poor skill levels and higher unemployment in such areas. In France, however, due to the different disposition of social housing construction after the war such magnet areas for immigrant populations tend to be on the city periphery, 'les banlieues'.

However, although the geography of problems and challenges may differ from the national/regional to the local the problems being confronted are similar. Social exclusion, unemployment, congestion and rural and environmental problems are almost all similar in their structural manifestation. What is the core interest of this volume is to assess how the policies for tackling these problems and their practical implementation are shaped within different cultural environments of legal, administrative and economic traditions and whether these contexts are influential in shaping their success or failure. In looking at these contexts the authors have examined the basics of land law, administrative structures and financial management structures and have uncovered quite specific differences in the nature of these which not only influence the operation of the planning system but also define its scope and purpose.

Since 'planning' in both countries is at its core the intervention of the public interest in the private interests of landowners to control how that land should be used, it seemed logical to begin this contextual review with a comparison of the systems of land law and land rights. Galey and Booth (Chapter 3) point to the fundamental conceptual difference in the legal status of landowners in both countries. In the UK the system is derived from a feudal origin where ownership is conceived as a 'bundle of rights', which can be detached from each other, thereby allowing the State to 'own' the 'development' right and to intervene in its realisation, contrasting with a system where rights are indivisible and the State's control of land-use change being contained in legal codes which constrain individual rights in favour of the communal interest. This is best illustrated by the process of regulating 'change of use', an everyday simple task in the British system, but until a recent court decision an almost impossible task in France. Paradoxically, they note that the control over development by the State is more consistent in the latter model. This system is complicated by differing legal structures of inheritance law with regard to land which has resulted in a land ownership pattern of large farms and estates in the UK and small-holdings in France. These pose quite different land assembly problems for developers and may account for the absence of the classic land speculator/developer in France. As Booth, Nelson and Paris indicate (Chapter 5) this results in the planning process being dominated by quite different actors in each country. In France by different public authorities working in partnership to guide private development; in the UK as an almost adversarial conflict between public authorities seeking to restrain private developers and to obtain some agreed consensus among a variety of parties interested, in both the normal and the legal sense, in the future development of an area.

In respect of the administrative structures within which planning operates there are stark differences which again have an impact on development and other policy areas. The issue of devolution in the UK is of considerable interest to French observers but what it does is bring home to them the true nature of the 'United' Kingdom in that it is in essence a State composed of four separate cultural areas each with a different attachment to the unifying institution, the Crown. Thus the devolution of responsibility for planning to the Scottish Parliament and executive is merely an extension of a long-standing separateness based on its different legal and government systems. No such historic variety remains within the unitary French State. The result is that in the UK there is the scope for the development of several responses to problems and the possibility of intra-national policy evolution which is a stimulus to all. This is particularly true in areas such as regeneration and urban policy and the management of rural problems. The movement to a regional structure in England, however slow, meets the same problem as the that of regional government in France, how to deal with large and powerful metropolitan areas. Thus in both cases the recent changes to planning legislation leaves the door open for the existence both of regional plans if desired and, in England sub-regional plans and in France SCOTs for metropolitan areas. Thus in both countries no satisfactory resolution of the city/region conflict has been achieved either in administrative structures or in the levels at which plans are prepared and operated.

The UK system is perhaps more stable at the local level where local authorities are usually of sufficient size to deal with urban-wide problems and to resolve conflicts between poorer areas and more affluent ones within one jurisdiction. The constitutionally guaranteed position of the communes in France and their universally small size and social cohesion has meant that such wider area planning has relied on more *ad hoc* agencies with less democratic answerability, such as Communautés de Communes, Communautés d'Agglomération and Communautés Urbaines. However, as Booth, Nelson and Paris also indicate, the decentralisation process in France is leading to more innovation *within* the existing system of 'collectivités' than in England where central government regulates all local government activity very tightly.

The problems these two models pose for planning in metropolitan areas are described by Verhage, Baker and Boino (Chapter 6) and it is clear that neither city has the perfect answer to metropolitan planning and indeed both demonstrate that planning is usually dominated by major regeneration projects at the heart of metropolitan areas than by a metro-wide process.

The problem of administrative fission recurs in the French rural environment and has been seen as a fundamental barrier to rational planning since power is retained within the government structure and therefore with the mayors of small communes. Recent coalescences into Communautés de Communes, reducing the number of decision-making bodies to a tenth of their former number, may begin to change this fragmentation. By contrast in the UK despite recent moves to give more power to parish councils, the larger units of government and the greater inclusion of non governmental and voluntary agencies outside the 'political structure' in Britain gives greater scope to tackle the problems of small towns and rural areas (Carrière, Farthing and Fournier, Chapter 8).

However, the consequences are even more marked in the attempts to tackle more intractable urban problems such as bad housing, race relations and unemployment. It is clear from the recent developments in 'urban policy' in each country that while in the UK, in each of its constituents, there has been progress in tackling such issues cohesively at a city-wide scale, recent legislative measures in France (Loi Chevènement and Loi Voynet) to break down commune independence of policy implementation in urban and city-wide complexes has been thwarted by the intransigence of communes in spreading the responsibility for tackling social exclusion. The term 'urban policy', invented by the French and originally intended to be an attempt in the 1980s to cover policy in all these areas, is now synonymous with the problem of social housing and problem areas (Fraser and Lerique, Chapter 9). The French process appears to have stagnated since the heady days of the creation of DIV and the problems remained as intractable. In Britain the three constituent administrations have developed innovative responses and the period both before and after devolution has been marked by the establishment of a degree of cohesion between the policies of policy departments, e.g. employment, education, and those responsible for their coordination at a local spatial level. However, as Fraser and Lerique note, the recent English 'State of the Cities' report highlights the same problems as were noted in the unpublished White Paper of 2001. The problems may be just as intractable in the UK as in France.

A further major context within which planning operates is the economic and financial and here the French system appears to be a much more benign one for planning to operate in. As Fraser and Hoffmann point out (Chapter 10), the final stages of the implementation of any plan or project is its construction and that involves its financing. Thus while every British town, unless in an area of high development pressure by private interests, seems to have areas of dereliction or underuse of land, because the public authorities have neither the political will nor the finances to assure development (they *do* have the tools), such wastelands are almost considered an affront to the public and communal will in France and seldom stay undeveloped for long. This is achievable because of the existence of strong long-standing mutual funding organisations such as the Caisse des Dépôts independent of both the government tax base and the corporate financed development industry. Thus the planning process in France *delivers* development in addition to proposing it.

A final area is that of the transport network, which is influential in many land development decisions. There are clear differences between the two countries in how this is managed and operated. The public transport system is planned integrally with other factors in France, particularly at the metropolitan and regional levels. However, apart from London which is breaking new ground in developing models of public regulation of private operators, other areas of the UK present very unsatisfactory models of public transport operation suffering from what Harman, l'Hostis and Ménerault (Chapter 12) describe as 'micro management from the centre' (a reflection of the process of plan regulation). This allows transport to be an integral aspect of plan development at regional or metropolitan level in France but one which has a separate process in the UK.

Transferability

Historically the examination of foreign practices has had the objective of trying to find 'better' ways of doing things. In the 1970s the Community Land Act in the UK drew some of its ideas from the ZUP land development process in France. Early French urban policy initiatives drew on the 'Educational Priority Areas' initiative in the UK and on contemporary US ideas. Despite the failure of these transplants, policy makers will continue to use comparative examples to find panaceas for their country's troubles. From the analyses explored in this volume a few areas can be identified where the possibility of transplanting some ideas could be pursued.

As previously referred to, in the urban policy field there is clear evidence that in the UK as a whole the variety of initiatives developed in England, Scotland and Wales and the central measure which have been put in place to combat poverty by the Treasury ensure an environment where policies to tackle major social problems can begin to yield results both nationally and at a local level. In France recent riots speak of a failure to get to grips with the malaise of the socially deprived. What is the key difference? The analysis would seem to suggest that it is not the nature of particular programmes which is the key factor; indeed these often seem curiously similar in both countries, but the administrative and political climate in which they are devised and implemented. In England, and separately in Scotland, there is a cohesion of administrative direction across disparate departments delivered through a major senior department, the ODPM in England, the Executive itself in Scotland which ensures that policies and programmes are funded and implemented and have the support of the Executive. In France when the DIV was first created such cohesion existed but has sadly been lost. At that time the DIV and the programme it was in charge of were of considerable interest to British authorities and merited close study, the work of Mawson and Le Galès being the proof. The related Contrat de Ville programme attracted equal analysis by Parkinson and Le Galès. The lesson is that the French government must discover its former cohesion of purpose between the executive and various ministries; an analysis of why the British examples now seem to be yielding better results would be of value.

On the other hand there is clear evidence that the weakness of the physical planning system in England and to a lesser extent in the other two national entities is at the implementation stage, compared with France and several other European countries. The new Planning and Compulsory Purchase Act still does not address this, neither did the Barker Report in respect of housing. Instead the UK tamely relies on the private sector development industry to implement plan proposals because of a lack of public finance to achieve this. In France the existence of mutual funding specifically raised for the purpose of implementing projects which are in the public interest means that it is possible to deliver renewal, infrastructure and housing as planned. Thus from a UK point of view the examination of the possibility of reviving an independent non-government and non-'City' run investment sector is an imperative. The creation of a Caisse des Dépôts in the UK would seem to be worth exploring. Equally, the reluctance to engage with the new world of 'globalised' finance in France must change if more investment is to be brought to deliver regeneration in French cities. Each country has something to learn from the other in this field.

At the various levels of plan preparation and delivery there are again balances of trade which could be effected. The larger size of UK local authorities means that more comprehensive local plans are prepared and there is a need to reinforce the emerging coordination among small communes in France to achieve similar results and not least in the suburbs of the larger metropolises mitigating the effects of 'social exclusion'.

However, conversely, British local authorities suffer from 'micro-management from the centre' in this field also and devolving more responsibility for local innovation to them as in the French model could be advantageous. The new devolved administrations in Scotland and Wales and the emerging English regional structures present a contrast to the unitary nature of the French State but it is here that policy innovation may prosper in the UK. However, the possible realisation of such importations will pose a challenge to the traditional constitutional status of French communes, etc. and an equal challenge to the centralist, financially-derived 'dirigisme' of the UK government. Finally, the two countries have much to learn from each other in the management of public transport systems and their relationship to the planning process. Again the French are faced with an investment challenge and the British with that of delegating more responsibility to local, certainly metropolitan, levels.

The European dimension

What has become evident from a number of chapters is the extent to which supra-national forces are having an impact on planning structures and processes. This is most evident from the analysis of the way in which both countries are adjusting their systems to integrate with EU initiatives in the ESDP. As Sykes and Motte (Chapter 7) demonstrate this has been far easier for the French system than the British. It has a long tradition of national planning through the process of Aménagement du Territoire and budgeting through the Contrat de Plan as well as close co-operation in cross-border infrastructure development with countries such as Belgium and Spain. In Britain this cross-border element only appears in Ireland where much progress has been made, although Interreg programmes for cross-border working such as the Transmanche and the North Sea programmes are also integrating many aspects of the physical environment from bicycle routes to freight transport. Recent moves in Scotland and Wales to produce their own national plans has pushed the English authorities in ODPM to think more nationally in terms of development and to begin to integrate regional strategies as they emerge into more cohesive strategic 'plans' for wider areas which link into the ESDP structures. The 'Strategy for the North' which covers three regions is such a document. Thus the concept of a British national plan linking in to continental strategies across the Channel and the North Sea is not too distant a prospect.

The influence of wider forces is however also more subtle. The reforms of the Common Agricultural Policy (CAP) have put similar pressures on rural and agricultural communities in both countries to change and create a new rural economy. This is reflected in the pressures being put on small and market towns which serve such areas to develop new economic strategies if they are not either to decline totally or to become mere suburban and retirement dormitories. Equally, the urban strand of EU programmes from DG XVI, V and II have assisted in the reshaping of many decaying urban cores and the tackling of urban social problems. The attempts to tackle deprivation are undertaken within a pan-European strategy to combat urban deprivation.

The spectre of globalisation allied to EU initiatives to open up markets in services and finance also has an emerging influence on several aspects of physical development. This is especially notable in the financial structures used to assure development. In France the mutual banking sector, a unique and invaluable tool for backing up and ensuring the delivery of housing and other urban development must face up to the increasing pressure of growing choice in the investment market for French investors and a slow decline in profitability. This is occurring at the same time as British authorities are looking for further, more local, sources of finance, having been forced since the early 1980s to become more and more dependent on corporate capital as the main engine for property development. The conclusion by Fraser and Hoffmann in Chapter 10 is that neither extreme model will serve to balance economic and social needs in planning strategies and that encouragement should be given by the EU to the development of local 'social finance' systems to serve and deliver planning strategies among other things if a 'social Europe' is to mean anything.

More recently it is evident that in both countries the comparative position of their major cities at a European level has given cause for concern and occasioned an official response. This emerged first in France with the DATAR (DIACT) programme to assist city regions to improve their competitiveness at a European level. Fifteen cities are now working on major schemes to improve their image and advance their economic standing. This, as pointed out by Fraser and Lerique (Chapter 9), has shifted urban policy concerns in France in particular away from traditional concern with disadvantaged urban areas. In Britain the recent report by the ODPM, 'The State of the

English Cities, 2006', is also likely to lead to future policy being influenced by European concerns as well as national and local ones.

Social theory

A major similarity which pervades all of the comparisons is the extent to which the political leaning of the government in power has shaped the objectives and direction of policy and practice. Here a myth in the British world, that the French system is and has always been 'technocratic' and 'above' the machinations of politicians is well and truly laid to rest. Just as the political swing in the UK from the left in the 1970s through the long period of liberal right-wing government until 1997 and then into a more complex period of New Labour can be detected in the shifting emphases of British planning and itinerant policy areas, so too does the French system reflect the change to a Socialist government in 1982 and the shifts and changes from right to left and into 'co-habitation' since then. Technocracy may have held sway in the early postwar years but recent policy analysis indicates that it too has passed into history; the French planning, urban policy, transport, etc. systems are as politically directed as they are in the UK.

Here and there in the text of the various chapters contrasts emerge between the two systems which point to their quite different constitutional and cultural roots. While this can glibly be summarised as being due to the fact that one country is a monarchy and the other a republic there is more to it than this. After all there are other monarchies in Europe whose constitutions are closer to the French than to the British, e.g. the Netherlands, and other republics, e.g. Ireland, which are in most aspects of planning very close to the United Kingdom. It is in the nature of these forms that the difference lies and this can be seen from certain details of the context and process of planning.

Galey and Booth identify the clear feudal roots of the land tenure system in the UK, even more feudal in Scotland than in England, and to the effect that this has on land rights and the ability of the State at large to intervene in these in the interests of the community. The fact that inheritance laws are a derived function of this feudal origin merely emphasises the power of landowning classes in the structure of the country and the origin of the large estates and farms which give an advantageous development opportunity to the property sector. The land-holding structures, which were created in the early nineteenth century as France began to reshape national institutions, and the egalitarian inheritance laws have led to the evolution of a very different relationship between State and individual in respect both of the State's right to act in the interests of the citizen and in the type of land market confronting the 'promoteur' which resulted paradoxically in the creation of a weak development industry compared with Britain and a strong State rationale for intervention in the development process.

One of the fundamentals of the French constitution is the guaranteed existence of certain government institutions, particularly the commune. It is the bedrock of popular involvement in the democratic process and there are no powers available to the State to alter this. Thus in many aspects of plan preparation and implementation the ultimate power lies at this level and a wider spatial perspective is lost or subverted. This has had a profound effect in recent years in the field of urban policy where the State has found it difficult to spread the burden of dealing with the many problems of the disadvantaged social housing estates in 'les banlieues'. These are often concentrated in only one commune with neighbouring communes declining to share the burden of dealing with them (Breuillard, Stephenson and Sadoux in Chapter 4 and Fraser and Lerique in Chapter 9). There is thus a constitutional barrier to the creation of greater units to dissipate this problem. By contrast in the UK local government is the creature of the sovereign parliament and is based on the principles of administrative efficiency. Frequent variations in structure and boundaries to meet new challenges are common, perhaps too common, but they allow for the creation of larger more functional units although the people's involvement in local democracy seems less enthusiastic.

Another set of institutions derived from the Republic's origins is the system of mutual banks and financial agencies such as the Caisse des Dépôts et Consignations, which, so far, have remained independent of the commercial banking sector or direct government control; they are the people's banks to deliver their communal programmes and the State or the corporate financial world could not easily undermine their constitutional position. Such institutions have withered on the vine in the UK and local development in regeneration and even now for social housing relies on this powerful, often international financial machine. While this may not appear to be part of the British constitution it is derived from the sovereignty of parliament which has steadily since the early 1980s opened up the opportunities for such free market financial systems and not given as much attention to the development of a more local investment process.

The direction of change

In trying to gauge whether the two countries are drawing closer together in their planning systems or remaining distinct from one another, one has to understand that they have begun with different basic problems and have moved in different time scales. Thus the urbanisation process which had begun in an unplanned way before 1939 in France was more formally guided in the postwar years. This process was, in fact, almost over in the UK before the World War I. This left a legacy of different rural and urban problems for each system to deal with as they progressed to manage such problems in the latter part of the twentieth century. Thus the problems of social disaffection were detected much earlier in British urban areas. The consequences of mass immigration from outside Europe were evident sooner and the beginnings of urban policy were laid down in the early 1970s. In France this process did not make itself evident until the late 1970s and policy did not begin to take shape until the 1980s. The reverse is the case in rural areas. The CAP in France began to cushion rural areas from change in the early 1960s whereas a new set of rural problems did not emerge in Britain until the 1990s. However, in both cases as is demonstrated by Carrière, Farthing and Fournier (Chapter 8) there is much common ground in their approaches to dealing with similar problems of rural depopulation, decline of services and the 'suburbanisation' of the countryside.

In the globalising world there is more than a hint of paradox in the situation where one country (France) is being forced towards opening up its financial markets, which may destroy valuable institutions honed to serve the public interest over two centuries, while the other (the UK) is attempting to escape the influence of a corporate financial system which is suffocating the development of local financial initiative.

There does not appear to be even a minimum movement in the structure of the land tenure system in either country. Thus although some government ministers and the 'Barker Report' suggested measures which look like historic 'betterment levies', land in Britain is likely to continue to be viewed as a commodity to be developed and changed in response to economic and social forces. Equally in France the system of land rights will continue to be as rigid as ever and the process of development will continue to be controlled by a combination of public direction and individual rights.

Where this cocktail of profound change to certain factors such as economic development and social evolution and rigidity of land tenures and administrative systems leaves the 'planning' systems is interesting. In the core chapters which deal with the system itself the various recent changes following the SRU in France and the 2004 Act in England and changes in Scotland and Wales are described. The conclusions by the authors reflect their views that the revisions may make the systems more responsive to changing conditions in the world's economy, in Europe and within their national frameworks, but that they are essentially the same systems. They are still two-tier with strategic decisions at one level and local decisions at the other; they are still managed by local politicians even if local groups are given more say, and most importantly they are still given a purpose by the political direction of the governments which control them. Thus as Farthing and Carrière point out (Chapter 2), the use of the planning system in the UK to sustain economic growth in the south-east of England and facilitate economic regeneration in other areas such as the north of England is the dynamic behind the reshaping of the structure. It is not a coincidence that 'development controllers' will become 'development managers'. In France the colossal challenge facing the government to deal with a combination of social exclusion and economic stagnation means that the planning system through the Loi SRU allied to regeneration projects and the 'competitivity of cities' agenda spearheaded by DIACT are oriented to serve the effort to turn these issues around. Here the constitutional barriers such as the rigidity of local government power may be difficult to overcome. Thus the dynamism in the system will only ensure change if it is accompanied by change in some of the contextual frameworks within which planning operates. The few ideas put forward as possible for transfer from one society to the other might assist in this process. Until then the possibility of the two becoming similar remains so near, but still so far away.

Index

Ogden, P.E. and Hall, R. 24
ONS *see* Office for National Statistics
Opérations Eté-jeunes 139
OPQU *see* Office Professionel de
    Qualification des Urbanistes
OREAM *see* Organisation d'Etude et
    d'Aménagement
Organisation d'Etude et
    d'Aménagement (OREAM) 86
'Our Cities are Back' (2004) 146
*Our Countryside: The Future. A Fair
    Deal for Rural England* (2000) White
    Paper 8, 123, 125, 127, 130
Our Towns and Cities: The Future
    (2000) White Paper 8, 144–5, 148,
    163, 176
Pacte de la Relance de la Ville 141

PADD *see* Projet d'Aménagement et de
    Développement Durable
PADOG *see* Plan d'Aménagement et
    d'Orientation Générale
Parkinson, M. 22; and Le Galés, P. 140
passenger transport authority (PTA) 193
passenger transport executive (PTE)
    193, 199
Patault, A.M. 38
PDUs *see* plans de déplacements urbains
'People, Places and Prosperity' report
    146
Périmètre des Transport Urbains (PTU)
    194
Peyrony, J. 105, 106
Plan d'Aménagement et d'Orientation
    Générale (PADOG) 86
Plan d'Occupation des Sols (POS) 70,
    74, 80, 83, 85, 165
Plan Local de l'Habitat (PLH) 142
Plan Local de l'Urbanisme (PLU) 29, 41,
    60, 72, 80, 87, 89, 164, 197
planning *see* metropolitan planning;
    spatial planning; strategic planning
planning actors 80–1, 84; central
    government/national politicians
    75–6; developers 79; development
    agencies 77–9; local authorities 76;
    the professions 76–7
Planning Advisory Group 8
Planning and Compensation Act (2004)
    7, 92
Planning and Compulsory Purchase Act
    (2004) 84, 89, 146, 212

planning instruments 79–80, 84;
    and discrete-area planning 73–4;
    origins/meanings of 73; and reform
    of systems 71–2; and UDCs 74; and
    use of agreements/obligations 74
Planning Policy Guidance notes (PPGs)
    58, 69, 103, 108
Planning Policy Statements (PPS) 58,
    109, 110
Plans de Déplacements urbains (PDUs)
    105, 197, 204
PLH *see* Plan Local de l'Habitat
PLU *see* Plan Local de l'Urbanisme
*Polarisation and Social Housing: The
    British and French Experience* 5
pôles de competitivité 27
'Policy for the Inner Cities' (1977)
    White Paper 170
Politique de Villes Moyens 75
*Politiques Foncières Comparées - Grande
    Bretagne* (Renard & Vilmin) 5
Pontier, J.-M. 162
population *see* demographics
POS *see* Plan d'Occupation des Sols
Power, A. 2, 4, 20
private finance initiative (PFI) 159–60,
    165, 166–7, 174, 176
the professions 76–7
Programme Local de l'Habitat 70
project planning 95–6
Projet d'Aménagement et de
    Développement Durable (PADD) 72,
    80, 85, 113
Projets d'Agglomération 80
'Propositions pour l'aménagement du
    territoire' report (1986) 101
Prud'homme, R. 19; and Nicot, B.-H.
    24; and Terny, G. 173
PTA *see* passenger transport authority
PTE *see* passenger transport executive
Public Health Acts 44
Public Value Management 178
public-private partnership (PPP) 2,
    6, 8, 9–10, 63, 157, 160, 206;
    and additional funding 179; as
    alternative approach to delivery
    178–9; areas of interest 180–2,
    184; attractions of 176, 178–80;
    budget enlargement model 177; and
    changing working practices 178; as
    contractual agreement 173, 176;
    development of 174–5; dynamics